Number and Nightmare

Forms of Fantasy in Contemporary Fiction

Number and Nightmare

Forms of Fantasy in Contemporary Fiction

Jean E. Kennard

ARCHON BOOKS   •   1975

Library of Congress Cataloging in Publication Data

Kennard, Jean E   1936-
    Number and nightmare, forms of fantasy in contemporary fiction.

    Bibliography: p.
    Includes index.
    1. American fiction—20th century—History and criticism. 2. English fiction—20th century—History and criticism. 3. Existentialism in literature.   I. Title.

PS379.K4   823'.9'1409   74-28448
ISBN 0-208-01486-1

© 1975 by Jean E. Kennard
First published 1975 as an Archon Book,
an imprint of The Shoe String Press, Inc.
Hamden, Connecticut 06514

Printed in the United States of America

CREDITS AND ACKNOWLEDGEMENTS

Chapter one, "Joseph Heller: At War with Absurdity," in a revised form, and parts of chapter two, "John Barth: Imitations of Imitations," originally appeared in *Mosaic: a Journal for the Comparative Study of Literature and Ideas* published by the University of Manitoba Press.

Permission to include quotations from the works of authors considered in this study have been granted as follows:

John Barth
From *Chimera*, copyright 1972 by John Barth. Reprinted by permission of Random House, Inc.
From *End of the Road*, copyright 1958, 1967 by John Barth. Reprinted by permission of Doubleday and Co., Inc. and Lurton Blassingame.
From *The Floating Opera*, copyright 1956, 1967 by John Barth, published by Doubleday and Co., Inc. Reprinted by permission of Lurton Blassingame.
From *Giles Goat Boy*, copyright 1966 by John Barth. Reprinted by permission of Doubleday and Co., Inc. and Lurton Blassingame.
From *The Sot-Weed Factor*, copyright 1960, 1967 by John Barth. Reprinted by permission of Doubleday and Co., Inc. and Lurton Blassingame.

Anthony Burgess
From *MF*, copyright 1971 by Anthony Burgess. Reprinted by permission of Alfred A. Knopf, Inc.
From *Re Joyce*, copyright 1965 by Anthony Burgess. Reprinted by permission of W. W. Norton and Co., Inc. and Faber and Faber, Ltd. Published in the British Commonwealth under the title *Here Comes Everybody*.
Excerpts from the following books are reprinted by permission of W. W. Norton, Inc. and William Heinemann, Ltd: *A Clockwork Orange*, copyright 1962 by Anthony Burgess, *Enderby*, copyright 1968, 1963 by Anthony Burgess; *Tremor of Intent*, copyright 1966 by Anthony Burgess; *The Wanting Seed*, copyright 1962 by Anthony Burgess.

William Golding
From *Lord of the Flies*, copyright 1954 by William Golding. Reprinted by permission of Coward, McCann and Geohegan, Inc. and Faber and Faber, Ltd.
Excerpts from the following books are reprinted by permission of Harcourt Brace Jovanovich, Inc. and Faber and Faber, Ltd· *Free Fall*, copyright 1959 by William Golding; *The Inheritors*, copyright 1955 by William Golding; *Pincher Martin*, copyright 1956 by William Golding; *The Spire*, copyright 1964 by William Golding.

Joseph Heller
From *Catch-22*, copyright 1955, 1961 by Joseph Heller. Reprinted by permission of Simon and Schuster and A. M. Heath and Co., Ltd. for Jonathan Cape.

Iris Murdoch
Excerpts from the following books are reprinted by permission of The Viking Press, Inc. and Chatto and Windus, Ltd.: *The Bell*, copyright 1958 by Iris Murdoch; *A Fairly Honourable Defeat*, copyright 1970 by Irene Alice Murdoch; *Flight from the Enchanter*, copyright 1956 by Iris Murdoch; *The Sandcastle*, copyright 1957 by Iris Murdoch; *A Severed Head*, copyright 1961 by Irish Murdoch; *Under the Net*, copyright 1954 by Iris Murdoch; *The Unicorn*, copyright 1963 by Iris Murdoch; *The Time of the Angels*, copyright 1966 by Iris Murdoch.

For Gail

Contents

This book is a study of the fantasy techniques of some British and American novelists who gained their reputations in the sixties. Specifically, it is an examination of the relationship between these techniques and the Existentialist premises defined in the early work of Jean-Paul Sartre and Albert Camus. It is also an attempt to define two major forms of fantasy in contemporary fiction, *number* and *nightmare*, on the basis of the novelists' response to a Post-existential world view.

Many of the commentators on contemporary fiction have found it necessary to discuss Existentialism in order to define the intellectual climate of the post-1945 world. Neither they nor I mean to suggest that every novelist is an attentive reader of *The Myth of Sisyphus* or of *Being and Nothingness* nor that all those who have read early Existentialist philosophy necessarily agree with its premises. But few would deny that the postwar atmosphere has been permeated with Existentialist concepts since the notion of the absurd seems to define the contemporary situation so well.

We have not, though, done a very thorough job of defining the relationship between Existentialism and fiction. We have tended to consider it only in terms of American fiction, although it originated as a European philosophy, and have made little or no attempt to compare its influence on even British novelists. That is one of the things I wish to rectify with this study.

It is perhaps even more serious that we have, to a large extent, treated the absurd hero as Existentialism's sole contribution to postwar fiction.[1] This approach tends to assume the conventions of realism, an awkward term I shall attempt to define later; it is very difficult to discuss a novel in terms of the protagonist's experience without talking about him as if he were a living person. The approach, thus, overlooks the fantasy techniques which are anti-realistic and which, perhaps, most of all characterize contemporary fiction.

Recently, before it has really been thoroughly examined, some commentators seem ready to dismiss the influence of Existentialism on contemporary fiction as no longer relevant. For example, Raymond Olderman claims "Existentialism does not explain what is central to the novel of the 1960s."[2] But what he is dismissing turns out to be that vision which produced "the individual's existential encounter with the facts of experience";[3] in other words, the novel of the absurd hero. Olderman goes on to define a Post-existential sensibility which is, he says, different from the Existentialist view in that it sees man in relationship not to a world of chance but to a world where "all things are malevolently ordered."[4]

It is certainly true that the Post-existential world view appears more nihilistic than the sort of humanism found in some novels with absurd heros. But it springs from precisely the same Existentialist root; it merely stresses the premises of the absurd dilemma rather than the more palatable notion that man is free to create himself, an idea Sartre and Camus have themselves used to construct a humanistic, moralistic philosophy. From the point of view of the individual, a world of accident, of chance, *does* appear malevolent because it ignores man. The early work of Sartre and Camus emphasizes this. In Sartre's *Nausea*, Roquentin feels objects are actively opposed to him because he can no longer control them; in *The Myth of Sisyphus*, Camus claims that in the experience of the absurd "the primitive hostility of the world rises up to face us across millennia."[5]

Olderman does, however, correctly associate this nihilistic Post-existential sensibility with the mode of black humor. Unfortunately, this is another of the vague terms that have plagued discussions of the technical aspects of contemporary fiction.[6] Like such labels as *absurd novel* and *anti-novel*,[7] black humor has been used in a rather loose manner by critics. They seem to have in mind a novel similar to an absurd play where horror is treated as comic and the audience "is confronted with actions that lack apparent motivation, characters that are in constant flux, and often happenings that are clearly outside the realm of rational experience."[8] But the techniques of this kind of novel have not been adequately compared to those of the theater of the absurd. Although this study is not the place for a detailed comparison of that kind, I shall attempt to illustrate in my introduction the direction such a comparison might take.

What is worse, this loose use of labels has allowed novelists to be discussed as illustrations of the same phenomena when they really have very different aims. For example, in an essay on *Catch-22*, John Hunt claims that Heller shares with Bellow, Malamud, Styron, Durrell, Beckett, and Golding a distinctly modern way of writing about the fantastic.[9] This, surely, is a group of novelists who use fantasy for a variety of ends. Similarly, Vonnegut and Burgess are often inaccurately treated as philosophical blood brothers because they both frequently set their novels in fantastic future worlds.

The major differences between the fantasy novelists of the sixties can perhaps best be described in terms of their responses to the Existentialist premises, to the notion of the absurd dilemma. This is not to deny that many of the techniques I shall describe can be found in novels predating the work of Sartre and Camus, particularly in the fiction of such novelists as West, Céline, and Kafka. Nevertheless, since 1945 these techniques have undoubtedly become more widespread; indeed in the 1960s they became the rule rather than the exception. This is probably because the view of man's relationship to his world as irrational and absurd, a view, of course, also predating Sartre and Camus, has been confirmed and strengthened by the postwar experience.

I have chosen to discuss seven novelists: four of them—Joseph Heller, John Barth, James Purdy, and Kurt Vonnegut, Jr.—accept a Post-existential world view; three—Anthony Burgess, Iris Murdoch and William Golding—refute the Existentialist premises. They are all writers of fantasy but represent opposing forms of the novel.

The two forms they represent can be conveniently defined by the labels Ihab Hassan has used to distinguish between the language of Beckett and that of Joyce: *number* and *nightmare*. In a recent lecture at the Second International James Joyce Symposium, Hassan said: "If Joyce and Beckett divide language between them, they also polarize it, as Elizabeth Sewell would say, between Nightmare and Number. The language of Nightmare is that of confusion and multiple reference; it creates a world in which all is necessary, all significant; everything is there at once. But the language of Number empties the mind of reference; it creates a world of pure and arbitrary order; nothing there is out of place."[10] This distinction was, as Hassan points out, originally the distinction Elizabeth Sewell makes between Rimbaud and Mallarmé in *The Structure of Poetry*.[11] He has applied it to Joyce and Beckett and I have appropriated it, adapted it slightly, and use it to describe two forms of the contemporary novel, one which employs the techniques of Beckett and the other many of the techniques of Joyce.

Number, the form of fantasy used by Heller, Barth, Purdy and Vonnegut, is a dramatization of the Post-existential view of the human condition, of "The exile of consciousness from both word and flesh . . . The alienation of consciousness . . . from the earth."[12] Its most significant characteristic is that it is anti-literature, anti-myth, destructive of form. The novel of number does not construct a pattern but turns pattern on itself, often through self-parody. "In Beckett," Hassan says elsewhere, "literature rigorously unmakes itself."[13] The novel of number takes the reader systematically and logically towards nothing, towards the void, by breaking down one by one his expectations of realism.

Although I shall define these expectations of realism more thoroughly in my introduction, it is worth noting here that in calling this form of fantasy a deliberate violation of the conventions of realism, I have in mind basically what Ian Watt has called "the primary convention, that the novel is a full and authentic report of human experience";[14] that is, that a reality exists prior to the novelists' attempts to describe it. Arthur Mizener defines ordinary fiction as operating on the assumption "that the objects of perception are real—exist independent of the observer and that events occur in a space-time in a cause-and-effect, historical pattern for which the ideal model is a set of equations."[15] This definition of realism applies both to novelists who precede the Jamesian notion of dramatic scene, of showing rather than telling, and to those who follow.

To a large extent, though, the novelists of number depend on the pre-existence of the Jamesian conventions for their effects. These conventions are summarized in Ford Madox Ford's contention that the aim of good modern novelists was "to take the reader, immerse him in an Affair so completely that he was unconscious either of the fact that he was reading or of the identity of the author."[16] James's dicta became so thoroughly accepted by early twentieth-century novelists that readers have come to expect an author to remain, in Joyce's words, detached, like God, paring his fingernails. The novelists of number, however, deliberately draw our attention to the fact that we are reading and, beyond this, to the fact that they are creating, not describing, a reality. They appear to agree with Ionesco that "the authentic nature of things, the truth, can only be revealed to us by fantasy, which is more realistic than all the realisms."[17]

The novel of number works rationally, although one of its premises is a distrust of reason, to destroy illusion. It turns logic against language to expose the inadequacies of words. It is always, in a sense, ironic, "the mirthless laugh in the face of unhappiness, that is, the human condition."[18] The novel of number dramatizes Beckett's belief that art is fidelity to failure. It shows the impossibility of its own creation. "The end of a sentence cancels its beginning."[19]

Nightmare is the form used by those writers who offer answers to the Post-existential dilemma, or rather deny its existence. Burgess, Murdoch and Golding all believe that the world has order even if man cannot discover its meaning and even if it does not contribute to his happiness. The novel of nightmare is fantasy in the sense that it often presents us with events which are not possible given the present state of human knowledge. It often employs the realistic methods of characterization. It is fantasy also in the sense that it draws attention to its own pattern. Henry James says that when we think we see life without rearrangement in fiction, we feel we are touching the truth; when we see it with rearrangement, we feel we are being put off with a convention, a substitute, that it is not realistic. The novelist of nightmare wishes us to be aware of his re-arrangement.

Nightmare is basically a constructive form; each of these writers creates myths. They move the reader towards recognition of an all-inclusive world, a puzzle in which all the pieces fit. The novel of nightmare is usually a fable; that is, to use John Peter's defini-tion, it gives the impression that the author began with some initial thesis or contention he wished to embody in concrete terms. A fable gives the impression that it is preceded by the conclusion that it is its function to draw. Its pattern is obvious because the satisfaction in reading it lies in making the whole out of the parts, in solving the problem. The reader is supposed to be detached, observing, rather than involved and identifying.

In attempting to refute the Post-existential view of the world, the novelist of nightmare draws on an older tradition of fantasy, that of myth. Its most recent influence, claims Hassan, is Joyce. "Joyce renders the collective experience of mankind in puns of infinite reverberations, yet reduces all that experience to a single utterance, a seamless unity."[20] The reader is taken towards infinity where there is mystery rather than a void. The language of the novel of night-mare, unlike that of the novel of number, is highly metaphoric, sometimes comic but not ironic.[21] Art itself is seen as evidence of redemption, as a reflection of that order which denies the Post-existential world view. The novelist of nightmare "values art supremely. For him the artist is a Promethean figure who ends by usurping the place of Zeus."[22]

To fit seven novelists into such a distinction as this too closely would inevitably be to distort. Each novelist responds differently to the Post-existential sensibility; the fantasy techniques of each are therefore different. Similarly, each novel has its own flavor which is bound to escape any net one attempts to catch it in. I am also aware that my selection of novelists may raise some objections. Everyone is likely to have his own candidates for inclusion. I realize I could have included Pynchon, Hawkes, Beagle, Barthelme, Lessing, Ellison, and Fowles, to name a few. The existence of so many other novelists who fit these categories tends to support my thesis and I hope that the analysis of the seven novelists I have chosen will suggest ways of approaching the others.

My choice is, of course, partly personal preference. Beyond this, although I am not claiming direct Existentialist influence as a prerequisite for these fantasy techniques, awareness of Existentialist theory can, in fact, easily be documented in the cases of these seven. I have chosen them also because they are all very much contemporary novelists although they gained their reputations in the 1960s. As I write this, Heller's new novel, *Something Happened*, has just been published; Murdoch and Purdy have new novels about to appear; Burgess threatens another. Like Tristram Shandy's, so many of whose creator's experiments in fictional technique foreshadowed those of the contemporary novel, my subject tends to grow faster than I can discuss it.

The Post-existential World:
Image and Counter-Image

This chapter is intended to give an overview of the major fantasy techniques of the novels of number and nightmare and to show the relationship between these and the Post-existential world view. I shall not be primarily concerned with the later humanistic doctrines of either Sartre or Camus because these have little relevance to the more nihilistic novel of the sixties. Of major importance is the definition of the absurd dilemma from which the Post-existential view derives. It finds its philosophical roots primarily in Sartre's *Being and Nothingness* and Camus' *The Myth of Sisyphus*, though its definition is assisted by a consideration of the early novels of both writers, particularly of Sartre's *Nausea* and Camus' *The Stranger*. The novelists of number share the Post-existential view; the novelists of nightmare refute its basic premises.

This philosophical disagreement is responsible for the major differences in their use of fantasy. The novel of number employs many of the techniques of the theater of the absurd which derives from the same philosophical base. Since the techniques of the drama of the absurd have been discussed elsewhere in much more detail than those of fiction, I shall assume greater familiarity with them and use them merely as points of comparison to clarify my comments on the novel of number. The novel of nightmare, which remains closer to realism and uses fewer fantasy techniques than the novel of number, necessarily receives less attention here. I inevitably find myself defining it as much by what it does not do as by what it does.

The starting point of Existentialism is an act of perception, a view of the world as it is; its first conclusion is that man's relationship to this world is absurd. The experience of the absurd is illustrated in *The Stranger* and in *Nausea* and is explained in *The Myth of Sisyphus*. But, unlike much of the Post-existentialism of the novel of number, Existentialism is not primarily a philosophy of despair, neither Sartre nor Camus stops at explaining the absurdity of man's relation to his world. Camus' *The Rebel, The Plague, The Fall*, and the three novels of Sartre comprising *Roads to Freedom* are all concerned with living after the experience of the absurd, in the knowledge of absurdity. These works are humanistic and often didactic; the novel of number is not. Neither Sartre or Camus employs any of the fantasy techniques which characterize the drama of the absurd and the novel of number; their novels and plays are essentially realistic.

Both Sartre and Camus begin with a definition of the world as it is familiar to us most of the time. This familiar world is ordered, has meaning which can be rationally discovered, is peopled with human beings who have definite and discernible identities, and contains objects that can be named and thus controlled by man. Values may differ, but the possibility of absolute truth exists even if no one has yet discovered it. The individual feels, therefore, that this relation to the world is meaningful, that his actions in it have a purpose, even if this purpose has not yet been achieved.

This is the view of the world reflected in the realistic novel and in naturalistic drama. Realism assumes, as Robbe-Grillet, among others, points out, that there is a reality which exists prior to the writer's attempt to portray it, and that this reality is accepted as reality by readers and writer alike. The technical aspects of such literature imply a logical and consistent world. Writing about Balzac, Robbe-Grillet says: "All the technical elements of the narrative—systematic use of the past tense and third person, unconditional adoption of chronological development, linear plots, regular trajectory of the passions, impulse of each episode toward a conclusion, etc.—everything tended to impose the image of a stable, coherent, continuous, unequivocal, entirely decipherable universe. Since the intelligibility of the world was not even questioned, to tell a story did not raise a problem."[1] Similarly, in an article entitled "Spatial Form in Modern Literature," Joseph Frank claims that writers who find themselves in harmony with their environment produce realistic literature.

A familiar form of the realistic novel is that in which we follow the "development" of a character from childhood to something called "maturity." This "maturity" generally involves the learning and acceptance of "true values" and adjustment to the "reality" of society.[2] In Dickens's *Great Expectations*, for example, the structure of the novel follows chronologically the stages in Pip's maturing. Pip's maturity consists in recognizing and accepting that material success not worked for and the outward trappings of rank are no substitutes for true affection and hard work. He learns to abandon his fantasy world for the real one.[3] There is no question raised about which world is real nor about the absoluteness of the values Pip adopts at the end of the novel. In spite of the recent comparisons between Dickens and Kafka,[4] Dickens never really questions the intelligibility of the universe.

The world as it appears to us most of the time is, according to the early work of Sartre and Camus, an illusion. The universe has no meaning, no reason for existing; there is, therefore, no reason for accepting one value rather than another. The world merely exists, is merely there, gratuitous and contingent, an accumulation of objects. Human beings are merely other objects in this world and at certain times the inhuman aspect of others can be brought home to us by a sudden change in our angle of vision. Camus writes: "Men, too, secrete the inhuman. At certain moments of lucidity, the mechanical aspect of their gestures, their meaningless pantomime makes silly everything that surrounds them."[5]

This aspect of Existentialist theory and the modern stress on the dangers of technocracy have reinforced one another. They are perhaps equally responsible for the dominance of the theme of dehumanization in contemporary literature. In Kurt Vonnegut's novels, for example, the willingness of scientists to treat human beings as objects and the elevation of machines to the status of human beings are constantly recurring ideas. Samuel Beckett's characters become machines, adapting bicycles to serve as legs when the body gradually disintegrates, or living as objects in ash cans. Our willingness to value the system rather than the individual ends with each of us seeing others as inanimate. So Lieutenant Scheisskopf in *Catch-22* can consider nailing all his men together for the sake of a perfect parade.

Although other human beings may appear as objects to him, the individual man differs from the objects in his world in his desire to find meaning for his existence, in his need for absolute values. It is a given in *The Myth of Sisyphus* that man has "a nostalgia for unity," an "appetite for the absolute,"[6] a drive towards objective understanding which is the one quality Sartre and Camus see as innate to man. Camus points out that this quality alone separates man from the rest of the world: "If I were a tree among trees, a cat among animals, this life would have a meaning, or rather this problem would not arise, for I should belong to this world. I should be this world to which I am now opposed by my whole consciousness and my whole insistence upon familiarity."[7]

It is neither man nor the world which is absurd. What is absurd is the confrontation between man's desire for meaning and a silent, unreasonable universe. Man cannot but ask something of the world, which the world by its very nature cannot provide. From the point of view of the individual, the experience of the absurd, or nausea as Sartre calls it, is a separation of himself from all that was previously familiar to him. He feels bereft even though the familiarity was simply with his own illusory view of the world. Camus explains that "a world that can be explained even with bad reasons is a familiar world. But, on the other hand, in a universe suddenly divested of illusions and lights, man feels alien, a stranger. . . . This divorce between man and his life, the actor and his setting, is properly the feeling of absurdity."[8]

This "divorce," this experience of the absurd, is described by both Sartre and Camus as a sudden experience, one that can happen anywhere to anyone, but which is sensed initially as alienation for the individual from a hostile world, a world with which he can no longer deal. This notion of alienation, of course, is fundamental to the Post-existential world view of the novel of number. For a moment we cease to understand the world because "for centuries we have understood in it solely the images and designs we had attributed to it beforehand."⁹ The world does not change in the experience of the absurd, but the stage scenery created by our imaginations slips momentarily and the world "becomes itself again."¹⁰ It is this experience Sartre describes in *Nausea*. Roquentin attempts to establish a relationship between the trees, the gates, the stones that he sees, to come to terms with the chestnut trees by counting them and by measuring their height, only to find that "each of them escaped the relationship in which I tried to enclose it, isolated itself and overflowed."¹¹

There are experiences of the absurd described in many contemporary novels, just as there are innumerable alienated heroes. What is more interesting is the way in which the fantasy techniques of the novel of number bring about the experience of the absurd in the reader. The novel itself serves as the world about which the reader has illusions or expectations. He expects those aspects of realistic fiction that reflect a stable, coherent universe.

In spite of all the experiments in form in twentieth-century literature, most readers still undoubtedly approach a novel with expectations of what they think of as "life-likeness," but which are really conventions of the realistic novel: a causally related plot, characters who exhibit familiar human emotions, language which is largely referential, logical argument. Since Henry James, they also expect the apparent absence of the author's voice, though, as Wayne Booth says, the author can never really choose to disappear.¹² Northrop Frye points out that our initial tendency in picking up a novel is to relate it to life and that this tendency has been fostered in us by critics; we have, he says, an expectation of plausibility.¹³ This can be demonstrated by some of the early reviews of contemporary novels. For example, in a 1963 review of *Catch-22*, Roger Smith complained that "the book tells no story. . . . There are no characters . . . its author cannot write."¹⁴ The review makes clear that Smith has misunderstood Heller's techniques because he expected a realistic novel.

When his expectations of the novel are frustrated, the reader has an experience of the absurd. It is worth noting the relationship between the experience of the absurd and the nature of humor. If Bergson is right and laughter depends on incongruity, in other words also on a frustration of expectations, it is not surprising that the experience of the absurd frequently produces a laugh of ironic detachment. Purdy's novel, *Cabot Wright Begins*, for example, ends on just such a laugh. Nor is it surprising that the literature producing an experience of the absurd in the reader is usually defined as comedy, albeit black comedy. Laughter, indeed, is often the only resolution of the Post-existential dilemma that the novel of number provides.

One of the methods by which audiences' or readers' expectations are frustrated is by drawing attention to the fictional nature of the play or novel. One of the conventions of post-Jamesian realism is the assumption that for the duration of the novel one is participating in "real life." Even in novels which predate James, where a narrator addresses the reader directly, in *Tom Jones* or *Tristram Shandy* for example, although the illusion that we are participating in "real life" rather than reading is broken, the illusion is maintained that the narrator is telling us a true story. The narrator in such novels is, of course, a character himself; as Booth points out, he cannot be assumed to be the author.[15]

When John Fowles gives us three possible endings to *The French Lieutenant's Woman* and lets us choose our own, when we find Beckett's characters writing Beckett's novels, when Robbe-Grillet gives us many possible versions of one event and refuses to tell us "the truth," even the illusion of hearing a true story is shattered. We are shown the process of creation and doubt is thrown on the existence of any reality. The importance of this technique to the contemporary novel has been discussed recently by Richard Poirier in his essay "The Politics of Self-Parody." Poirier defines "a literature of self-parody which makes fun of itself as it goes along. It proposes not the rewards so much as the limits of its own procedures; it shapes itself around its own dissolvents; it calls into question not any particular literary structure so much as the enterprise itself of creating literary form."[16] This is an accurate description of one of the major characteristics of the novel of number. Since the novelist of nightmare believes in an ordered reality, he does not use this technique.

The major forms that this self-conscious art technique takes can be illustrated from the drama of the absurd. The fact that in *Victims of Duty* Ionesco introduces a discussion of the very kind of drama he is presenting and even uses his own name is typical both of him and of other playwrights of the absurd. He closes *Amédée* with the words "Let's close the shutter, Eugène, the show's over."

Gide used this device in *The Counterfeiters*, of course, before Ionesco employed it on stage and before the appearance of the novel of number. It is an example of one of those techniques which predate Existentialist theory, but which have nevertheless since become a fashionable tool for dramatizing it.

An important subdivision of writers' allusions to their art is the insistence on an actor's playing his role self-consciously, a technique fundamental to an understanding of Genet and important in the plays of Beckett, Gelber, and Albee. In Beckett's *Endgame* we see the simpler form of this self-consciousness, a character who plays the role of a performer within the play. Hamm's consciousness of himself as story-teller leads him to make such comments as "I feel rather drained. The prolonged creative effort . . ." and "I'm warming up for my next soliloquy" which have meaning within the context of the play and also an ironic significance since Hamm is an actor playing a role.

In the plays of Jack Gelber and Jean Genet a deliberate ambiguity is established in the minds of the audience as to what is "real" and what is art. In the work of both dramatists theatrical illusion is shattered but from opposite directions. Genet presents us with highly stylized drama in which one role is uncovered to show another role, which in its turn reveals yet a third masquerade, so that in the end the audience believes that it is seeing "real life," only to be reminded that "real life" itself consists merely of role playing. In Gelber's play, *The Connection*, the actors play the role of actors putting on a play so that the illusion is created that what we are watching is "real life." While the form of Genet's drama suggests, then, that life is as artificial as art, that of Gelber's only proves that art can appear as improvised and spontaneous as life. The equivalent technique in fiction can be found in Vonnegut's *Breakfast of Champions* and Barth's *Giles Goat-Boy* where the authors self-consciously play the role of authors.

In almost all plays of the absurd there are direct comments made to the audience. These comments are invariably of an antagonistic nature, inviting the audience to compare what they see on the stage with their own life, challenging them to prove their own lives more meaningful. Irma's final words in Genet's *The Balcony* are to the audience: "You must now go home, where everything—you can be quite sure—will be even falser than here."

In these three ways, then, by ironic allusions to the fact that the play is art, by self-conscious role-playing by the characters, by direct addresses to the audience, the dramatists of this kind of theater take from us any assurance that we know what drama is. It is certainly not what we are used to or what we expected. These plays seem fantastic at first, but we are finally forced to realize that drama which does not pretend to be other than drama is not less real but more real than a play that creates the illusion of being a "slice of life." Our expectation of reality is shown to have been an expectation of illusion. The shattering of these illusions brings about in the audience an experience of the absurd.

The experience of the absurd as described in the early work of Sartre and Camus is accompanied by certain realizations about the nature of man's identity, his actions, his relationship to objects, and his use of logic and language. Indeed it is invariably an experience in relation to one of these which produces the feeling of absurdity. In the experience already referred to from Sartre's *Nausea*, it is clear that Roquentin's nausea is brought about by a realization of the nature of the objects surrounding him, or more properly by a realization that he cannot fathom their nature. In Camus' *The Fall*, the judge has an experience of absurdity, characterized for him by mocking laughter, when he realizes that the identity or role upon which he has built his life is an illusion. But whatever brings it about, the significance of the nausea to each of the other facets of man's life rapidly becomes apparent.

We usually think of other human beings and of ourselves as having definite identities, as a combination of certain characteristics which make us recognizable to others and to ourselves. Iris Murdoch claims that the "myth of the 'ghost in the machine' is so deep in our language we inevitably think of the person as composed of psychic forces."[17] Thus we can talk of someone being "selfish," "good tempered," "shy," as if these qualities were both innate and fixed in the individual whom they described. In the novel this attitude is reflected in the convention of character creation. Robbe-Grillet explains that our expectations of character are based on the realistic nineteenth-century novel; we expect a character to have a proper name, a profession, qualities reflected in his face, and a past which has molded his personality. We expect his character to determine his actions and the consistency of his reactions. "His character permits the reader to judge him, to love him, to hate him,"[18] Robbe-Grillet says. Similarly, Wayne Booth claims that one of our chief pleasures in reading fiction is our strong concern for the characters as people.[19]

In opposition to the view of identity that this convention implies, Sartre explains in *Being and Nothingness* that an individual has no innate characteristics, that he chooses and makes himself, that he is only what he wills himself to be. The individual human consciousness, called by Sartre *le pour-soi* or being-for-itself, is nothingness, and it can only recognize itself in so far as it perceives itself not to be the objects around it or *l'en soi*, being-in-itself. In the experience of nausea or the absurd, the individual, recognizing that he has no relation to the world about him, is thrown back upon his own nothingness.

It is only to other people that the individual has a definite identity, not to himself. Sartre talks of his attempt to define himself as being-seated and the impossibility of this without an observer: "I myself shall never succeed at realizing this being-seated which I grasp in the Other's look. I shall remain forever a consciousness."[20] For this reason, in his constant effort to create identity for himself, the individual frequently looks to other people. As Camus says in *The Rebel*, he can only assure himself of his own existence by seeing its reflection in the faces of others.

A novelist who accepts Sartre's premises about human identity is likely to reject the realistic method of characterization, which, as Robbe-Grillet says, implies the existence of innate characteristics. But the reader, who still expects nineteenth-century "characters," fully developed, firmly anchored in their settings, tends to evaluate characterization according to E. M. Forster's distinction between "flat" and "round" characters. The "round" character is judged superior, because it is considered more "life-like."

If man has no innate identity, then the narrator of Barth's *End of the Road* is right when he tells us that he is only "in a sense" Jacob Horner. If there is no such thing as consistency of character, then why should Barth not have Burlingame reappear in *The Sot-Weed Factor* in multiple disguises, any one or all of which might be his "true identity." If human beings are not composed of sets of character traits, but define themselves through illusory views of the meaning of their existence, then the caricatures of *Catch-22*, each of whom is defined by his obsession, are better illustrations of

Heller's view than any "round" character could be. If there is no causal relationship between man's character and his actions, then there need be no more indication of motivation than there is in Purdy's *Malcolm*. But since all these techniques frustrate our expectations for "round" characters, are anti-realistic, we consider them untrue to life and thus fantastic.

Similarly what we face on the stage in the plays of the absurd is a group of puppets who display no emotions with which we can identify and who appear to be manipulated by the dramatists with little consideration of motivation. They are differentiated for us, like the characters in *Catch-22*, by their particular illusions or by their situation in life. In some of the plays the characters' lack of identity is shown by their changing places like Pozzo and Lucky in Beckett's *Waiting for Godot*. In *The Bald Soprano*, Mr. and Mrs. Martin become Mr. and Mrs. Smith by repeating at the end of the play the words Mr. and Mrs. Smith have used at the beginning. In this play Ionesco also emphasizes the sameness of his characters by giving a whole family the same name, Bobby Watson.

The novelists of nightmare, who refute Sartre's premises about identity, tend to employ, at least partially, the traditional methods of characterization even in a fantasy fable. This is particularly true of William Golding who claims, in complete opposition to Sartre, that human nature has an essence. *Lord of the Flies*, for example, suggests that man is innately violent. Much of the success of this novel depends, therefore, on the extent to which the characters are psychologically convincing. One can employ the old criteria of literary criticism.

Golding's view of human nature limits both the possibility and the significance of human action. Sartre and Camus, on the other hand, claim that once an individual has realized that the role by which he normally identifies himself can be changed at will, that he can choose others, then the burden of this choice, this freedom, is upon him. He is free to act but has to discover a direction in which to act. Under ordinary circumstances most human action is habitual. Camus writes: "Rising, streetcar, four hours in the office or the factory, meal, streetcar, four hours of work, meal, sleep and Monday Tuesday Wednesday Thursday Friday and Saturday according to the same rhythm—this path is easily followed most of the time. But one day the 'why' arises and everything begins in that weariness tinged with amazement."[21] Once the "why" has arisen, a man can no longer rationalize his actions by depending on the future—"We live on the future: 'tomorrow,' 'later on,' 'when you have made your way,' 'you will understand when you are old enough' "[22]—but he still has no reason for acting in any particular way.

Since the absurd teaches that there are no absolute values, all human action is, in any ultimate sense, futile. Man can depend on no outside authority to give meaning to his actions and has first to choose his criteria of judgment before he can decide what action he should perform. Nevertheless, Sartre and Camus move forward from this position to construct modes of action they consider valid. The premises about action defined in their early work are not, for them, at least, a reason for despair.

The action of a realistic novel mirrors a world in which event is not only motivated by character but is causally related to subsequent events. Action in this world is justified by absolute moral laws and can therefore be judged by external criteria. Thus it is true that the plot of a realistic novel frequently progresses to a resolution in which lessons are learned.

The moral satisfaction of meaning is suggested in the aesthetic satisfaction to be derived from the completeness of a realistic novel of plot. Frederic Jameson points out in his essay "Metacommentary" that "the novel of plot persuades us in a concrete fashion that human action, human life is somehow a complete, interlocking whole, a single, formed, meaningful substance. . . . Our satisfaction with the completeness of plot is therefore a kind of satisfaction with society as well, which has through the very possibility of such an ordering of events revealed itself to be a coherent totality, and one with which, for the moment, the individual unit, the individual human life itself, is not in contradiction."[23] Jameson's comments can be usefully applied also to the novel of nightmare which, although not a realistic novel of plot, nevertheless brings its reader to acceptance of its meaning through his aesthetic satisfaction in the completeness of its pattern.

The novelist of number or dramatist of the absurd who accepts the premise that human action is ultimately futile and, unlike Sartre and Camus, sees this as cause for despair is likely to treat the action of his novel or play very differently. The form of many of the plays of the absurd is circular to suggest the futility of human action: *The Bald Soprano* ends with a repetition of scene one; the second act of *Waiting for Godot* is almost a repetition of the first. The different stages of the action of such plays often follow each other with a dream-like rather than logical connection. In Ionesco's play, *Victims of Duty*, the probing of Choubert's mind by Madeleine and the Detective merges gradually into a sexual fantasy, linked to the preceding events only by the sexual connotations of the words used to describe Choubert's descent into his memory. There is a similar sense of a dreamlike connection between episodes in Purdy's *Malcolm* and Pynchon's *V.*

The action of many plays of the absurd and novels of number starts as familiar and becomes fantastic gradually in one of three ways. In Ionesco's *The Chairs* the old man says to the old woman, "But it's monotonous. . . . For all of the seventy-five years that we've been married, every single evening, absolutely every blessed evening, you've made me tell the same story, you've made me imitate the same people, the same months . . . always the same . . . let's talk about something else."[24] The old man's habit of doing imitations, not in itself absurd, becomes absurd in the three ways.

First, he has done the same imitations repeatedly, "every blessed evening" for seventy-five years. The repetition of ordinary action to a point of absurdity is used similarly in Ionesco's *The New Tenant* where so much furniture is moved into an apartment that there is no room for the tenant, and in *Catch-22* where Milo Minderbinder's business enterprises gradually involve the whole world. Second, he imitates months as well as people, so an absurd action develops from the familiar one, as it does in *The Lesson* where the lesson turns into a murder, or in Vonnegut's *Cat's Cradle* where a meeting of souls turns into a meeting of soles. Third, although he is annoyed at having to repeat his performance, he treats the absurdity of imitating months as if it were a normal form of behavior. In the same way the characters in *Amédée* treat the growth of the dead body in the apartment as if it were in no way unusual. This discrepancy between an event and the tone in which it is treated is a major technique in absurd plays and in the novel of number. When what is usually considered horrific is treated calmly or disinterestedly as it is by Beckett, Heller, Purdy, and Vonnegut, it may suggest the inhumanity of man's relations with his fellow, but it also inevitably implies the meaninglessness of human life and hence of human action.

One of the most important fantasy techniques concerning the action of the novel is the use of divergent accounts of the same event. Both Heller in *Catch-22* and Barth in *Giles Goat-Boy* employ it. The technique dramatizes, of course, the impossibility of establishing anything for certain, one of the Existentialist premises. The impossibility of the reader's establishing the truth about the action of the novel is simply an illustration of the novel's statement. There have been a number of contemporary novels that use history to illustrate this concept: Barth's *Sot-Weed Factor*, which takes place in seventeenth-century England and Maryland; John Fowles's *The French Lieutenant's Woman*, a "Victorian" novel, Thomas Berger's *Little Big Man*, which is set in nineteenth-century America, are examples. Each of these novels shows us that history is merely a series of subjective reports, the truth of which can never be established.

Since the world is irrational, it has no meaning that can be rationally determined. In *The Myth of Sisyphus* and *Being and Nothingness*, man's traditional tool for discovering meaning, his reason, has very limited value. Sartre and Camus point out that reason can never transcend the fact that it is a man-made tool; it is therefore powerless to discover "truth" or "reality" and can only perpetuate man's own illusory view of the world. If man attempts to find the meaning of life through reason, he rapidly reaches "those waterless deserts where thought reaches its confines."[25]

On the other hand, reason functions usefully within the boundaries of the actual. Both Sartre and Camus stress the necessity for man to make his choices according to reason. If a fire is burning down the building in which I am writing and has already blocked exit by the door, then reason tells me to estimate the distance to the ground and if possible exit by the window. This use of reason is not incompatible with what Camus calls the "absurd spirit." Camus distinguishes between these two aspects of reason: the psychological and the metaphysical. The psychological concept of reason limits itself to describing apparent reality and excludes values as incapable of rational determination. Reality can plan a journey but cannot prove the existence of God.

This dethroning of reason, for which the early work of Sartre and Camus is largely responsible, has probably created the contemporary novel's concern with the definition of sanity. The impossibility of distinguishing between madness and sanity, which concerned Pirandello in *Henry IV*, appears to have led in many recent novels to suggestions of the superiority of "madness." Ken Kesey in *One Flew Over the Cuckoo's Nest* says that those whom society defines as insane are in fact not really distinguishable from the so-called sane. In *Four-Gated City* and *Briefing for a Descent into Hell* Doris Lessing goes one stage further, claiming that "madness" may be a higher state of consciousness, a way to perceive truths the "sane" man has no knowledge of. Obviously Doris Lessing is not a novelist of number since she believes in a transcendent world beyond individual consciousness, but her interest in sanity is part of the same general questioning of the rational which Sartre and Camus provoked.

One of the defining characteristics of the novel of nightmare is its acceptance of a transcendent world which cannot be rationally discovered. The novelists of nightmare recognize that our world appears to be chaotic and irrational, but choose to have faith that it makes ultimate sense. They admit, then, that the world looks as if it is the world defined by the early work of Sartre and Camus, but they do not draw from that the same conclusions as the novelists of number. The distinction is in many ways reminiscent of that E. M. Forster makes in *A Passage to India* between "muddle" and "mystery".

The attack upon man's faith in his reason has been made through a variety of techniques in novels of number and plays of the absurd. In these works the very process of reasoning seems to break down before us. Thus not only is our illusion that life has meaning taken from us, but even the means, reason, by which we think we can find meaning. These techniques contribute more than any others perhaps to bring about the experience of the absurd, the experience of disillusionment, in the audience and reader.

The causal relationship between the clauses of a standard sentence and between the sentences of a standard paragraph implies the rational and coherent universe the Existentialists deny. In many speeches or passages of dialogue in absurd plays and novels of number this expected relationship does not take place and one word is related to the previous one through association of sound or meaning rather than to the overriding intent of the sentence. Lucky's speech in *Waiting for Godot* is a good example of this: "I resume flying gliding golf over nine and eighteen holes tennis of all sorts in a word for reasons unknown in Feckham, Peckham, Fulham, Clapham."[26]

A more frightening technique is the use of logic or apparent logic to arrive at an absurd conclusion. Sometimes this effect is achieved within the space of a short sentence, simply by the introduction of a familiar phrase where it does not fit. So in *The Lesson* the professor says, "Soon you'll know all the seasons, even with your eyes closed. Just as I do."[27] More often the dialogue becomes absurd more slowly and the appearance of logic is sustained through words and sentence structure which suggest a reasoned argument.

Occasionally, as in this passage from N. F. Simpson's *One Way Pendulum*, not only the appearance of logic but logic itself is used to make nonsense out of sense. Mr. Groomkirby has taken an oath that he will lie in court:

Judge: You mean, in other words, that you intend to lie to the court.
Mr. Groomkirby: That is so, m'lord, yes.
Judge: A frank and honest reply.
Defense Counsel: . . . The witness says he is lying, m'lord, but we have every reason to believe that in saying this he is lying.
Judge: And that he is in fact telling the truth?
Defense Counsel: That is the dilemma we are in, m'lord.
Judge: No very great dilemma. This is clearly a witness of candid integrity upon whom it would be perfectly proper to place the utmost reliance.[28]

That other instrument with which man has traditionally given meaning to his world, language, is seen in the early work of Sartre and Camus to be as worthless as reason. Language cannot define what is contingent and chaotic because in the very act of labeling or grouping it implies relationships the things themselves surpass.

Roquentin sees language and the world as hopelessly divided from one another. The word remains on his lips and refuses to go and rest upon the thing, he claims. Watt, in Samuel Beckett's novel, has a similar experience with a pot: "It resembled a pot, it was almost a pot, but it was not a pot of which one could say, Pot, pot and be comforted."[29] If man cannot describe his world, then there is no reality which men agree upon. One can indeed, as Jacob Horner explains to his freshman class in Barth's *End of the Road*, call a grammar book a horse. I do not mean, of course, to suggest that this view of language derives solely from Sartre and Camus. Wittgenstein's questioning of the relationship between word and fact is, for example, obviously relevant here.[30]

In the theater of the absurd, particularly in the plays of Ionesco, Beckett, Pinter, and Albee, our preconceptions about language as an adequate tool for communication are broken down completely. We are forced into a position from which we must look at language and are made aware of the value of each word. The most obvious way in which this is done is through attacks on the banality of everyday speech with its juxtaposition of the trivial and the important, its vague generalities, its repetitions.

We are also shown that our belief that we say what we mean is an illusion in passages which take a figure of speech literally, as in this one from Pinter's *The Dumb Waiter*:

Ben: Go on, go and light it.
Gus: Eh?
Ben: Go and light it.
Gus: Light what?
Ben: The kettle.
Gus: You mean the gas.
Ben: Who does?
Gus: You do.
Ben: What do you mean, I mean the gas?
Gus: Well, that's what you mean, don't you? The gas.
Ben: If I say go and light the kettle, I mean go and light the kettle.
Gus: How can you light a kettle?
Ben: It's a figure of speech: light the kettle. It's a figure of speech.[31]

The novelist of number works chiefly, like the dramatist of the absurd, with the actual meanings of language; his aim is to dramatize for us that what we mean and what we say are often very different. The novelist of nightmare, on the other hand, works primarily with the connotations of language, with metaphor and symbol. The multiple meanings of a given word and the relationship that this suggests between apparently disparate objects are for him evidence of pattern and therefore of mystery rather than muddle.

The methods by which one can live in a world in which the only meaning is that which one attributes to it are suggested by the novels of Sartre and Camus and discussed in Camus' *The Rebel*. The experience of the absurd has shown that all truth, all reality is relative, and it has raised certain questions. If in order to create identity from nothingness one must act, how does one choose to act? What action is meaningful when there are no absolutes? How can one act in relation to objects, including other human beings, from whom one is eternally alienated? Of what function are reason and language in a contingent, chaotic world? In other words, why live at all and if one chooses to live, by what values can one do so?

The fantasy techniques employed by novelists who accept Sartre's and Camus' premises, the novelists of number whose world view is Post-existential, serve primarily to bring about the experience of the absurd in the reader by frustrating his expectations of realism; such novelists as Heller, Purdy, Barth, Vonnegut, and Beckett have this in common. Yet, in spite of a shared sensibility, each writer responds differently to the knowledge of the absurd, and the differences in the atmosphere of the novels seem to me to reflect these various responses. Hence what for Barth is sometimes a reason to enjoy the momentary pleasures while one can, may be for Purdy a cause of pain and despair, for Beckett a reason for ironic detachment. None of these novelists responds in the same way as Sartre and Camus; none moves forward to a moral, humanistic position where, for example, political action is possible. A knowledge of the response of Sartre and Camus to the absurd dilemma is, in fact, more important to understanding the novelists of nightmare, Murdoch, Burgess, and Golding, who provide answers to the Post-existential dilemma.

Although the experience of the absurd is in a literal sense an experience of disillusionment, in which one is separated from one's illusions about the world, it is not, according to Sartre and Camus, a cause for despair. On the contrary, it is the first necessary step on the road to a genuine way of life. After this experience one has the choice of continuing to live in the spirit of what one has seen or of ignoring it and returning to one's habitual existence. If one chooses to recognize what one has seen, "the return to consciousness, the escape from everyday sleep represent the first steps of absurd freedom."[32] Awareness is in itself a value, then, and to keep this awareness alive is one of the responsibilities of the man trying to live in the spirit of the absurd: "Living is keeping the absurd alive. Keeping it alive is above all contemplating it."[33]

This awareness is not in itself enough. Iris Murdoch asks, "Can the self-aware, unillusioned consciousness take itself as a value or must the valuable be always the transcendent something by which it is haunted?"[34] The "unillusioned consciousness" is the first value, but neither Sartre nor Camus ignores the desire for "the transcendent something" which is fundamental to man. It is in fact in the name of a transcendent value that the individual must act in opposition to the irrationality of the world, seek his freedom or rebel.

The only valid form of action in an absurd world is, to Camus, rebellion. The metaphysical rebel, he explains in *The Rebel*, "opposes the principle of justice which he finds in himself to the principle of injustice which he sees being applied in the world."[35] The rebel expresses an aspiration towards order, albeit an order he knows can never be achieved. He is fighting for what should be against what is. Ironically, if he could succeed in establishing an absolute value he would only have succeeded in establishing a tyranny. The individual can be as oppressed by an absolute moral value, by absolute justice or absolute freedom, for example, as by total chaos. The value for which the rebel acts differs with each individual and is as variable as the oppression against which he revolts.

Although this value is relative, it is transcendent to the individual himself and thus a value which applies to all men. Camus explains how the individual experience of absurdity becomes collective in rebellion: "Therefore the first progressive step for a mind overwhelmed by the strangeness of things is to realize that this feeling of strangeness is shared with all men and that human reality, its entirety, suffers from the distance which separates it from the rest of the universe. The malady experienced by a single man becomes a mass plague."[36] Rebellion, then, remains individual but springs from a sense of collective oppression.

Although Sartre differs from Camus in pointing out more forcefully that the sense of collective experience can only be felt by the individual and cannot have any exterior verification, the difference is one of emphasis and is not really fundamental, for Sartre, like Camus, stresses the existing individual who acts in the name of all men. To choose to be something is to affirm at the same time the value of what one chooses. Nothing can be good for the individual without being good for all.

The most important value for Sartre is freedom which, as he explains it, includes authenticity and excludes "bad faith." To act in "bad faith" is to ignore what the experience of absurdity has taught about the nature of the world and to retreat into old habits or hide behind old absolutes, in other words to attempt to escape from freedom. Freedom to Sartre is not only the condition in which man lives, the fact that it is possible to act in any given way, but something to be chosen and worked towards. It is the choice to act in a certain way with reference to no forces beyond one's self. One could say that it was being true to oneself, except that the self is, according to Sartre, created in freedom and there is no self to be true to before the choice of freedom.

It is obvious that the choice of freedom is not easy in as much as it requires total personal responsibility for the selection of the values upon which one acts. For this reason man is always tempted to escape from freedom, to return to his habitual state, even after the experience of the absurd: "we are always ready to take refuge in a belief in determinism if this freedom weighs upon us or if we need an excuse. Thus we flee from anguish by attempting to apprehend ourselves from without as an other or a thing."[37] In other words we will often claim we cannot help how we act or how we are because we refuse to recognize the fact that we are free to choose and make ourselves.

Sartre's idea of freedom, then, differs very little from Camus' concept of rebellion. Both are individual choices to act in opposition if need be to the moral and social absolutes of their world, in the name of a value important to oneself and significant to all men. The

Existentialism of Sartre and Camus is, finally, a form of humanism, optimistic rather than pessimistic. The novelists of nightmare, William Golding, Anthony Burgess, and Iris Murdoch, refute Sartre and Camus primarily through attacks on this idea of freedom. For each of these novelists some absolute truth, some unalterable fact about human nature or the universe, often both, precludes the possibility of freedom. Golding and Burgess, who retain a belief in essence, have a deterministic view of the human condition which is in many ways more pessimistic than the Existentialism of Sartre and Camus.

Even in an irrational and meaningless world Sartre and Camus find it possible, then, to affirm in freedom and rebellion values which, although relative, make a moral and ethical life possible. One of the values they have both chosen to affirm is that of artistic creation, particularly the writing of novels. As one would expect, Camus describes the writing of fiction as an act of rebellion, Sartre as an exercise of freedom. Any work of art, explains Camus, involves choice and selection and therefore imposes limits upon and creates an order from the gratuitousness of reality. Rebellion is also a demand for order, so the writing of a novel can be seen as an act of rebellion: "The novel is born at the same time as the spirit of rebellion and expresses on the aesthetic plane, the same ambition,"[38] because "artistic creation is a demand for unity and a rejection of the world."[39]

Sartre sees the creation of a novel in basically the same way as Camus, but stresses the fact that it is a cooperative act, that the creation of order is as dependent upon reader as upon author. The artist exercises his freedom in choosing to present the world in a particular way, "by introducing order where there was none, by imposing the unity of mind on the diversity of things."[40] But a novel needs a reader in order for this creation to have the objective existence it can never have to its author who finds only himself in his work. "To write is to make an appeal to the reader that he lead into objective existence the revelation which [the author] has undertaken through language"[41]; it is an appeal to the reader's freedom.

Sartre and Camus, whose descriptions of the absurd show us that our usual view of the world is mere fiction, claim the writing of fiction as one authentic method of dealing with the absurdity of existence. Man needs to feel that his life has order and meaning; the production of a novel, which claims to be no more than an illusion, can fulfill this need. It is not surprising, then, that in an atmosphere so permeated with the Post-existential sensibility a dominant theme of the contemporary novel should be the writing of novels. As Howard M. Harper, Jr., says in a recent essay on contemporary fiction, "When subjectivity itself becomes the subject, the writer himself becomes the only real character and his own feelings and actions the only valid plot."[42] It is a theme that concerns both the writers of fantasy and such realistic novelists as Bellow, Roth, Joyce Carol Oates, and Bernard Malamud.[43] It has, of course, been the subject of earlier writers, though rarely so directly or in such large numbers. In the Romantic tradition, as Bloom points out, poetry is always, in a sense, the subject of the poem.

But although the subject of art is significant to both the novelists of nightmare and the novelists of number, their attitudes toward it are very different. The novelists of nightmare, in this instance, come close to adopting Sartre's and Camus' position, except that they see the order created by a work of art as a reflection of the essential pattern in the universe. The novelist of nightmare, under the influence of Joyce, suggests through the intricate patterning of his novel that everything is related, that the universe has meaning. The novel thus becomes a microcosm of the world; the reader accepts that the mystery of the universe is meaningful because he has been forced to construct the meaning of the novel.

The novelist of number, whose Post-existential world view denies the significance of any act, uses literature to dramatize its own impossibility. The novel of number is, therefore, self-destructive; it unmakes itself. But even an attempt to bring about an experience of the absurd in the reader is a moral gesture, an attempt to communicate one's own position. So the novelist of number in a way also affirms writing as a value. Purdy's characters may discuss the impossibility of writing today, but Purdy continues to write. Even Beckett, each of whose works is shorter and uses fewer words than the one before, cannot quite "go silent." The protagonist in the title story of John Barth's *Lost in the Funhouse* perhaps comes closest to explaining why novelists of number continue to write. If there is no absolute reason to write, there is equally no absolute reason not to. Ambrose has recognized the dual symbolic signifi-

cance of the funhouse as life and as art. The final words of the
story are: "He wishes he had never entered the funhouse. But he
has. Then he wishes he were dead. But he's not. Therefore he will
construct funhouses for others and be their secret operator—though
he would rather be among the lovers for whom funhouses were
designed."[44]

Part One

Number

Joseph Heller:
At War with Absurdity

Catch-22 is a novel about the irrationality and absurdity of war and of one man's private war against this absurdity. Heller describes a group of American fliers stationed on a fictional Italian island called Pianosa towards the end of the second world war. Each of them, like Captain Yossarian, is in some way a victim of the way his world is organized. The action of the novel concerns Yossarian's realization of this and his eventual rebellion against it in an act of freedom. The central situation is Yossarian's attempt to save his own life by avoiding any more flying missions. The experiences he undergoes in his attempt to deal with the system—interviews with Colonel Cathcart, the administrator Wintergreen, and the doctor; visits to the hospital with imaginary illnesses; brief adventures in Rome with prostitutes; a temporary involvement with a fellow officer's business ventures—only reveal to him the impossibility of saving himself while remaining within it. One must either join the system or reject it, and with his refusal to fly more missions Yossarian chooses to reject it.

Catch-22 is, however, much more than an antiwar novel. Heller's vision of the horrifying absurdity of service life in World War II is, as the constant references in the novel to its wider implications indicate, merely an illustration of the absurdity of the human condition itself.[1] *Catch-22* reflects a view of the world which is basically that defined in the early work of Sartre and Camus.[2] The world has no meaning but is simply there; man is a creature who seeks meaning. The relationship between man and his world is therefore absurd; human action having no intrinsic value is ultimately futile; human beings have no innate characteristics. Reason and language, man's tools for discovering the meaning of his existence and describing his world, are useless. When a man discovers these facts about his condition, he has an experience of the absurd, the experience which Sartre calls "nausea." But there are innumerable contemporary novels which share this Post-existential world view. What is interesting about *Catch-22* is that the fantasy techniques Heller has developed have a direct relation to the Post-existential sensibility; they are an attempt to dramatize his view of the human condition rather than merely describe it.[3]

The treatment of the soldier with convulsions Yossarian witnesses in Rome is a heightened example of many futile actions which take place throughout the novel. A group of observers lifts the soldier from the street to the hood of a car and then, because they can think of nothing else to do, back on to the street again. Pointless repetition is characteristic of almost everyone's work in the service. Major Major, for example, is involved in signing a useless proliferation of documents. Pfc. Wintergreen digs holes in Colorado and then fills them up again; he recognizes that this is not a bad assignment in wartime. It is, as he points out, "a matter of duty . . . and we each have our own to perform. My duty is to keep digging these holes."[4]

But for whom or what is one to perform this duty? The question of authority is central to the novel. God certainly no longer runs the organization, though He lingers on in certain distorted images some characters still have of Him. Colonel Cathcart wishes to use Him when it is convenient, when prayers before missions, for example, might help him get his name into the *Saturday Evening Post*, a project which he only gives up when he discovers that the enlisted men do not have a God and a chaplain of their own and would have to be included in the prayers. Mrs. Scheisskopf is too modern a woman to believe in God, but is distraught when Yossarian suggests that God might be evil and malicious. The God she does not believe in "is a good God, a just God, a merciful God" (p. 185). To Yossarian, "He's playing. Or else He's forgotten all about us"

(p. 184). As Dunbar repeats from time to time throughout the novel, "God is dead" (p. 129).

Duty is now due to such vague abstractions as patriotism and free enterprise, which have become exactly the tyrannous absolute values that Camus talks of in *The Rebel*. The old man in the brothel in Rome exposes patriotism as illogical: "Surely so many countries can't *all* be worth dying for" (p. 253). Capitalism and free enterprise lead Milo to bomb his own unit and he excuses his action with the old slogan that what is good for money-making interests is good for the country. "Incentive" and "private industry" are "goods" and their evil results cannot change anyone's attitude to them.

Such absolute values as patriotism, then, are merely words, words which have become divorced from the implications of their meaning. Heller's awareness of the separation of word and idea, which Sartre talks of, is apparent in several places in the novel. General Peckem has lost all sense of what words mean and writes his communications in a manner that combines impeccable grammar and trite adjectives: "He was always 'augmenting' things. Approaching events were never 'coming,' but always 'upcoming'" (p. 328). Language no longer communicates but serves to confuse things further. When Yossarian makes a game of censoring letters, declaring one day, "death to all modifiers," the next declaring a "war on articles," and finally blacking out everything except *a*, *an*, and *the*, he finds that it creates "a message far more universal" (p. 8).

In the world of the novel the authoritative values which determine the rules of behavior are man-made, but it would be false to suggest that they are the creation of any specific men, for example, of superior officers to trap the less fortunate, as Yossarian so often imagines. "Maybe they should give him three votes, said Yossarian. Who's they? Dunbar demanded suspiciously" (p. 15). It is this indefinable "they" who organize the world, and everyone is trapped in the organization; everyone is caught by Catch-22.

Catch-22 is, of course, Heller's symbol for the irrational nature of the world. Any attempt to argue logically and reasonably ends in a paradox; one reaches that point where thought reaches its confines, which Camus talks of. The most frequent example of Catch-22 is the argument over being "crazy" and its relation to flying more missions. Yossarian asks whether Orr can be grounded if he is "crazy," and the doctor replies that Orr has only to ask to be grounded. However, to ask to be grounded is evidence of sanity, proof that Orr is not crazy; it is Catch-22. Further examples of Catch-22 occur over the rules for asking questions in the education session and during Yossarian's visit to Pfc. Wintergreen.

Catch-22 is composed of rules apparently designed to make it impossible for a man to find a reasonable way out of them. They do not exactly contradict each other, but are continually inadequate to the occasion and always disregard the individual human life. They are intended to impose order upon chaos, but life exceeds the rules which only serve in the end to create more chaos. One of the clearest examples of this is the firemen's leaving the blaze at the hospital in order to obey the rule that they must always be on the field when the planes land. Another is the case of Doc Daneeka who is declared dead and treated as such because his name was on the flight log of a plane that crashed, although he was never in the plane and is, as everyone knows, still alive.

Such critics as Lehan and Patch who take the world of *Catch-22* to be malevolent and distinguish between this view and the world of Camus and Sartre are, I think, missing the point. Heller makes it clear that Catch-22 does not exist: "Catch-22 did not exist, he was positive of that, but it made no difference. What did matter was that everyone thought it existed" (p. 418). It is, as Thomas Blues says, "an illusion that controls the minds of men . . . a disease of the eyes."[5] An irrational world appears malevolent to man who needs meaning and rationality, just as the world frequently appears sinister to Roquentin in *Nausea* and to Rieux in Camus' *The Plague*. Heller emphasizes this through the many references to one versus all in the novel; Yossarian takes as a personal affront what is merely a general design which ignores him.

In a world where philosophical ideas, traditional morality, and reason itself are apparently useless, all man has to hold on to is his own physical body. The value which Heller supports throughout the novel is that of human existence, the individual human life. "Clevinger was dead. That was the basic flaw in his philosophy" (p. 107), and the secret which Snowden reveals to Yossarian is that "man is matter" (p. 450). Dunbar, questioned about his habit of cultivating boredom to increase his life span by making time pass more slowly, replies that, even if life this way is not very enjoyable, "what else

is there?" (p. 40). There is no talk of love or even of close friend-
ship in the book; the pleasures of life are purely physical—food,
liquor, sex—just as the only real horror is physical pain and ultimately death. "In an absurd universe," writes Frederick Karl, "the
individual has the right to seek survival . . . one's own substance
is infinitely more precious than any cause."[6]

The view of the world in *Catch-22*, then, is the same view as that
presented in the early work of Sartre and Camus, and the aware
individual in this world comes to very much the same realization
about it as does Roquentin in Sartre's *Nausea*. He realizes that there
is no ultimate reason for doing one thing rather than another. He
realizes, too, that there is "no way of really knowing anything"
(p. 274). The chaplain sees or thinks he sees a naked man in a tree
and finds it impossible to decide whether he actually saw him or
whether it was an hallucination. Colonel Cathcart becomes involved
in the same complex maze of possible interpretations when he
attempts to evaluate other people's attitudes to him, and at the end
of the novel we learn that there are always two widely divergent
official reports for every event that takes place.

When everything is questionable, it is a small step to questioning
one's own identity, and Heller gives several illustrations of the effect
of this problem on his characters. Yossarian proves with admirable
logic that the second soldier in white is the first one, because all his
identifiable characteristics, bandages and tubes, are the same. The
colonels in the brothel in Rome find they have no identity without
their uniforms. When he enters kindergarten, Major Major discovers he is not Caleb Major, but "some total stranger named Major
Major Major about whom he knew absolutely nothing and about
whom nobody else had ever heard before" (p. 87). Names, uniforms,
marks of identification are all a man has in Heller's world to assure
him of his own identity.

Yossarian and the chaplain, probably the two most aware characters in the novel, both have experiences of the absurd very similar
to those of Roquentin in Sartre's *Nausea*. The chaplain experiences
terrifying moments when familiar objects and people "took on an
unfamiliar and irregular aspect that he had never seen before and
made them seem totally strange" (pp. 209-210). Yossarian's experiences also have the effect of alienating him from his environment,
but are less concerned with the strangeness of objects than with their

profusion and gratuitousness. When he is walking in the woods, he sees "dozens of new mushrooms the rain had spawned poking their nodular fingers up through the clammy earth like lifeless stalks of flesh, sprouting in such necrotic profusion everywhere he looked that they seemed to be proliferating right before his eyes" (p. 147). In spite of all the aspects of this passage that link it to the specific situation of *Catch-22*, the suggestion of Yossarian's numerous dead friends, for example, and the rapid increase in their numbers, it would not be out of place in *Nausea*.

Like Sartre and Camus, Heller does not, however, have a totally pessimistic outlook. Unlike some other novelists of number, he believes that valid action is possible for the individual; there is even the suggestion of a sane universe for which Sweden is a symbol. The hope of Sweden is perhaps a false note in the novel,[7] but it is important to remember that it is a state of mind rather than a real place. Heller, himself, has stated that he does not see Sweden as an ideal society, but has used it in the novel to represent "a kind of Nirvana."[8] Although Orr has, at least reportedly, reached Sweden, ironically by pretending to be "crazy," Yossarian at the end of the novel does not really expect to get further than Rome, to be subject to the same pressures as on Pianosa. In the interview with Krassner, Heller points out that Yossarian is going the wrong way to get to Sweden, that he knows he is not going to get there, and that his action is important as "an act of protest."[9]

Frederick Karl describes Yossarian as "the man who acts in good faith," and claims that all he can "hope to recognize is that the universal or collective force can never comprehend the individual." He goes on to call Yossarian's final decision "a moral act of responsibility," conscious and free, while the other characters are not free because they are unaware.[10] This is all true; it is obvious that Yossarian is a man of whom Sartre would approve, but it does not go far enough. Certainly awareness is a prerequisite to the right action as Heller sees it. It is proved useless to be simply good like the chaplain or merely innocent like Nately. And certainly Yossarian acts in freedom, but in the name of what? I do not think that it is only in the name of his own individual life, although this is his starting point. What many critics have overlooked is that Yossarian changes, is the one character who learns from his experience in the novel.

At the beginning of *Catch-22* Yossarian attempts to exercise his reason to escape from the situation he is in. "Everywhere he looked was a nut, and it was all a sensible young gentleman like himself could do to maintain his perspective against so much madness" (p. 21). He soon learns, however, that everyone considers everyone else "a nut" and that when he attempts to argue logically against flying more missions he comes up against Catch-22. He realizes that to use reason in the face of the irrational is futile and that the way out of Catch-22 is simply to rebel, in Camus' sense, to take a stand, to say no. He refuses to fly any more missions. This is, of course, the way the problems of Catch-22 have been solved earlier in the novel: the young officers solve the problem of the "dead man" in Yossarian's tent simply by throwing out his possessions; Major de Coverley solves the "great loyalty oath" Catch, which is preventing the men from getting their meals, simply by saying "Give everybody eat" (p. 120).

Up to the final episode in the book, Yossarian is the great supporter of individual right. He explains to Clevinger that someone is trying to kill him and answers Clevinger's explanation that they are shooting at everyone with "What difference does that make?" (p. 17). Yossarian indeed realizes, as Karl suggests, "that one must not to be asked to give his life unless everybody is willing to give his,[11] but by the end of the novel he has come to realize the logical extension of this concept, that, if what is true for one must be applied to all, then one cannot attempt to save one's own life at the expense of others. One cannot give tacit acceptance to other people's deaths, without giving everyone the same right over oneself. One must not, as Camus says, join forces with the pestilences.

This is surely the significance of the episode in which Nately's whore tries to stab Yossarian and its relevance to his change of mind. Yossarian is given the chance to save his own life if he lies about Colonels Cathcart and Korn to their superior officers. He will, in accepting the offer, probably act as an incentive to his fellow officers to fly more missions in which many of them may be killed. After accepting the offer he is stabbed by Nately's whore and realizes perhaps that by joining those who are willing to kill, he has given everyone the right to kill him. If one rebels, one must rebel in the name of a value which transcends oneself; human life is the value for which Yossarian rebels and runs off to Rome, and it is no longer merely his own human life.

This point is stressed by Heller in Yossarian's declaration that he is going to try to save the kid sister of Nately's whore, is going to perform an unselfish act, though we obviously do not expect him to find her. If we look back at the novel in the light of what Yossarian's decision reveals, we can see that Heller has presented us with a series of character studies of selfish men and has shown how their actions for their own gain have involved death for others. They are all like Major Major's father, "a long-limbed farmer, a God-fearing, freedom-loving, rugged individualist who held that federal aid to anyone but farmers was creeping socialism" (p. 85). Milo, another "rugged individualist," bombs his own men; Colonel Cathcart, aiming at impressing the Generals to obtain promotion, keeps raising the number of missions his men must fly. To claim, as Karl does, that these characters "are not really evil in any sinister way" but just "men on the make"[12] is to miss the point. The "man on the make" is evil to Heller, since he gains at the expense of others and asks them to do what he is not willing to do himself.

The last ten pages or so of the novel may be sentimentally handled, as critics have suggested, but they present the key to a full understanding of what Heller is saying. In an irrational and gratuitous world the aware individual has to rebel, but his rebellion must be a free act and in the name of a value which can be applied to all men and does not limit their freedom. Heller's final position is, then, a humanistic one. He alone of the novelists of number comes this close to the moral positions of Sartre and Camus. It is perhaps noteworthy that the final section of the novel, developing this view, is far more realistic in technique than the major portion of it.[13]

In a discussion of the techniques Heller has employed to convey his basically Post-existential view of the world it would be easy to ignore the obvious. *Catch-22* is a very funny book. It would be easy to ignore this because, in spite of the laughter it evokes, the overall impression one is left with is as much of horror as of humor.[14] The laughter evoked is not of the kind that unites us warmly in sympathy with the human race as we enjoy its foibles, but rather serves to alienate us by exposing the bitter ironies of existence. It is laughter of which Beckett would approve. Nevertheless, I believe that humor is a way of understanding the techniques of the novel. Laughter, as Bergson suggests, is caused by incongruity, by a frustrating of our expectations of a certain result, and it is a failure to fulfill certain of the reader's expectations which is the link underlying the fantasy techniques of the novel.

What is the basis of these expectations? When we discover that Milo has become mayor or civic leader of almost every town in Europe and North Africa, we are amused because that is impossible. We do not expect that to happen to anyone in life. It is not lifelike, not realistic. But when the reader is confronted with the juxta-position in one sentence of references to several unrelated events about which he so far knows nothing, we cannot say that it is not like life. Actually it is; we often overhear conversations which are meaningless to us because we do not understand to whom or to what the references apply. Yet we are surprised to find it in a novel. In this instance, obviously, it is our expectations about the nature of the novel, not about life, that are not fulfilled. In some way each technique Heller uses plays against and frustrates the reader's expectations of a novel, the illusions, one could say, that he has about the nature of the novel. The techniques are, then, techniques of the novel of number, designed to alienate the reader's con-sciousness, to take him to the void.

It is obvious that the narrative technique of *Catch-22* does not fulfill the expectation of the reader for a continuous line of action with one episode related to the next, at the very least chronologically, and with events life-size and probable. Situations initially familiar enough to the reader may be gradually exaggerated to the point of absurdity. Oil was always discovered wherever Chief White Halfoat's family pitched their tents, Halfoat explains, and the oil companies began sending out representatives to follow the family. Suddenly the whole action becomes incredible; the representatives begin to guess where the family is going, arrive there first, and prevent the Halfoats from pitching their tents. Captain Black's "Glorious Loyalty Oath Crusade" gets out of hand in a similar way when he makes everyone sign "two loyalty oaths, then three, then four" and introduces "the pledge of allegiance and after that 'The Star-Spangled Banner,' one chorus, two choruses, three choruses, four choruses" (p. 117), as do Dobbs's plans to murder Colonel Cathcart, which end in his planning to murder almost everyone. Many of the descrip-tions of exaggerated action concern Milo, whose activities become increasingly complex as the novel progresses. In this way each action parodies itself by suggesting the possibility of its endless progression.

The futility of all human action is suggested by Heller in the number of times events or conversations are repeated so that the reader, like Yossarian, eventually has the feeling that he has "been through this exact conversation before" (p. 455).[15] The dialogue that concludes with the realization that "crazy" men can be grounded but only "crazy" men will fly occurs numerous times, as does the pattern of Yossarian's conversations with the chaplain in which comments are punctuated continually by the phrases "that's bad" or "that's good." Colonel Cathcart's comment to Major Major when he tells him that he is the new squadron commander is similarly repeated. There are two trial scenes in the novel, one concerning Clevinger and the other the chaplain, and each follows the same pattern and comes to the same conclusion: "Clevinger was guilty, of course, or he would not have been accused, and since the only way to prove it was to find him guilty, it was their patriotic duty to do so" (p. 82).

The same sense of the futility of human endeavor is conveyed by circular actions like the episode of Hungry Joe and Huple's cat. Hungry Joe dreams that Huple's cat is sleeping on his face, suffocating him, and when he wakes up Huple's cat is sleeping on his face. Yossarian organizes a fight between Joe and the cat, but the cat flees and Joe is declared the winner, goes to bed victorious and dreams that Huple's cat is sleeping on his face, suffocating him.

The narrative technique serves to confuse the reader about time and to destroy any certainty he may have about what has taken place, thus creating in him the same doubts about reality that Yossarian experiences and that Sartre and Camus speak of.[16] Heller employs three basic methods of disrupting the expected chronological flow of the action. The first is a simple one. He often makes a statement about an event which has taken place and deliberately omits the clarification the statement requires. Therefore many of the major events in the novel are referred to two or three times, sometimes in increasing detail, before the full account is given. There are two references to Milo's bombing his own squadron before we are given the details; two to his ability to buy eggs at seven cents and sell them at a profit at five cents. The first reference to Snowden comes in the question Yossarian asks in the education session, and we learn simply that he was killed over Avignon. Half of the scene in which Snowden dies is described some twenty pages later, and it is almost two hundred pages before that scene is picked up again and continued to the point at which Yossarian sees Snowden. In the next reference we learn that Yossarian treated Snowden for the wrong wound and then finally, almost at the end of the novel, we are given the whole account. Occasionally the initial statement may be about an apparently impossible event, like the casual reference to the "dead man in Yossarian's tent" who "was simply not easy to live with" (p. 22). It is a hundred pages before we discover that this really refers to the possessions of a man who has been killed in action.

The second device creates confusion in the mind of the reader by presenting him with two apparently contradictory statements about the same event before providing a clarification. For example, Doc Daneeka tells Yossarian that he was drafted just when his business was beginning to show a profit. Later he describes himself as fortunate that the war broke out when things were at their blackest. Finally the explanation is given: the war initially improved his business, but being drafted prevented his profiting from it. A similar effect is created by the apparently absurd coincidence of Major Major and Yossarian independently signing Washington Irving's name to official papers, until it is revealed that Major Major obtained the idea by hearing about Yossarian's activities from a C.I.D. man.

The third method is an extension of the second; contradictory accounts are given of an event and no solution is provided. The reader is left uncertain of the truth and in some instances asked to believe the incredible. The C.I.D. man is supposed to have caught a cold from the fighter captain who, we are told, did not have a cold; Milo claims that he did not direct the antiaircraft fire upon his own planes, then that he did. Chief White Halfoat's incredible story about his family being moved every time oil is discovered is called a lie by Yossarian, but Halfoat is transferred to Pianosa from Colorado at the first mention of oil. Some of these techniques of action resemble, superficially at least, those found in certain novels of nightmare. Burgess's *Tremor of Intent*, for example, contains scenes which are exaggerated to absurdity. But while the novelist of nightmare may initially confuse the reader, he eventually takes him forward to the solution. He never leaves him, as the novelist of number does, with an insoluble contradiction.

As well as confusing the reader about the time or exact nature of the events in the novel, Heller also frequently shocks him by adopting attitudes to subjects or situations opposite to the expected ones. By introducing these unexpected attitudes in a very casual way, he not only challenges the traditional value system but suggests through his tone that nothing unusual is being said, thus doubling the shock effect. Nately, we are told, "had a bad start. He came from a good family" (p. 13), and "did not hate his mother and father, even though they had been very good to him" (p. 255). Yossarian is sorry to hear that he and the chaplain have a mutual friend, because "it seemed there was a basis to their conversation after all" (p. 12). The Texan is "good-natured, generous and likable. In three days no-one could stand him" (p. 10).

The disparity between tone and subject matter is exploited by Heller most successfully in his treatment of horrific situations, particularly those involving death or human suffering. Lieutenant Scheisskopf, anxious to have his men march in perfect formation in parades, wishes to nail his men together, but has to abandon the plan because he cannot obtain the necessary nickel-alloy swivels and does not believe the surgeons will cooperate. The plainness of the description of the soldier-in-white's death in the hospital suggests both that the loss of life has become a mere matter of routine and that language is doomed to failure when it attempts to convey the major human experiences. The language of this section is bald, without metaphor and almost completely lacking in adjectives and adverbs. The soldier-in-white has apparently been kept alive by having his urine pumped back into his body; this is treated as normal medical practice.

Heller's methods of characterization, like his narrative techniques and his use of tone, depend upon a frustration of the reader's expectations of realism.[17] According to the traditional view, as Robbe-Grillet claims, a character has to have a proper name, parents, heredity, profession, and a personality which permits the reader to judge him, love him, or hate him. There are two possible ways of failing to fulfill a reader's expectations about character in a novel: one is to change the character's identity, provide multiple personalities for the same name, or one name for various figures, and thus disturb the reader's whole conception of identity, as do John Barth and Samuel Beckett; the other is to provide caricatures, figures who are no more than puppets and in whom the reader is not expected to believe. Heller occasionally appears to experiment with the first method, as, for example, in the scenes where Yossarian pretends to be a dying officer whose parents fail to recognize him and where Yossarian and Dunbar discover they can change identities by changing hospital beds. But although in these scenes the characters experience doubts about their identities, the reader is always quite clear about the identity of the character and no real confusion is created.

Most of the characters in *Catch-22* are, however, caricatures, cardboard figures who are distinguished for the reader by their particular obsessions. Each lives with an illusory view of the world that isolates him and makes the results of his actions very different from his expectations. Each is, in his way, the unaware individual who, as Camus illustrates in *The Myth of Sisyphus*, believes that he can operate in the world as he imagines it and that his actions will achieve their purpose. So Hungry Joe devotes his life to taking pictures that never come out, Scheisskopf to conducting parades, Major Major to avoiding everyone. General Peckem, continually writing memoranda recommending that his Special Services Division be placed in control over the combat forces, finds that by the time he has succeeded he has been "promoted" to head of combat forces and someone else is now his superior. Colonel Cathcart, anxious for promotion to General, institutes a variety of plans to make himself popular with his superiors, but each of them leaves him less popular than he was before.

Most of these characters are introduced to us in deceptively explanatory paragraphs which appear to sum up their personalities in a few adjectives, but which really provide the reader with irreconcilably opposite traits. Colonel Cathcart, for example, was a "slick, successful, slipshod, unhappy man of thirty-six who lumbered when he walked and wanted to be a general. He was dashing and dejected, poised and chagrined" (p. 191). Gradually the characters become increasingly absurd as the personality traits of each are seen to be one, an obsession. It is believable that one of Milo's moral principles was that "it was never a sin to charge as much as the traffic could bear" (p. 66), but by the time his activities, which are centered in Palermo, have taken over Europe and North Africa in one vast Mafia-like syndicate and he has bombed his own men, he has become little more than a personification of greed. These characters may have names, parents, heredity, professions, and faces, but we cannot very long sustain the illusion that they are "real" human beings. I do not mean to suggest, of course, that all contemporary fantasy novels in which the characters are flat are novels of number. Novelists of nightmare, for different reasons, often employ flat characters, which are typical, after all, of the fable form.

The most important device a novelist has to suggest an irrational world is, of course, the treatment of reason itself.[18] Reasoning, in *Catch-22*, invariably ends up in some variation of Catch-22; apparent logic is used to destroy sense. The reader is led into following an argument which progresses logically, but which arrives at an absurd conclusion. Clevinger is on trial for attempting to disrupt Scheisskopf's parade:

> "In sixty days you'll be fighting Billy Petrolle," the colonel with the big fat mustache roared. "And you think it's a big fat joke."
> "I don't think it's a joke, sir," Clevinger replied.
> "Don't interrupt."
> "Yes, sir."
> "And say, 'sir,' when you do," ordered Major Metcalf.
> "Yes, sir."
> "Weren't you just ordered not to interrupt?" Major Metcalf inquired coldly.
> "But I didn't interrupt, sir," Clevinger protested.
> "No. And you didn't say 'sir' either. Add that to the charges against him," Major Metcalf directed the corporal who could take shorthand. "Failure to say 'sir' to superior officers when not interrupting them" (p. 77).

A similar conversation takes place between Yossarian and Luciana, who will not marry Yossarian because he is "crazy" and knows he is "crazy" because he wants to marry her.

Occasionally a statement which seems perfectly reasonable is invalidated by a subsequent statement, often a premise rendering it superfluous: Nurse Duckett, we are told, was "one of the ward nurses who didn't like Yossarian." A sentence or two further on we read, "None of the nurses liked Yossarian" (p.7). The end of the paragraph cancels its beginning in a manner characteristic of the novel of number.

Individual sentences in the novel may appear to be absurd when they are in fact completely logical: "I didn't know there were any other Captain Yossarians. As far as I know, I'm the only Captain Yossarian I know, but that's only as far as I know" (p. 13). In other instances the structure and tone of sentences suggest meaning where in fact there is none: "He had decided to live for ever or die in the attempt" (p. 30). "You're American officers. The officers of no other army in the world can make that statement. Think about it" (p. 28), says Colonel Cargill to his men.

Sentence structure is used throughout *Catch-22* to add to the reader's confusion about characters and events and contributes to the impression of an irrational world.[19] The novel is full of complex sentences with the individual clauses and phrases unrelated to each other or related at a tangent: "McWatt wore fleecy bedroom slippers with his red pajamas and slept between freshly pressed colored bedsheets like the one Milo had retrieved half of for him from the grinning thief with the sweet tooth in exchange for none of the pitted dates Milo had borrowed from Yossarian" (p. 61). As the sentence progresses each new clause or phrase does not clarify what has gone before but adds new complications: "Immediately next door to Yossarian was Havermeyer, who liked peanut brittle and lived all by himself in the two man tent in which he shot tiny field mice every night with huge bullets from the .45 he had stolen from the dead man in Yossarian's tent" (p. 18). A lack of subordination in sentence structure suggests that in a universe without values everything is of equal importance.

Heller's frequent use of lists similarly implies a contingent universe consisting of things which are simply there: "Hungry Joe ate voraciously—stammered, choked, itched, sweated, salivated" (p. 53); "There were diseases of the skin, diseases of the bone, diseases of the lung, diseases of the stomach, diseases of the heart, blood and arteries. There were diseases of the head, diseases of the neck, diseases of the chest, diseases of the intestines, diseases of the crotch" (p. 177).

A statement is often qualified by a negative clause that gives the appearance of clarifying but, of course, adds nothing: Nately "had gone every free day to work on the officers' club that Yossarian had not helped to build" (p. 18); "on the other side of Haver-meyer stood the tent McWatt no longer shared with Clevinger, who had still not returned when Yossarian came out of the hospital" (p.18). Heller's favorite stylistic device is the use of double or triple negatives in one sentence. This gives that effect of language constantly trying, but always just failing, to describe or define, which the reader is aware of throughout the novel. "And if that wasn't funny," we are told, "there were lots of things that weren't even funnier" (p. 17). "But Yossarian couldn't be happy, even though the Texan didn't want him to be" (p. 16). And Major Major's father has learned that "the more alfalfa he did not grow, the more money the government gave him, and he spent every penny he didn't earn on new land to increase the amount of alfalfa he did not produce" (p. 85).

The style of *Catch-22*, like the narrative technique, the tone and the methods of characterization, serves to frustrate the reader's expectations. Each of the techniques I have discussed depends for its effect upon a preconception of the reader that a novel tells a story, is peopled with recognizably human beings and is written in a style which justifies Ian Watt's claim that "the function of language is much more largely referential in the novel than in other literary forms."[20] The reader expects to be drawn into the world of a novel, but *Catch-22*, while initially providing him with familiar human situations, ends by rejecting him. It is anti-literature, a novel of number. The novel itself becomes an object providing the reader with the experience of the absurd, just as the trees provide it for Roquentin in Sartre's *Nausea*. After attempting to relate his preconceptions about novels, his "illusions" about the form, to this novel, the reader is finally stripped of them. *Catch-22* simultaneously shows man's illusory view of the world, employs techniques to suggest the irrational nature of the world, and is itself an object against which the truth of its statements may be tested.

Chapter Two

John Barth:
Imitations of Imitations

The direct influence of the early ideas of Sartre and Camus upon the work of John Barth[1] is probably more clearly marked than upon that of any other contemporary American novelist. There are several overt references to Existentialism in the novels. In *End of the Road*, the doctor advises Jacob Horner to "read Sartre and become an Existentialist" (p. 68); in *Chimera*, Polyeidus gives a lecture "on what he called the proto-existentialist view of the ontological metamorphosis" (p. 167). Barth's first two novels deal with central Existentialist problems: *The Floating Opera* with the question of suicide in a meaningless world which is, of course, Camus' concern in *The Myth of Sisyphus*; *End of the Road* with the possibility of action when there is no absolute reason for doing anything. In his discussion of *The Sot-Weed Factor*, Leslie Fiedler claims that Barth "finds in history not merely the truth, not really the truth at all . . . but absurdity," [2] and call him an "existential comedian."[3]

Although Barth's philosophic stance has not changed noticeably since his first novel, it is only since *End of the Road* that the Post-existential world view appears to have had a marked effect upon his techniques. In a 1967 article entitled "The Literature of Exhaustion," Barth gives a few unclarified clues about his intentions as a novelist.

Although they are only clues, it is possible to piece together from them a coherent theory closely related to Post-existentialist ideas. In his article Barth praises the work of Jorge Luis Borges, who claims that "the world is our dream, our idea, in which 'tenuous and eternal crevices of unreason' can be found to remind us that our creation is false or at least fictive." [4] The idea that there is no reality that can be apprehended by man, that all the absolute meaning man thinks he finds is subjective and therefore "false"—a concept fundamental to the early work of Sartre—underlies Barth's most recent techniques. Attempting to remind the reader constantly that life is as fictional as art, he has written two novels which, he claims in this article, are imitations not of life but of novels: "If you were the author of this paper, you'd have written something like *The Sot-Weed Factor* or *Giles Goat-Boy*: novels which imitate the form of the Novel, by an author who imitates the role of Author."[5]

What exactly Barth means by this is not stated in the article but, if one bears in mind also his concern with novels as images of exhaustion, his meaning becomes clearer. There seem to me to be three ways in which a novel can be an imitation of "the form of the Novel, by an author who imitates the role of Author." On the simplest level Barth is talking of parody. A novel that deliberately exaggerates the characteristics of a certain type of novel, as *The Sot-Weed Factor* exaggerates the characteristics of the picaresque, is an imitation of a form. And, since any work of art is an imitation, in the sense of being an imitation of life, any work of art which parodies another is an imitation of an imitation.

But exaggeration of formal characteristics is not essential to achieve ironic effect. If an eighteenth-century picaresque novel were presented, without exaggeration, to a twentieth-century audience as a twentieth-century work, it would be differently understood. It would, in fact, suggests Barth, mean something different, because the twentieth-century audience would react from a different philosophic and artistic viewpoint. Barth could have merely "rewritten" *Tom Jones*, for example, as Borges "rewrites" *Don Quixote* in his short story "Pierre Menard, Author of the Quixote," using exactly the same words as Cervantes, and the sole fact that it was written in 1960 would have made its effect entirely different from that of the original: "I mentioned earlier that if Beethoven's Sixth were composed today, it would be an embarrassment; but clearly it wouldn't necessarily, if done with ironic intent by a composer quite aware of where we've been and where we are. It would have then, potentially, for better or worse, the kind of significance of Warhol's Campbell's Soup ads; the difference being that in the former case a work of art is being reproduced instead of a work of non-art, and the ironic comment would therefore be more directly on the genre and the history of art, then on the state of the culture."[6] Hence works of art can become imitations of themselves, without change, simply by being transported into a different environment.

The same effect can be achieved, of course, by an author imitating the role of an eighteenth-century novelist and writing an imitation of an eighteenth-century novel in the twentieth century. The possibilities are endless since, as time progresses, works of art can be repeated and repeated, and their changed environment will make them different. It is an image of exhaustion. Barth, like Beckett, offers us "a segment in an endless series . . . a comedy of 'exhaustive enumeration.' "[7]

The third implication in Barth's article is a question of self-conscious art. Barth says he is an author imitating the role of an author. In *Giles Goat-Boy* there is a writer, J.B., who is presenting a novel about Giles. But there is also, of course, a novelist John Barth who is writing about J.B. writing about Giles. As in Beckett's novels each "author" invalidates the previous ones, by revealing the fictional nature of his statements. The reader is taken towards the void as the novel gradually unmakes itself. This is also an image of exhaustion, since there could be another John Barth playing the role of John Barth, novelist, writing about J.B., who is writing about Giles. "When the characters in a work of fiction become readers or authors of the fiction they're in, we're reminded of the fictitious aspect of our own existence,"[8] explains Barth. Imagine a camera, focused upon a film, itself an imitation, which moves back to show a viewer watching the film. Another camera then shows the camera filming the viewer watching the film. An endless progression of illusions is possible. The second and third implications of Barth's statement are related to each other, of course: one is an infinite movement forward in time; the other an infinite movement backward in space. They are both techniques of the novel of number.

The interest in the relationship between fiction and reality links Barth to Purdy, who deals with the theme in *Cabot Wright Begins* and whose *Eustace Chisholm and the Works*, can also be considered an imitation of a novel. It links him even more closely perhaps with dramatists of the absurd like Jean Genet and Jack Gelber in their attempt to break down the expected audience/actor relationship by making the audience part of the play. What Barth is attempting to do in his novels is what Genet does when he has Irma in the final speech of *The Balcony* tell the audience to go home where everything will be just as false as it has been on the stage; or what Gelber does in *The Connection* when he has his actors behave as if they were spontaneously creating the play they are in. And just as in order to understand the techniques at work in the theatre of the absurd, it is necessary to realize that the theatrical expectations of even a contemporary audience are still those of realistic drama, in order to understand what Barth is doing one must realize that readers of novels still expect the conventions of the realistic novel.

In his first novel, *The Floating Opera*, Barth is concerned with the problem Camus claims is fundamental to living with the absurd, the problem of suicide. Todd Andrews, hero and narrator, relates the events of one day in his life when he decides to commit suicide and then chooses not to. His account of this day involves him in flashback descriptions of his relationship with a friend, Harrison Mack, and his wife, Jane, with whom Andrews has been having an affair. Jane had a child, Jeannine, who may be Andrew's daughter. It is the familiar triangle with a twist; the affair was originally suggested by Harrison as a way of showing his freedom from such false values as sexual fidelity. Mature people are not jealous, he argues. Andrews is also Harrison's lawyer in a very involved suit over his father's will.

Andrews suffers from a heart condition which may kill him at any moment, and his life has been a series of attempts to come to terms with this fact: "This fact—the fact that having begun this sentence, I may not live to write its end . . . this for thirty-five years has been the overwhelming condition of my existence, the great fact of my life" (p. 57). This condition, as Barth points out at the end of the novel and Andrews comes to realize, is the great fact of every man's life. Death, as Camus claims in *The Myth of Sisyphus*, is the one certainty.

In order to come to terms with this fact of his life, Andrews has adopted a series of attitudes, a series of approaches to the world: "Each stance, it seemed to me at the time, represented the answer to my dilemma, the mastery of my fact; but always something would happen to demonstrate the inadequacy of my conclusion" (p. 22). None of Andrew's conclusions about the world is final, of course, because the world in its gratuitousness and irrationality always intervenes, just as it does in the novels of Vonnegut and Purdy. But Andrews, unlike most of the heroes of Vonnegut and Purdy, realizes that his conclusions are necessarily subjective and therefore always false.

Barth uses two symbols in the novel to convey this Post-existentialist view of the human condition. The first is the metaphor of the floating opera itself, a show boat drifting up and down a river on the tide, so that the audience on the banks sees only what is going on when it happens to pass: "Most times they wouldn't understand what was going on at all, or they'd think they knew, when actually they didn't. Lots of times they'd be able to see the actors, but not hear them. Need I explain? That's how much of life works" (p. 13). The second symbol is the Inquiry which Todd Andrews is undertaking into his father's suicide. To collect and understand the causes of any human act, Andrews finds, is a lengthy process since one can never be sure that one has discovered all the facts. Then he realizes his interpretations of the facts will be subjective and therefore biased, and this realization inaugurates an inquiry into his own motives. The task, obviously, is endless, as is any attempt to understand human existence. Nothing can ever be established for certain in the world as Barth sees it. Andrews cannot even establish for certain whether the day upon which these events happened was June 23 or June 24. There is no absolute meaning in life, as Andrews tells his reader: "The truth is multiform" (p. 245).

If there is no absolute truth, Todd Andrews realizes, there is then no reason for doing anything. "Everything, I'm afraid, is significant, and nothing is finally important" (p. 12). In a conversation with Andrews, old Mr. Haecker, a resident of the hotel in which Andrews lives, claims that there is at least an absolute value to human life and Todd replies, "I deny it . . . there's no reason why you shouldn't believe that, but you can't prove it" (p. 178). It is following this conversation that Todd reaches the conclusion upon which his determination to kill himself is based: "*nothing* is intrinsically valuable; the value of everything is attributed to it, assigned to it, from outside the thing itself, by people" (p. 180). If there is no ultimate reason for valuing anything, no reason for action in any form, there is no reason for living, Todd argues.

When his suicide attempt is accidently interrupted, Todd finds himself paralyzed, unable to speak or explain, because he can see no reason to do so. In the first published edition of the novel, revised on an editor's advice to make it less pessimistic, it is the sickness of the small child, who is perhaps his daughter, that rouses him from the paralysis: "The first desperate sound of Jane's voice had snapped me out of a paralysis which there was no reason to terminate" (p. 266).[9] This incident leads Todd to reach the logical extension of his previous arguments: if there is no reason to live, then equally there is no reason for suicide; even if the value of a little girl's life is only relative, there are, after all, relative values.

Todd Andrews's position at the end of *The Floating Opera* is, then, very similar to that of the early Sartre and Camus. Man may be simply another gratuitous object in an irrational world, his actions may be ultimately futile and therefore ridiculous, but it is possible to go on living without absolutes. Man is free to choose his own values—"there is little need for weakness, reader: you are freer, perhaps, than you'd be comfortable knowing" (p. 108)—and to live by them even in an absurd world.

Unlike Sartre and Camus, however, Barth appears to feel that these values can be entirely personal, as Todd Andrews's are when he invests value in the life of his daughter. Nowhere does Barth suggest that in choosing values, man must choose for all men by holding valuable something which transcends personal interest. Todd Andrews goes on living to enjoy the immediate pleasures, and this attitude illustrates Barth's response to the dilemma of the absurd. It is perhaps wrong to say Todd "chooses" any values. In the end his heart does betray him and all his carefully argued reasons for suicide collapse before his spontaneous feeling for Jeannine. Similarly, earlier in the novel Harrison Mack's intellectual exercise of his freedom has collapsed before his jealousy over his wife's affair with Todd, and a German soldier has died because Todd feels he must trust his reason, which tells him this is an enemy, rather than his heart, which tells him this is a brother. This novel is the only one of Barth's to end on a humanistic note; it is worth remembering that the changes were made on an editor's advice.

Barth's interest in the relationship between the content and form of fiction, which he discusses in his article "The Literature of Exhaustion," is made apparent twice in *The Floating Opera*. He explains to the reader that the symbol of the floating opera showboat applies not only to life but to the structure of his novel: "And that's how this book will work. I'm sure. It's a floating opera, friend . . . you'll catch sight of it, then lose it, then spy it again" (p. 14). Although *The Floating Opera* is in fact quite easy to follow, the concept of a novel reflecting the irrational world and as impossible to interpret as life itself—a concept realized in *The Sot-Weed Factor* and *Giles Goat-Boy*—is implicit in this early statement. He discusses his inability to "stick to the straight highway of the plot, when there's half a world on either side" (p. 182), thus implying that the conventional form of a novel fails to imitate the gratuitousness and irrelevancies of life. He feels that he will not escape "the reckless charge of disorganization from those who would prefer our world to be a rational one, in which single chapters have single introductions and all chapters are relevant" (p. 182).

In spite of this interest in form, however, Barth's first novel remains fairly close to a traditional realism. It is not itself a novel of number, although it experiments with some of the techniques of the novel of number. Only twice does he hint at the exaggeration of action to absurdity he uses in his later novels to suggest the futility of human action. The first time is in the conversation among Captain Osborn and his friends on the "loafer's bench," which has no real relevance to the novel but is allowed to continue for a whole chapter, mirroring the irrational comments typical of senile old men. The second is in Andrews's description of the lawsuit between the Butlers and the Mortons which exaggerates the complexities of legal reasoning and terminology.

Once Barth also employs the technique of reasoning logically to absurdity, which he calls in this novel reasoning "to the end of the line." In *The Sot-Weed Factor*, where it is used much more frequently, it is called "the pit." In *The Floating Opera* this conversation takes place between the little girl Jeannine and Andrews:

"Why do the actors act funny?"
"They do that so the people will pay to some to see them. They want to earn money."
"Why?"

"So they can eat. They like eating."
"Why?"
"You have to eat to stay alive. They like staying alive."
"Why?"
"That's the end of the line again" (p. 210).

What is most interesting in the form of *The Floating Opera* is the first indication of the techniques Barth develops for *The Sot-Weed Factor* and *Giles Goat-Boy*. Throughout the novel Todd Andrews "plays the role of author," constantly commenting on the problems of writing, and thus makes the novel very self-consciously a work of fiction. In this way Barth reminds the reader that he is reading, much as Genet, Gelber, and Ionesco remind their audiences that they are watching a play. The difference here is that it is the narrator who is self-conscious, not the author; these comments to the reader can therefore be taken as realism rather than as a fantasy technique. Nevertheless, the effect of this is to separate the reader from the experiences described in the novel, to frustrate his expectations of involvement in a "slice of life."

At the very beginning of *The Floating Opera*, Andrews addresses the reader: "Good heavens! How does one write a novel? I mean, how can anybody possibly stick to the story, if he's at all sensitive to the significance of things?" (p. 8). After springing the surprise introduction of the heroine of the novel, Andrews again comments on what he is doing: "either you're familiar with the business of climaxes and anti climaxes, in which case no explanation is necessary, or else you know even less about story telling than I do, in which case an explanation would be useless" (p. 26). The interplay between fiction and reality is suggested in Andrews's comments on symbolism, comments which imply, like Princeton Keith's remarks on coincidence in *Cabot Wright Begins*, that the conventions of novels fail to mirror life by insisting on probability: "One is constantly being confronted with a sun that bursts from behind clouds just as the home team takes the ball; . . . So, reader, should you ever find yourself writing about the world, take care not to nibble at the tempting symbols she sets squarely in your path" (pp. 116-117).

Once in the novel Barth extends this technique by having Todd comment on his own comments on his own writing, a method he exploits more fully in *Giles Goat-Boy*: "And I lose even by explaining

my discomfiture concerning these juxtaposed mirrors—the one on the
street and the one in the bedroom—because the explanation itself is
arch, painfully so, and my pointing out its archness archer still, until,
like any image caught between facing mirrors, this conclusion loses
itself, like a surrealist colonnade, in an infinite regress of archness. I
apologize" (p. 123). Ironically, Barth adds one final "archness" to
his comments on archness, by apologizing for linking his chapters
with the image of two mirrors and including in that apology the
simile of facing mirrors. This technique is, of course, an image of
exhaustion, as is the metaphor used within it, that of facing mirrors.
It is also the sort of self-parody Poirier talks of in *The Performing
Self,* characteristic of the novel of number.

End of the Road, Barth's second novel, presents three different
approaches to the Existentialist dilemma in the form of three characters, Jacob Horner, Joe Morgan, and the Doctor. Jacob Horner,
paralyzed because he can see no reason to act, is discovered by a
self-styled doctor on a railway station bench. The doctor suggests
Horner try teaching as a form of therapy, and in a teachers' training
college in Maryland Horner meets Joe Morgan and his wife Rennie.
The action of the novel concerns Horner's relationship with the Mor-
gans, his affair with Rennie and a subsequent abortion. It ends with
Horner's return to an institution, where he writes his experiences. The
novel has the same basic situation as *The Floating Opera* and can be
seen as an "imitation" of it.

The first sentence of the novel gives the key to Jacob Horner's
problem. "In a sense, I am Jacob Horner" (p. 5). Jacob has no real
identity. The Doctor accuses him of having a "vacuum" for a self
and Rennie says to him: "I think you don't even exist at all. . . . You
cancel yourself out. You're more like somebody in a dream. You're
not strong and you're not weak. You're nothing" (p. 55). Jacob
knows this to be true of himself, since he has long been aware of what
he calls his "weatherless days," days in which he has no mood and
therefore no identity. Jacob realizes, too, that any character we attribute to other people is bound to be at least partly false and that "he
is wise who realizes that his role-assigning is at best an arbitrary
distortion of the actors' personalities" (p. 25).

Jacob's problem is not, however, just that he has no innate character—Barth, like Sartre, feels that the self has no intrinsic qualities—but
that he cannot form one, cannot adopt a personality, because he is

incapable of action most of the time. He is subject to fits of total paralysis because, realizing that there are no absolute reasons for doing anything, he cannot make a decision. Jacob even has difficulties over so small a matter as the position in which he sits when talking to the Doctor. Similarly, he can see a host of reasons for applying for a job at Wicomico State Teachers' College and a host of reasons not to, for having the interview on Monday or on some other day, for approving of the Doctor and for disapproving of him, for agreeing with Joe Morgan and for refuting his arguments. Jacob is able "to maintain with perfectly equal unenthusiasm contradictory, or at least polarized, opinions at once on a given subject" (p. 96), because, he claims, he suffers from cosmopsis, the cosmic view, in which "there is no reason to do anything" (p. 60).

The Doctor, who recommends that he read Sartre, sets out to cure Jacob by imposing order upon him. He tells him to teach grammar "No description at all. No optional situations. Teach the rules. Teach the truth about grammar" (p. 8)—and to make all decisions arbitrarily on an alphabetical or chronological basis. The Doctor realizes that there is no such thing as truth, that the world is arbitrary, is "everything that is the case, and what the case is is not a matter of logic" (p. 66). In this world, the Doctor claims, like Sartre, human beings have only a chosen identity, that therefore "Choosing is existence: to the extent that you don't choose, you don't exist" (p. 67).

The Doctor is the one character who survives in the novel, but this is not because he avows Existentialist premises but because he recognizes the dangers inherent in any generalizations, even Existentialist ones: "Those are both good Existentialist premises, and whether they're true or false is of no concern to us—they're useful in your case" (p. 71). He explains to Jacob that he does not treat paralysis, but paralyzed Jacob Horner. What the Doctor does in fact is to apply the Existentialist premise that there are no absolutes to Existentialist premises themselves.

Joe Morgan's life is destroyed because he fails to do this. Joe is the antithesis of Jacob; he has reasons for everything he does. Joe knows that "Nothing matters one way or another ultimately" (p. 36), that his own values are relative, and that "the only demonstrable index to a man's desires is his acts " (p. 42). The trouble with Joe is that he has made reason an absolute, believes that "intelligence will solve all problems" (p. 99), and applies his chosen value to all circumstances. He can defend his position logically, but cannot solve his problems with it. He insists on knowing why Rennie and Jacob committed adultery even when it becomes increasingly clear that they had no reasons. Life destroys his world through a chance accident during an abortion: "What the case is is not a matter of logic" (p. 66).

Barth thinks, then, that reason is an inadequate tool for dealing with the world, and language is inadequate to describe it. Jacob Horner explains: "Assigning names to things is like assigning roles to people: it is necessarily a distortion" (p. 114). Once we describe anything, give it a name, or classify it, we have already falsified it: "To turn experience into speech—that is, to classify, to categorize, to conceptualize, to grammarize, to syntactify it—is always a betrayal of experience, a falsification of it" (p. 96).

End of the Road may not be experimental in its techniques, but it is certainly a clear statement of those ideas upon which the techniques of Barth's later novels of number are based. The statements on language, for example, as well as being reminiscent of Sartre's, are the clue to the techniques of Barth's third novel, *The Sot-Weed Factor*, in which he attempts to remind the reader of the illusory nature of his perceptions by a self-conscious imitation of those perceptions as they appear, falsified, in realistic fiction.

Although *The Sot-Weed Factor*, a picaresque novel set in seventeenth-century England and Maryland, is far more ambitious than his two earlier ones in its techniques, the ideas expressed in it have all appeared before in Barth's work in some form or another. At the beginning of the novel Ebenezer Cooke, hero of *The Sot-Weed Factor*, resembles Jacob Horner in his approach to life. He is unable to choose, unable to state a preference for anything: "Ebenezer could be persuaded, at least notionally, by any philosophy of the world (p. 21). For this reason, Ebenezer, like Jacob, is subject to periods of immobility, and, as in *End of the Road*, Barth suggests that failure to choose a role to perform means absence of identity. Ebenezer is a virgin at the age of thirty because he can imagine any kind of a man taking a woman, bold, bashful, boy or lecher, but since "he felt himself no more one of these than another and admired all, when a situation presented itself he could never choose one role to play over all the rest he knew" (p. 57).

Ebenezer adopts a role, that of idealistic poet laureate of Maryland

and virgin, but he invests absolute value in his chosen role and has no knowledge at first of the "real" nature of the world. The action of the novel is Ebenezer's discovery of the world's true nature, is his disillusionment. The process of becoming disillusioned involves him in a series of wild adventures in Maryland, both helped and hindered by his ex-tutor Henry Burlingame, his twin sister Anna, a transported London prostitute Joan Toast, and his father. Burlingame is searching for his own identity by attempting to discover the facts about his origins, a situation reminiscent of *Tom Jones* or *Joseph Andrews*. Burlingame's search requires him to find an ancient journal, the diary of Captain Smith, and involves both him and Ebenezer in political intrigue connected with the government of Maryland.

Ebenezer learns that reason can prove anything, as his answer to Burlingame's questions on gambling indicate. He realizes that the gambler may be saying "God hath no hand in things" or, since no man gambles who does not believe in luck and to believe in luck is to deny blind chance, he is perhaps saying "Yea to God." It is one of those questions "that have many sides" (p. 227). He finds that it is impossible to establish the facts of human history and equally impossible to discover whose values are right and whose wrong. One chapter heading reads: "The poet wonders whether the course of human history is a progress, a drama, a retrogression, a cycle, an undulation, a vortex, a right-or-left-handed spiral, a mere continuum, or what have you. Certain evidence is brought forward, but of an ambiguous and inconclusive nature" (p. 725). Ebenezer decides that he cannot write an idealistic poem glorifying Maryland because conditions in Maryland are far from glorious, and so he writes a satire instead. For all this he blames "the nature of Reality, which had failed to measure up to his expectations" (p. 229).

It is Burlingame, Ebenezer's tutor and friend, who sees man's relation to the world as absurd and who points this out to Ebenezer. Burlingame explains that we have only our own perception to depend upon to establish reality and therefore everything is subjective and cannot be absolute: "In fact, you see a Heraclitean flux: Whether 'tis we who shift and alter and dissolve; or you whose lens changes color field, and focus; or both together. The upshot is the same, and you may take it or reject it" (p. 349). There are only two ways to survive in this world as Burlingame sees it: either be "dull-headed," which he feels, like Camus, is far the more common, or recognize that the world is meaningless and chaotic and force one's own patterns upon it: "One must assert, assert, assert, or go screaming mad" (p. 365). The true nature of the world and the purposeless of any human action, is symbolized in Ebenezer's dream, a dream in which he arbitrarily selects a mountain to climb, overcomes many obstacles to reach its top, only to find the people on top do not know what mountain it is they are on and admit there is nothing there to climb for.

The world, as Barth sees it, then, simply exists and man's usual view of it is an illusion. When Ebenezer recognizes this he has an experience of the absurd. He looks up at the night sky and finds it to be different from his expectations; he is suddenly stripped of his illusions about the world and experiences a feeling of alienation: "Viewed in this manner, the constellations lost their sense entirely; their spurious character revealed itself, as did the false presupposition of the celestial navigator, and Ebenezer felt bereft of orientation" (p. 366).

Just as Ebenezer's expectations of the night sky are frustrated in the preceding scene, the reader's expectations of a novel are frustrated by the techniques Barth employs in *The Sot-Weed Factor*. Perhaps the most obvious of these techniques is the one employed by Barth to suggest that man has no absolute identity. Unlike the consistent characters of a realistic novel, Barth's characters adopt so many disguises during the course of the novel that doubt is thrown on the original personalities in which the reader meets them. In "The Literature of Exhaustion," Barth praises Borges for using this technique, saying, "The doubles that his characters, like Nabokov's, run afoul of suggest dizzying multiples."[10]

Ebenezer Cooke hears, just before he embarks for Maryland, that someone else bearing his name has recently been taken to jail. He learns, too, that Slye and Scurry have already escorted a man they think is Cooke to Plymouth. Bertrand, Ebenezer's servant, also disguises himself as the poet and on board ship they deceive Captain Pound by reversing roles until Pound announces a second or possibly a third impostor claiming to be Cooke. Joan Toast, the prostitute from London, with whom Ebenezer is in love, reappears as the girl on the mast of the Cyprian and as Susan Warren. When Ebenezer sees the girl on the mast, she reminds him of Joan, but since Miss Robotham has already reminded him of Joan, the reader is inclined to dismiss this resemblance. It is some two hundred pages later that he discovers that the girl on the rigging was indeed Joan. When we first meet Susan Warren, she talks of Joan as a newly arrived prostitute from London; later they turn out to be the same person. As in the case of all these disguises, no recognition is apparently possible from physical appearance. When Ebenezer does attempt to penetrate disguises, he is invariably wrong. He argues a good case for Miss Bromly's being Joan Toast, only to discover that Miss Bromly is his sister Anna. By the time the reader is half way through the novel, Barth has him expecting characters to reappear in disguise. At this point he confuses him further by encouraging him to penetrate the disguise and outguess the author and by then frustrating his expectations.

There are many minor disguises: Miss Russecks turns out to be Roxane, Eben and Anna's nurse; Ben Avery is also Ben Long; Drakepecker is Dick Parker; but the figure in the novel who carries the weight of Barth's ideas on identity is Burlingame, originally tutor to Eben and Anna. Burlingame's first reappearance is as Peter Sayer, who reveals his earlier identity to Ebenezer by continuing a poem that only the two of them know. Scurry and Slye capture Eben and take him to John Coode who turns out to be Burlingame, whom this time Eben recognizes immediately. It takes him a little while to discover his tutor is Timothy Mitchell, who in this disguise reveals to Eben that he also played the part of Charles Calvert, Lord Baltimore, during their interview before Eben left for Maryland. Barth raises the suspicion that Charley Mattassin, a half-caste whom Ebenezer meets in Maryland, is also Burlingame, but Charley Mattassin turns out to be Burlingame's brother. Burlingame's final disguise is actually as the traitor, Nicholas Lowe.

The technique of disguise, of course, raises the question of the relationship between fiction and reality. Burlingame suggests that Baltimore and Coode, historically antagonists for power in Maryland, perhaps do not exist at all, except as others have impersonated them: "it may be they're naught but the rumors and tales themselves" (p. 753). Ebenezer suggests that if that is so, then fiction perhaps has more substance than reality: "When I reflect on the weight and power of such fictions beside my own poor shade of a self, that hath been so much disguised and counterfeited, methinks they have tenfold my substance" (p. 753).

One of Barth's most interesting techniques involves bringing his reader to what he calls "the Pit." "The Pit" is that mental state of absolute confusion in which all points of certainty have been removed —another name for the experience of the absurd. One way of doing this is to bring home to the reader that everything is subjective by proving to him that he has no way of ascertaining the truth about any given event in the novel. This technique suggests to the reader the equal impossibility of ascertaining the truth about any event in history or his own life. Ebenezer recognizes Burlingame disguised as Sayer because he can complete a quatrain known only to them, but Burlingame points out that this is not necessarily proof of his identity: "Suppose today I'd claimed to be Burlingame, for all my alteration, and composed a line to fit your quatrain—nay, a whole life story—which did not match your own recollection; and when you questioned it, suppose I'd challenged your own identity, and made you out to be the clever impostor" (p. 143). Ebenezer refuses to consider the matter further since "such casuistical speculations lead only to the Pit" (p. 143). "The facts avail one naught in making judgments" (p. 515) and "things are not as they seem" (p. 465), Ebenezer and the reader are forced to concede.

The second way of bringing the reader to the Pit is to expose him to the infinite possibilities of variations upon an idea, to suggest to him the gratuitousness and endless variety of things in the world, by confronting him with the gratuitousness and variety of things in the novel. The first example of this in *The Sot Weed Factor* is Ebenezer's experience when trying to buy a notebook. Bragg, the bookseller, offers him so many kinds of notebooks that Ebenezer cries, "Stop . . . 'Tis the pit" (p. 125). Heller uses lists for the same purpose in *Catch-22*. Historical events are treated in a similar way. When the supposed Lord Baltimore relates the history of Maryland to Ebenezer, the details and twists in the story become so numerous that it is all but impossible to follow what is happening.

Burlingame's lecture on twins in history and religion and their symbolic significance becomes an interminable list of strange names: "I have learnt of a nation called the Zuni, that worship Ahaiyuta and Matsailema, . . . of another called Awikeno, that worship Mamasalanik and Noakaua—all of them twins" (p. 525). The effect upon the reader of the sound of these names and the great number of parallel clauses is like that of a chant, hypnotic and dizzying. Ebenezer calls it Burlingame's scheme to drive him mad. Lists of words of a similar kind occur in two other places in the novel: once when Ebenezer and Burlingame have a rhyming match; once when the two prostitutes exchange insults for six pages. This is a technique used frequently by Beckett in *Watt* and recalls the last scene of Ionesco's *The Bald Soprano* in which dialogue breaks down into a series of meaningless sounds. Barth, too, I think, is making a comment on the divorce of language from sense through this technique, by giving instances in which words are not used in any way to communicate meaning.

Techniques which serve to undermine the reader's expectations of logic, language, and character in the novel are present in all novels of number, as I shall demonstrate. But Barth differs from many of the other novelists by making his latest novels complete parodies of particular literary forms, imitations not of life but of art. In this way the form of his novels unmakes not only itself but the genre it is imitating. *The Sot-Weed Factor* is a parody of a picaresque novel, of the sort of work in which a hero in search of his origins experiences a series of adventures and finally becomes readjusted into the framework of his society. The method of parody is exaggeration.

Action in the picaresque novel is full of coincidental reappearances, is generally described so as to create the maximum suspense, and is frequently of a violent nature. The violent action typical of this type of novel is imitated and exaggerated in the chapter headings. Barth, as I have already shown, reintroduces almost all his main characters, Burlingame, Anna, Joan Toast, usually under new identities. Even some of the minor characters reappear in unexpected places: John McEvoy in the Indian village; Andrew Cooke as a suitor to Susan Warren. Barth also exaggerates the usual methods of creating suspense to the point of infuriating his reader. This is most obvious in his treatment of Captain Smith's journal, the lost book needed to reveal Burlingame's origins. The journal is actually a bawdy retelling of the Pocahontas story and is discovered by Burlingame in five sections, each of which ends at an exciting moment. Barth suspends the main action of the story five times to include the next episode of the journal, always leaving his reader to wait a hundred pages or more to find out what happens next.

Ebenezer, far from being readjusted into his society, loses his illusions about it, and writes a satire called *The Sot-Weed Factor* instead of his proposed *Marylandiad*. Since the title of Ebenezer's satire and that of Barth's novel are the same, and since we are told that Ebenezer writes of his own experiences which are also the subject of Barth's novel, it seems as though *The Sot-Weed Factor* is one of those novels Barth so much admires in which the characters become the authors of the works they are in. This technique, Barth explains, is a version of the *regressus in infinitum*, "is an image of the exhaustion, or attempted exhaustion, of possibilities—in this case literary possibilities."[11]

As I explained earlier, it is as an attempt at the exhaustion of possibilities that we must also see his technique of "imitating imitations." Barth claims that "Literary forms certainly have histories and historical contingencies, and it may well be that the novel's time as a major art form is up . . . No necessary cause for alarm in this at all, except perhaps to certain novelists, and one way to handle such a feeling might be to write a novel about it."[12] Barth, then, reproduces the picaresque novel with ironic intent, as an attack upon our preconceptions of the novel as a form. It is not only the exaggerations which indicate the irony, but the time and place of the reproduction. It is interesting to note that Barth has published a "revised" edition of *The Sot-Weed Factor* which makes no alterations in the original. The "revised" edition can thus be seen as an imitation of the first. Imitations of imitations are, of course, images of exhaustion in the same way as are characters becoming authors of the books they are in. They imply a starting again after everything is used up, and suggest an endless series of imitations. At the same time they are necessarily self-conscious works of art serving both to undermine the reader's illusion that fiction is a "slice of life" and more importantly to remind him that reality is no more "real" than fiction.

Giles Goat-Boy, Barth's fourth work, is, like *The Sot-Weed Factor*, an imitation of a novel; but whereas *Sot-Weed* is an imitation of a picaresque novel written in the twentieth century, *Goat-Boy*, which also parodies other genres, is primarily an imitation in that it is a series of illusions. It is also written by an author playing the role of an author.

Giles Goat-Boy consists of a series of tapes that form the body of the novel and tell the story of George, the Goat-Boy, who some legends claim was a spiritual leader. Playing an author, J. B., Barth claims that these tapes were brought to him by Stoker Giles, son of the goat-boy, and that he has sent them to his publisher in place of a novel called *The Seeker*, which he had promised but had been unable to write. J. B., like all men in Barth's Post-existential world, indeed like Giles himself, seeks meaning but cannot find it. Stoker Giles denies authorship of the tapes, claiming they were recorded by WESCAC, the giant computer. The publisher, in a "Disclaimer," states: "And the computer, the mighty 'WESCAC'—does it not too disclaim authorship? It does" (IX).

The novel is an allegory which conceives of the universe as a vast university campus[13] divided into East and West like the postwar world. New Tammany College, the U.S.A., is run by WESCAC, the giant computer, and is in opposition to Nikolay College, home of the Student-Unionists, run by EASCAC. Barth questions the possibility of a modern savior through the introduction of George, originally Billy Blockfuss, a sort of Christ-figure—goat-boy with a cloven hoof instead of shepherd—who attempts to prove he is Giles, the awaited grand-tutor, son of WESCAC and Miss Virginia Hector. The plot of the novel, which imitates many characteristics of epic, is George's search for his origins.

Giles Goat-Boy is in many ways similar to Burgess's *MF*; Burgess, like Barth, makes much use of the Oedipus myth. But the two novelists use similar material to entirely different ends. Myth in the novel of nightmare produces an answer, unites the apparently disparate parts of the Post-existential world together. In *Giles Goat-Boy*, Barth is in fact parodying this function of myth, just as he is parodying such other forms as allegory, epic, and Greek tragedy. *Giles Goat-Boy* unmakes itself; it is a novel of number.

George begins life as a goat among goats and as an animal does not question the meaning of his existence. When he comes to recognize his humanity through meeting Lady Creamhair, he conceives the notion that he may be the grand-tutor and leaves the goat pasture for the ambiguities of the campus. George, like Beckett's Watt, proceeds to question his world in a reasonable manner, but although many different ways of life are offered to him, there seems to be no reason for choosing one rather than another. Barth illustrates the inadequacies of all ways of approaching the world through the various people who inhabit the campus: Peter Greene, the WASP, is schizophrenic, blind to his own vices, inconsistent in his political and emotional life; Eierkopf, the scientific intellectual, is impotent; Croaker, the purely animal, is totally undisciplined and causes chaos; Kennard Sear, the psychiatrist, cannot help his own wife; the Living Sakhyan, a mystic, contemplates while others drown. In the world George enters, "Arrows flashed this way and that; signs commanded one on every hand to stop, to go, to turn" (p. 268).

This world is constructed of opposites, as is that of Burgess's *MF*: for Eierkopf there is Croaker; for Lucius Rexford, the "good" leader, there is Maurice Stoker, the "bad"; for Peter Greene, the capitalist, there is Leonid, the communist. For passage there is failure; for George, Harold Bray. But these opposites are not part of a great duality, as in Burgess's world; they simply negate one another, as Barth switches his satirical attack from one concept to its opposite, in a way typical of Vonnegut. The key to understanding Barth's use of opposites lies in Eierkopf's comments on refracted images: "Contrary to what one might suppose, he said, an image twice refracted in certain complementary ways was not always thereby restored to its original state, any more than a cat dissected and reassembled in the zoology laboratories was the same cat afterwards: sometimes it came out doubly distorted (as it always was in theory); sometimes it seemed to vanish altogether" (p. 478)

George is presented with seven assignments, all of which are "to be done at once, in no time" (p. 428); but the more George attempts to understand his tasks the more interpretations of each become possible. The ambiguity of language prevents any certainty of their nature. Does the assignment "see through your Ladyship," for example, mean "understand Anastasia; that is, to divine the inmost heart of one fellow human" (p. 519), or, as Kennard Sear suggests, "Understand the female elements in your psyche" (p. 524)? Language, as always in Barth's Post-existential novels, makes exact meaning impossible. So George develops two theses: that damnation, or failure and salvation, or passage are two different things; that "failure is passage" (p. 604). Neither of these succeeds because, as in *The Sot-Weed Factor*, "Some things that look alike, you'll see to be different, and some you thought were different will turn out to be the same. But you can look from now until the end of terms and you won't see anything but the natural University. It's all there is" (p. 379). There is no answer to be found, no meaning in an irrational world.

George may feel, as he does for a moment when sexually intertwined in WESCAC's belly with Anastasia, that there is "an entire, single, seamless campus" (p. 731), but it seems to me a mistake to take this as Barth's answer, as Scholes does. George's feelings bear no more relation to an outer reality than do Peter Greene's when he wakes up after making love and knows "Nothing had changed: there was still no Founder, no sense in the University . . . there was still no more reason, ultimately, to heed the summons of his bladder and children than not to. Yet all these truths had a different *feel* now" (p. 283). Barth allows, here as in *The Floating Opera*, for the value of human emotion, but does not offer it as an answer to the Post-existential dilemma. The Posttape in which an older George looks back, having found his experience impossible to teach, precludes the possibility of Barth's intending to offer us any final solution.

The reader never discovers whether or not George is in fact a grand tutor, and this, of course, is Barth's main point. He is both discussing and dramatizing the impossibility of establishing any truth for certain. *Giles Goat-Boy* is Barth's illustration of one of the premises of the Post-existential world that everything is ultimately subjective; we can interpret the facts anyway we choose. The novel is to the reader as the Bible is, for example, to anyone who attempts to understand it. In a 1965 interview Barth said, "Really what you want to do is re-invent philosophy and the rest—make up your own whole history of the world. . . . What *I* really wanted to write after *The Sot-Weed Factor* was a new Old Testament, a comic Old Testament. I guess that's what this new novel, *Giles Goat-Boy* is going to be. A souped-up Bible."[14] The warden of the library discusses the Old Scrolls (the Bible) with Giles: "All the texts are corrupt, you know, even these—copies of copies of copies, full of errata and lacunae —but we never could agree on a common reading, and of course the Old Scrolls acquired a great spurious authority for sentimental reasons, even though they contradict each other and themselves" (p. 720).

There are many ways, too, of interpreting the symbolism of *Giles Goat-Boy*. What, for example, is WESCAC intended to represent? WESCAC at first seems to stand for the atomic bomb. Max Spielman, Giles's early guardian, is guilt ridden because he pushed the button that caused WESCAC to EAT innumerable people. Yet WESCAC, according to Miss Virginia Hector, Giles's suspected mother, is Giles's father. Does WESCAC, then, represent God?

Was Giles the son of a virgin? There is no way of discovering if either is the correct interpretation. As the Posttape states: "If the GILES is WESCAC's son, and a Grand Tutor, is not WESCAC in a sense the Founder? Might being EATen not be equivalent to 'becoming as a kindergartner,' and hence the Way to Commencement Gate?" (p. 760).

The two levels of allegory, religious and historical, frequently contradict each other in this fashion. But there is no really clear line of allegory even if one takes the two aspects separately. Barth tempts his readers into identifying his characters as historical figures, but they ultimately escape identification, as Scholes's comments on Max Spielman indicate: "Max Spielman, for example, has overtones of Einstein and Oppenheimer specifically, but points dimly to other figures, mainly Jewish, who have shaped modern life: Freud and Jung certainly, Marx possibly."[15] *Giles Goat-Boy* is a parody of allegory just as *The Sot-Weed Factor* is a parody of the picaresque novel.

Barth also makes the novel a parody of epic and of Greek tragedy through the use of the self-conscious art technique. Early in the novel George and Max discuss types of hero; George's search for his parents is apparently ended when the traditional birthmark is discovered on his leg. But this mark of identification is invalidated when Harold Bray, George's rival who is as adept at disguise as Burlingame, is found to have a similar stain. George is taken to see a campus production of *Taliped Decanus*, a parody of *Oedipus Rex*, which openly discusses itself through reference to terms associated with Greek drama: "In the protasis, or prologue, / The protagonist exposed to the deuteragonist and choragos / Harmartia caused by hubris" (p. 346). The Taliped play is a miniature version of *Giles Goat-Boy* but comments on it through contrast. Whereas Taliped finds the truth, George does not. Barth ends the tapes with a final example of self-conscious art: George meets a girl who is reading *Giles Goat-Boy*.

Barth ends *Giles Goat-Boy* by creating doubt about the authenticity of the "tapes" which form the body of the novel. The Posttape, invalidating all the previous tapes, comes at the end of the novel. As J. B., Barth then points out in a Postscript the internal evidence against the Posttape's authenticity, stating that even the type of the pages is different. But, as a final footnote tells the reader, the type of J. B.'s Postscript is not the same as that of his "Cover-Letter to the Editors and Publisher." Which of J. B.'s letters is genuine, if either? In this way Barth suggests an endless series of doubts and inflicts upon the reader that inability to establish anything for certain which is the subject of his novel.

Chimera, John Barth's most recent work, appears to take his theory of a literature of exhaustion as far as it will go. It is, like the Chimera of myth, composed of three parts, in this instance three novellas, each a modern retelling of an older story: Dunyazadiad, Perseid, and Bellerophoniad. At least, it is usual to think of the story of Scheherazade, of Perseus, of Bellerophon as predating the 1970s, though by the time one has finished reading *Chimera*, it is hard to be certain. For as Barth shows us, illustrating his comments on Beethoven's sixth symphony, all tales are both endless and endlessly repeated. None of the novellas is really concluded, and Barth himself, in the form of a genie, tells Scheherazade who has asked him whether he invented the stories she told: "I won't be born for a dozen centuries yet! You didn't invent them either, for that matter; they're those ancient ones you spoke of, that 'everybody tells': Sinbad the Sailor, Aladdin's Lamp, Ali Baba and the Forty Thieves!" (p.21).

Chimera consists of three of the tales everybody tells and extends the experiments in narrative trickery begun in *The Sot-Weed Factor*. It constantly negates its own illusions in two principal ways: it employs a series of advanced forms of the tale-within-a-tale device; it takes the self-conscious art technique to such an extreme that Barth begins to write a critical commentary on *Chimera* within the book itself.

The "Dunyazadiad" is, in terms of its narrative, comparatively simple although Barth introduces in it a comment on the complex devices he will employ later in *Chimera*. The genie and Scheherazade speculate on "such questions as whether a story might imaginably be framed from inside, as it were, so that the usual relation between container and contained would be reversed and paradoxically reversible. . . .Or whether one might go beyond the usual tale-within-a-tale, beyond even the tales-within-tales-within-tales-within-tales" (p. 32). Commenting on *Chimera*, the genie tells Scheherazade that he has "set down two-thirds of a projected series of three novellas, longish tales which would take their sense from one another" (p. 36).

The story of Scheherazade's postponement of her murder by the cynical King Shahryar by teasing his curiosity with unfinished tales is apparently told in Barth's version by her little sister Dunyazade to the king's brother Shah Zaman. The careful reader learns that early in the novella from the references to "your brother." Barth relates the inner tale to the outer by having Dunyazade's position with Shah Zaman initially parallel to her sister's with Shahryar, and the story of Scheherazade's stories the story Dunyazade tells her husband. But the final paragraph reverses all the certainties the reader has carefully established for himself when Barth through the use of the terms "little sister" and "Dunyazade" suggests that Scheherazade is telling the tale of her sister telling the tale of her stories: "There (with a kiss, little sister) is the sense of our story, Dunyazade" (p. 64).

The parallelism between sex and writing emphasized in Dunyazadiad is used to suggest a philosophy perhaps more optimistic than that in Barth's other novels and very similar to Vonnegut's: that although the Post-existential world allows us no absolutes, we can act as if permanence were possible. Life like art is a matter of seeming, of acceptable illusions. "Let it be *as if*! Let's make a philosophy of that *as if*!" (p. 62), says Shah Zaman to Dunyazade.

"Perseid" shares this philosophy with the first novella as Perseus is immortalized with his love Medusa. Perseus endlessly repeats his tale, the facts of which he learns from a series of mirrored panels depicting his experiences: "Thus this endless repetition of my story: as both protagonist and author, so to speak, I thought to overtake with understanding my present paragraph as it were by examining my paged past and thus pointed, proceed serene to the future's sentence" (pp. 88-89). "Perseid" is apparently a story told to Calyxa during a brief visit to heaven by Perseus, but eventually proves to have a larger framework in which Perseus is relating his relating of it to his love Medusa. In this novella the reader is deceived as to audience rather than narrator.

In the modern version the action of the original story unmakes itself: Perseus attempts to return their eye to the Gorgons and discovers his enemy Medusa to be the woman he loves. Medusa is finally revealed as an idealized Andromeda, a fact revealed cryptically to the reader on the second page of the novella when Perseus prints on the sand PERSEUS LOVES ANDROMED and then adds the modern USA to form ANDROMEDUSA.

"Bellerophoniad" is, of course, the story of Bellerophon, grandson of Sisyphus, who destroys the monster Chimera just as his story, "Bellerophoniad," unmakes Barth's story *Chimera*. Bellerophon, in Barth's version an aging mythic hero, is a parallel to Barth himself, forty-year old "J. B. the Pretender" (p. 257), a writer who has suffered from writer's block and fears failure.

Barth, or rather a variety of Barth stand-ins, gradually dominates the tale he is telling by an increasing use of self-conscious art: "I can't keep straight who's speaking as I used to" (p. 154). Originally a commentator on the novellas of *Chimera*, he begins to discuss not only this but his earlier work, referring to *The Sot-Weed Factor*, to *Giles Goat-Boy*, to critical comments upon them, and to his current thematic concerns: "the mortal desire for immortality, for instance, and its ironically qualified fulfillment—especially by the mythic hero's transformation, in the latter stages of his career, into the sound of his own voice, or the story of his own life, or both. I am forty" (p. 207). Characters from earlier Barth novels appear: Harrison Mack, Jerome Bray, Todd Andrews, and the image of exhaustion is suggested in such proposed new titles as *The End of the Road Continued* and *Sot Weed Redivivus*.

"Bellerophoniad" is told as a description of a tale, a device which never allows the reader the luxury of an illusion of realism: "Bellerophon wishes he had never begun this story. But he began it. Then he wishes he were dead. But he's not" (p. 178). This new self-conscious art device is used, as self-conscious art always is, to remind the reader that "the truth of fiction is that Fact is fantasy; the made-up story is a model of the world" (p. 256). A speaker, B., ends "Bellerophoniad" with a comment upon it, appropriately left unfinished: "It's not at all what I had in mind for Bellerophon. It's a beastly fiction, ill-proportioned, full of longueurs, lumps, lacunae, a kind of monstrous mixed metaphor. . . . It's no *Bellerophoniad*. It's a— " (pp. 319-320).

Chimera, then, like *Sot-Weed* and *Giles Goat-Boy*, self-destructs. Each work takes the reader progressively closer to the void by means of those techniques which frustrate his expectations of the novel as a form. All of Barth's fiction is an illustration of the Post-existential sensibility, but only *Sot-Weed*, *Goat-Boy* and *Chimera*, I would claim, are novels of number. As imitations of imitations they are objects from which the reader becomes alienated, dramatizations of man's alienation from his world. Barth, then, employs a form of the novel which, like Borges's story "Tlon", is "a paradigm of or metaphor for itself; not just the *form* of the story, but the *fact* of the story is symbolic: 'the medium is the message!' "[16]

Chapter Three

James Purdy:

Fidelity to Failure

It is true that the world of James Purdy's novels[1] is the Post-existential one of Heller's and of Barth's: the world has no meaning which can be rationally discovered; human beings have no innate identity; human action is futile. It is true, too, that although Purdy's techniques appear at first to be closer to realism than Heller's and Barth's, in the sense that fewer obviously impossible events take place and that his settings are familiar places—Brooklyn, Chicago, towns in the Midwest—his intention is usually theirs: to reject the reader, to destroy his illusions about the novel as a form, and hence to bring about in him the experience of the absurd. Most of Purdy's techniques are, in fact, those of the other novelists of number. He deliberately omits the motivations of his characters and indicates no causal relationship between events. His tone frequently conflicts with his subject; his dialogue has few logical connections.

Nevertheless, Purdy differs significantly from Heller and Barth in the effect that the Post-existential dilemma has upon him. For him it is cause for despair rather than for ironic laughter.[2] The characters of Purdy's novels are human beings whose needs are desperate and whose agony is extreme. This agony is so apparent to us, perhaps, because of Purdy's emphasis on one aspect of the absurd dilemma: the failure of human communication which a purely subjective world and the lack of any innate human identity make inevitable.

The failure of communication is present in two forms in each of Purdy's novels. First, it is seen as a failure of all love relationships; for Purdy, love is primarily a matter of communication. Bettina Schwarzschild, among other critics, has pointed out that "Purdy's work is about love. Love between mother and child, brother and brother or sister, husband and wife, aunt and nephew, friends, neighbors, strangers. People stumbling, groping, towards each other, and failing. Always failing."[3] The progress in each of Purdy's novels is the same: it is a movement towards the loss of the hope of love that the central characters have held. Alma, in *The Nephew*, realizes she can never know anything about her dead nephew; Malcolm dies after failing in his many attempts at human contact; Daniel Haws and Captain Stadger destroy each other. Each of the characters moves towards nothingness.

The second, equally important failure of communication in Purdy's novels is the failure of art. More than any of the other novelists of number Purdy resembles Beckett in illustrating the concept of art as fidelity to failure. Beckett's comments on the Dutch painter, Bram Van Velde, applied by Hassan to Beckett himself, apply equally well to Purdy:

> To him, art is a fidelity to failure, and also "a kind of Pythagorean terror, as though the irrationality of pi were an offense against the deity, not to mention his creature." Art, then, is failure and frozen outrage. "I know," he says, "that all that is required now . . . is to make . . . this fidelity to failure, a new occasion, a new term of relation, and of the act which, unable to act, obliged to act, he [the artist] makes an expressive act, even if only of itself, of its impossibility, of its obligation." Obligation, we see, wrestles with impossibility, and the result is always pyrrhic. The artist, like so many heroes of Beckett, can neither continue nor desist. The work of art itself—painting or play—contracts to express the paradox of its own existence.[4]

Purdy's novels are full of failed writers: Alma fails to write the memorial to her nephew; Malcolm attempts to record his conversations when he is delirious; Bernie Gladhart cannot write the story of Cabot Wright since there is no story to tell; Eustace Chisholm abandons his career as poet. Each of them fails to communicate through words, finding either that the truth, being subjective, escapes him, or that language is inadequate to express it. Purdy's own novels give us precisely that sense of attempted expression which fails, of art struggling against its own impossibility. Yet they exist, expressions of the paradox of their own existence. Like all novels of number they take the reader towards nothingness; each novel, like its reader, struggles but fails to make sense of the experience it records.

"63: Dream Palace," Purdy's first extended work of fiction, is the story of Fenton Riddleway, a boy from West Virginia, who is introduced to the hope of a better life by a writer called Parkhearst Cratty and who apparently murders his younger brother Claire because he feels Claire is preventing the realization of this new life. The story is told as part of a conversation between two failed writers, Parkhearst Cratty and a woman called Grainger to whom Parkhearst has introduced Fenton. It is an interesting foreshadowing of the major themes that will dominate Purdy's later work.

Each character in the story has found some kind of illusory value to take the place of the God none of them, except perhaps Claire, can any longer believe in. In the absence of God, Parkhearst has his astrology and his "people," people whom he meets in parks and bars and whose stories he collects. But Parkhearst, Purdy indicates, never approaches reality and in truth is afraid he will become involved in something more than a story. All meaning for Grainger is centered in the shrine she has built for her dead husband Russell, a shrine she never enters and which she finally opens to provide some clothes for Fenton. Claire, the apparently retarded brother of Fenton, alone believes in God and claims to Fenton's annoyance that he can hear Him, but even he gradually loses hold of this faith and says finally, "I don't think about Him" (p. 153).

Fenton develops his dream during the course of the action. It is a version of the American dream and involves marrying a rich woman and living in a mansion. The loss of Fenton's dream forms the action of the novella. He realizes that the only real thing in his life is his brother Claire; but it is too late; he has already killed Claire to protect his dream of "living in a mansion." He is left with nothing. Ironically, the story of Fenton, the story of a boy with a dream, has become in its turn the only thing that matters to Grainger and Parkhearst; it has become their dream.

The illusory value each character adopts as a substitute for faith is always related to another human being. The repeated religious references in the novella emphasize this. The men in the park wander about "aimless and groping" like "shades in hell" (p. 132). The hope of human contact is the hope of salvation: Bella thinks of Parkhearst, her husband, as "younger than Christ" (p. 139); Grainger's shrine to Russell is called a "church"; Fenton says to Claire "You look Christ awful" (p. 153). Hayden Banks, whose acting indirectly contributes to Fenton's murder of Claire, is described as a devil, just as Grainger, who perhaps provided the motive by offering Fenton a new life, is called "Queen of Hell." But Claire, whose body in the cedar chest at the end of the novella is overlooked by a picture of Jesus among the thieves and a poem about Mother Love, is an ironic Christ figure. There is no hint of resurrection; he does not save Fenton.

Because each character is encapsulated in his subjective world, another's identity can never be apprehended, and communication is therefore impossible. Grainger tells Parkhearst that Fenton "is as vague as a dream" to her, and he replies, "that means he is more real to you than anybody" (p. 128). Parkhearst, the writer, is constantly trying to discover the true nature of others, but always failing. He stares at Grainger, hoping that her eyes "would yield him her real identity" (p. 128), just as he used to stare at Russell "to try to understand who he was" (p. 168). He cannot write about Fenton because "he never found out who he was" (p. 129). Parkhearst's wife Bella recalls that "there had been . . . scores, even hundreds of these people Parkhearst met in order to study for his writing, but the stories themselves were never put in final shape or were never written" (p. 136). Parkhearst's attempts are doomed to failure because identity is elusive and changes with name, clothes, and time. Fenton puts on a new suit of clothes and feels "that his soul had begun to change into another soul" (p. 176). The impossibility of human communication, which is the inevitable result of this absence of essential identity, is suggested symbolically in "63: Dream Palace," as in all Purdy's writing, by the constant references to drunkenness and "passing out."

All human action is seen as purposeless in "63: Dream Palace," reflecting the Post-existential position that there is no intrinsic value in any form of action. Grainger does not listen to the musicians she hires to come and play in her house; "she has the musicians come because there is nothing else left to do" (p. 156). The men in the park wander "without purpose away from the light" (p. 137). Fenton, who also attempts unsuccessfully to record his experiences, writes in his notebook: "Things don't go anywhere in our lives. . . . Sometimes somebody like Mama dies and the whole world stops or begins to move backwards, but nothing happens to us, even her dying don't get us anywhere except maybe back" (p. 150).

"63: Dream Palace" clearly demonstrates the impossibility of art. It opens deceptively with the establishment of certain facts in a manner characteristic of the realistic novel: " 'Do you ever think about Fenton Riddleway?' Parkhearst Cratty asked the great woman one afternoon when they were sitting in the summer garden of her 'mansion' " (p. 128). We know who is talking to whom, when and where the conversation takes place. But some of the facts seem strange and are never explained. Why is she called "the great woman"? Why is her house "a mansion"? Why are they both more intensely interested in Fenton Riddleway than any motive is adequate to explain? Purdy deliberately omits the motivations of his characters, in a way reminiscent of the plays of Harold Pinter. We therefore understand less and less of why the actions of the novel take place. Apparent realism is very soon revealed to be fantasy.

Purdy gives his readers much information about his characters; he seems almost obsessed with ages and names. It is as if he were demonstrating that one can know all the facts about someone and still know nothing of him. Fenton "told nearly everything as though in a police court, that he was Fenton Riddleway and that he was nineteen, that he had come with his brother Claire from West Virginia, from a town near Ronceverte, that their mother had died two weeks before, and that a friend of his named Kincaid had given him an address in a rooming house on Sixty-Three Street" (pp. 133-134). For all the information Fenton remains elusive. Why does he remain in that disintegrating house on Sixty-Third Street? Why does he carry a gun?

Since the impossibility of communication is one of the most important themes of Purdy's work, conversations among the characters are, as one would expect, fragmentary and often irrelevant. The effect of this is also to prevent communication between reader and author. The conversation between Parkhearst and his wife is typical. She says to him, "I suppose in the end you will let Grainger have

Fenton." After some thought, he replies, "Grainger won't get him," and adds a little later, "Fenton is different. . . . He has a gun for one thing" (pp. 137-138). The sense in which Grainger will or will not "get" Fenton, the history of the relationship between Parkhearst and Grainger, the difference made by Fenton's having a gun are never explained. This conversation is full of suggestions of a meaning never clarified for the reader.

As the novella progresses, one has the impression that language is less and less able to describe what is taking place. There is increasing use of such vague terms as "somehow" and "something." Parkhearst sees Grainger and Fenton together and comments, "Fenton looked somehow seedier than any living bum, but something about the way they were themselves, both together and apart, made them seem more real and less real than anybody living he had ever known" (p. 162). The deliberate vagueness achieved here is created elsewhere by the use of negatives and of adjectives suggesting limitlessness: "Fenton had soon found the taverns where his existence aroused no particular interest or comment. People occasionally noticed his accent or his haircut, but generally they ignored him. There was such an endless row of taverns and the street itself was so endless he could always choose a different tavern for each day and each drink" (p. 149).

The scenes of the novella follow each other with increasing lack of causal relation as Fenton seems to have less and less ability to control what happens to him. A theatre visit ends in a homosexual act resulting in the apparent murder of Claire. Fenton is stripped of his illusions. Similarly, the reader is stripped of his expectations of coherent form. All hope that he has received the "true" story is finally invalidated by the memory that what he has read is anyway only Parkhearst's version. The novella has unmade itself.

The themes of "63: Dream Palace" are more fully developed in Purdy's first full-length novel, *Malcolm*. Using the picaresque novel pattern of a young man setting out to learn about life through a series of adventures, Purdy ironically tells the story of a young man who is used by everyone he meets and learns nothing.

Purdy stresses the "nothingness" at the core of his central character; Malcolm is an illustration of the non-identity of Sartre's being-for-itself. He looks like a "foreigner" and appears to belong "nowhere and to nobody" (p. 7). He describes himself as "a cypher and a

blank" (p. 36), claims that he hardly feels he exists, and has no knowledge of such facts about himself as his date of birth. When he dies and
is buried, it is rumored that there is no corpse at the funeral.

Malcolm is an orphan; at least, his father has disappeared and is
presumed dead, but his relationship to his father, his need for him,
is central to the novel. It is clear that Malcolm's father's absence
is intended to represent the absence of God in the modern world.
Whether God ever existed or was simply a creation of man's desire
for meaning, as Sartre and Camus claim, Purdy never makes clear.
During the first interview between Mr. Cox and Malcolm, the boy
says simply that his father has disappeared. Mr. Cox assumes that
he is dead and is amazed that Malcolm has waited so long for his
return. After his meeting with Estel Blanc, Malcolm utters "his
usual silent evening prayer addressed to his father, wherever he
might be, dead or alive, lost or found" (p. 27). When Kermit insults
his father, Malcolm reacts violently and accuses him of insulting the
dead, though by this time "the image of his father was slightly blurred
in his own memory" (p. 59). Madame Girard claims that "nobody
thinks he exists or ever did exist," a comment Malcolm calls "blas-
phemy" (p. 59). Eloisa tells the boy that his "father will not return
from the dead" (p. 166), and Melba says "Who wants a father? It's
been old hat for years" (p. 212). Malcolm finally mistakes an old
drunkard in a nightclub for his father and after this disillusionment
is prepared to admit, "Maybe my father never existed" (p. 213).

In the absence of God man will seek to find his own meaning, and
Malcolm sets out to do this through visiting a series of addresses
provided by Mr. Cox, called significantly the astrologer. It is through
communication with people, then, that Malcolm first tries to come
to terms with life, but as always in Purdy's novels, this proves impossible. *Malcolm* can be read as an account of the failure of many types
of love. Each character with whom the boy comes into contact is
insulated from reality and genuine human communication by his
own obsessive illusion, by his own particular perversion of love.
Kermit, "the little man," indulges in constant self-pity. Madame
Girard, an exemplar of possessive love, collects young men about
her, telling Malcolm to leave Mr. Cox and "be my own, and not
his" (p. 62). Desperate for possessions, she insists on buying Kermit's
studio and Malcolm's portrait. Mr. Girard, her husband, is paternal
towards Malcolm, asking him to be his son, promising to be his

father; Madame Girard explains that all he wants is an heir to his fortune. Jerome, the homosexual ex-burglar, is evangelistic in his approach to people; "You're every confounded preacher and evangelist I have ever known" (p. 139), says Madame Girard to him. His wife, Eloisa, is a narcissist, an unsuccessful painter whose portraits always look like herself. Melba, whom Malcolm eventually marries, sees love only as sex and exhausts him with her sexual demands.

As in "63: Dream Palace," Purdy uses certain metaphors to suggest the impossibility of human communication. Drunkenness occurs frequently: at Madame Girard's chateau, at Eloisa's, and again with Melba. Letters go astray or are not given to the right person. In this novel, too, Purdy stresses the negative aspects of Sartre's theory that being-for-itself is nothingness, that we have objective reality only to others. Identity is elusive to all the characters in *Malcolm*, so they cling to labels: Estel Blanc, for example, wishes to be called a "mortician" not an undertaker; Madame Girard is prepared to lose her husband but not his name. Kermit, on the other hand, does not think of himself as a dwarf or midget, because no one has ever told him he is one. Language, they appear to feel, can create reality; Purdy knows better.

At the end of the novel, Malcolm comes to a realization that he has achieved nothing, that he left the bench for no reason and that now he has lost everything; " 'But I had everything until just a few days ago,' the boy cried. 'And suddenly, having left the bench entirely . . . for reasons I do not recall—I have nothing' " (p. 172). At first this statement seems ironic, for Malcolm appeared to have nothing when Mr. Cox first met him on the bench. But this is not so: Malcolm has lost something; he has lost his illusions, his hope of his father's return. On his deathbed he desperately turns writer in the vain hope that language will make some sense of his experience. He attempts to record his conversations with those he has met. This too is a failure; he is writing in a foreign language in delirium. *Malcolm*, then, is a novel of a young man's initiation into disillusionment. But unlike Yossarian in *Catch-22*, who learned to live after the experience of the absurd, Malcolm dies because there is no new direction to take. He has run out of addresses.

Malcolm, like "63: Dream Palace," opens deceptively: "in front of one of the most palatial hotels in the world, a very young man was accustomed to sit on a bench which, when the light fell a certain way shone like gold" (p. 7). The effect of providing such details as the gold color of the bench, when nothing else is revealed, is to suggest that these details are highly meaningful, to raise the reader's expectations of discovering the significance. The point of them in Purdy's fiction seems to be simply that they are completely irrelevant: the aim is to frustrate the reader's expectations.

Similarly, the introduction of Malcolm himself, which takes place in the second paragraph, is a parody of similar introductions to be found in realistic novels where the reader is given the necessary information to place the protagonist in his background. The paragraph develops through a series of negatives; we learn nothing about Malcolm except what he is not: he "seemed to belong nowhere and to nobody, and even his persistent waiting on the bench achieved evidently no purpose, for he seldom spoke to anybody, and there was something about his elegant and untouched appearance that discouraged even those who were moved by his solitariness" (p. 7). It is as if the novelist were attempting to begin but finding little he can say for certain; art is struggling with its own impossibility.

Purdy's description of the subsequent meeting with Mr. Cox contains many sentences suggesting meaning when there is none or emphasizing in contradiction to the sense. Mr. Cox, we are told, "felt obscurely that the young man on the bench offered a comment, even a threat, certainly a criticism of his own career and thought—not to say existence" (p. 8). Here the two sets of three parallel nouns—*comment, threat,* and *criticism* and *career, thought,* and *existence*—imply a progressive clarification of one noun by the others which does not take place. Mr. Cox, Purdy continues, "was at that period, in a sense, the city, the hotel, and in his own mind, civilization" (p. 8). In what sense, we are forced to ask, is Mr. Cox "the city" and "the hotel" if not "in his own mind," and yet the latter phase is used to qualify only "civilization." What troubles Mr. Cox is that "nobody had ever sat on this particular bench that persistently before, and, in addition, no one had really ever sat on it at all before" (p. 8). But the second reason is not "in addition" to the first, since the second precludes the possibility of the first. The bench is a display piece, even the old ladies "recognizing it by means of their worldliness and senility for the ornament it was" (p. 8). Is it possible to recognize anything by means of senility? What Purdy is doing in the first few pages of *Malcolm* is to suggest by means of such techniques the impossibility of establishing reality through words. He is attacking our preconceptions about language, is pointing out that language is that "absurd structure of sounds and marks" Roquentin sees it to be in *Nausea*.

The failure of communication is dramatized in *Malcolm*, as in "63: Dream Palace," through conversations in which characters reply to each other in a series of nonsequiturs. Although the characters frequently continue as if they had fully expected an illogical reply, their mutual lack of comprehension is obvious to the reader. When Malcolm explains to Estel Blanc that his father's disappearance has left him with very little with which to support himself, Estel replies, "It's nice, however . . . that speaking of comfortable, he left you in such pleasant circumstances" (p. 21). In a sense this is true; Malcolm's hotel is "comfortable" and could be considered "pleasant circumstances," but this was not, of course, Malcolm's meaning. Mr. Girard says to Malcolm, "Well, you see, I am thirty-seven, so that I am easily old enough to be your father," and the boy replies, "My father, however, looked older, though perhaps stronger, than you. He looked nearly forty" (p. 66). When Malcolm refers to Girard, Kermit exclaims, "Why he calls Girard by his first name" (p. 79), even though both Girard's names are Girard and it is therefore impossible to know which of them Malcolm is using.

Just as individual sentences cancel each other out, so too the action of the novel progressively unmakes itself. All relationships disintegrate: Kermit's and Laureen's, the Girards', Gus's and Melba's, Malcolm's and Melba's. As Malcolm follows up the addresses, each interview cancels the one before it; the new characters defame the old, as if, as Mr. Cox says about Madame Girard, they feel they exist only by defaming others. There is progressively less relationship between the scenes, and Malcolm is eventually found drifting aimlessly from one place to another.

Each scene also tends to disintegrate, the characters becoming increasingly grotesque, the action more extreme. Purdy's method is to describe his characters only after we are used to their names and have been listening to their conversation. We are lulled into what we take to be a familiar scene and are then suddenly forced to recognize its grotesqueness. Malcolm has been talking to Estel Blanc for some time before we are told that Blanc is wearing a puce jacket with diamond buttons and is the darkest person Malcolm has even seen. Laureen and Malcolm talk of Kermit Raphaelson before he enters; then we discover he is a midget. It is not that these characters are impossibilities; they can be met elsewhere in life and in fiction. But Purdy has so many of them in one novel that he leaves the impression that the whole human race is distorted and grotesque in some way or another.

The struggle between the necessity to write and the impossibility of writing is clearly demonstrated in the final pages of the novel. The action, the language, the characterizations have all unmade themselves, and Purdy heightens the effect of this by adding some paragraphs which parody the neat endings of realistic novels. He demonstrates the impossibility of imposing form upon life by doing so in an exaggeratedly tidy way. He gives an account of what happens to each of the characters after the the end of the novel. Kermit marries a wealthy film star; Eloisa and her husband take up social work; Estel Blanc runs an opera company; Girard Girard has six children; Melba marries Heliodoro, the Cuban valet; Madame Girard has a constant companion in a young Italian biochemist. Purdy has struggled towards a grotesquely happy ending.

In *The Nephew* Purdy extends the concept of elusive identity; the central character does not appear at all. Cliff Mason is missing in action in Korea when the novel opens and when it ends he is dead. We know nothing more of him at the end than at the beginning, in spite of the fact that the action of the book consists almost entirely of his Aunt Alma's attempt to write a "memorial" of his life. She asks Professor Mannheim to give her information about her nephew's college days but worries whether he will remember the things she wants to know. Halfway through the novel Alma discovers "there isn't a thing she knows for sure about him" (p. 72), and finally she puts the record book, which contains "only a few indecisive sentence fragments" (p. 98), away in a drawer. The only evidence that does come to light about Cliff, the existence of four thousand dollars he had been given by Vernon Miller and some large photographs of him in Vernon's room, has implications that Alma prefers to ignore. Cliff is so elusive in this novel that his death, like Mr. Barrington's, comes as a "mere corroboration to the public of the old suspicion that he had never existed at all" (p. 58).

The other characters in the novel are linked to each other only in that they are all inhabitants of Rainbow Center. As in "63: Dream Palace" and *Malcolm* there is no communication. The novel's dominant image is that of Alma and her brother Boyd sitting in their darkened house each evening unable to communicate because each is deaf. Everyone pursues his illusion or obsession as Alma pursues hers. Clara Himbaugh has her Christian Science, Mrs. Hawke her alcohol, Mrs. Barrington her garden. Clara attempts to convert Mrs. Hawke, who, having abandoned alcohol, tries suicide; Mrs. Barrington's garden is destroyed by storms. The dreams of these characters prove ultimately to have no more substance than the old flag Alma and Boyd raise each Memorial Day, which becomes, when Alma tries to repair it, "a tissue of rotted cloth, impossible to mend" (p. 133). The only faint glimmer of hope seems to be in the words of affection Boyd and Alma speak to each through the darkness in the final scene of the novel.

Although *The Nephew* appears to be more realistic than either "63: Dream Palace" or *Malcolm*, it employs many of the techniques of the other two novels. Rainbow Center is peopled with grotesques: a woman with a club foot, a mentally deranged mother, an alcoholic widow, and a professor who seduces students in graveyards. These characters are reminiscent of Beckett's; their bodies are gradually disintegrating. Alma's and Boyd's increasing deafness is not perhaps as extreme a form of disintegration as Malone's, but it has much the same effect.

The action of the novel is a movement towards the void: Cliff, reported missing at the beginning of the novel, is reported dead at the end; Alma gradually realizes that she never knew anything about her nephew. Similarly, the reader is taken towards nothing as each piece of information gleaned contradicts what has gone before. Alma, who believes that Cliff always wanted to spend his life at Rainbow Center, is told by Vernon that "Cliff hated Rainbow" (p. 130). This is subsequently refuted by Mrs. Barrington: "I don't think Vernon does lie. He's not very bright. He told you the truth as he heard it, but it wasn't the truth as your nephew felt it" (p. 138). Similarly, disparate accounts are given about the four thousand dollars found in Cliff's pocket the night before he left for the service.

Purdy occasionally employs another technique used by Heller in *Catch-22*: he gives accounts of people or events at different places in the novel, and only in retrospect does the reader realize that they could not have happened as described. We know, for example, that when Cliff was in college, Professor Mannheim was considered a good-looking European rake who had a reputation for seducing coeds. We are also told that Cliff went straight to Korea from college, at the most three years before the novel opens. Yet now Professor Mannheim is described as a doddering old man, his adventures with the coeds as happening many years ago. The effect of this is to prevent the reader's being fully able to place the events in the novel which resists any chronological organization.

But in spite of this use of some of the techniques of number and in spite of Post-existential world view of the novel, *The Nephew* is not, perhaps, fully a novel of number. Purdy makes no use here of the language techniques important to the other works and there is no dramatization of art's struggle with its own impossibility. It bears the same relation to Purdy's work as *The Floating Opera* does to Barth's.

Cabot Wright Begins has a double plot. Carrie Moore sends her husband, Bernie, to Brooklyn in search of facts that will enable him to write a novel about Cabot Wright, a young man recently released from prison after serving a sentence for raping more than three hundred woman. Zoe Bickle, a friend of Carrie, attempts to help Bernie. She meets Cabot only to learn that he has forgotten his own history. The second plot is the story of Cabot as reconstructed by Bernie and Zoe, and related to Cabot in order to help him establish his own identity. It is concerned with Cabot's relationships with his wife, Cynthia, with his supposed father and mother, with his boss Warburton, with his doctor, Bigelow-Martin, and with some of the women he rapes.

The world of *Cabot Wright Begins* is exactly the same world as that in Purdy's other novels. Here, too, everything is subjective—"No one knows how the arteries and nerves of the man next to you make him see you and the world that surrounds you both" (p. 11)—and each character has an illusory view of the next. Carrie Moore encourages her husband to believe that he is a writer, telling him he has "a great book inside him" (p. 12). Cabot Wright, the rapist, is described differently by each of his victims. It is a world where identity is impossible to maintain and where the labels one attaches to oneself have no basis in reality. Thus Curt Bickle is a "writer," although he does not write, and Bernie can accept the promise Carrie extends

that he will be a famous novelist even though he has never done anything but sell used cars. Human action is motiveless and purposeless
in this world. Cabot Wright apparently rapes for no reason. When
he hears the telephone ring, sometimes he answers it and sometimes
not, because he "didn't exactly see the point of answering" (p. 134).
It is the Post-existential world again, where all absolutes are necessarily illusions and a life built upon them ends in failure. Cabot Wright
reads Warburton's "Sermons" which talk of the "total failure of
human nature, history, government, the cosmos and god" and has
the "shattering feeling of entering into some kind of reality" (p. 178).

But although the themes of *Cabot Wright Begins* echo those of
the earlier novels, the emphasis here is different. Purdy is less concerned in this novel with the failure of human communication and
more interested in the relation between art, particularly fiction, and
reality. Purdy suggests that the usual concept of art as an ordering
and conveying of reality is simplistic. Bernie Gladhart is sent to
Brooklyn "with a mission to get the story of Cabot Wright from the
convicted rapist's own lips, and to write the truth like fiction" (p. 11).
This proves to be impossible because Cabot Wright has no recollection of the "truth" himself. He has read so much about himself that
he can no longer distinguish reality from fiction. Cabot Wright wants
Zoe Bickle, who has now taken over Bernie Gladhart's task, to tell
him the truth, so that he can find out who he is. Zoe attempts to do
this but the gratuitousness of reality, the impossibility of finding
the meaning in such a diversity of events, prevents her from com-
pleting the job. She finds that "Cabot Wright's life . . . was a
hopeless, finely-ground sediment of the improbable, vague, baffling,
ruinous and irrelevant minutiae of a life" (p. 109). Fiction cannot
capture reality and make sense of it, claims Purdy; the world is
irrational and has no inner meaning to be discovered. Life is no more
real than fiction, for to find a pattern in a life is to fictionalize it. Art
is impossible.

Cabot Wright's realization of this makes him give up the search
for who he is and brings him finally to laughter. What is described
at the end of *Cabot Wright Begins* is an experience of the absurd:
for the first and only time in Purdy's fiction a character laughs the
laugh of ironic detachment. Cabot describes it in a final letter to
Zoe: "Meaning is there no meaning, but the laughter of the moment
made it almost worth while" (p. 222). However, Cabot Wright does

not move from this realization of absurdity to find a way of living in rebellion or freedom, as Yossarian does. But there is the hint of a positive solution in Cabot's final letter to Zoe Bickle: "I don't have to ask those hard questions that nobody now or any of the other 77 billions ever found the answer to, What Makes Me Tick? I don't care about that now, Mrs. Bickle, but I do know, hear it any way you want, I am ticking as of this letter, anyhow, and I'll write the symbol for the way I feel now, which is HA!" (p. 233). Cabot's solution, then, as far as one can determine, is closer to that of Todd Andrews in Barth's *The Floating Opera* than to anyone else's; it is merely to continue, to live in the present, with the full realization that there is no meaning, no intrinsic value in anything, always before him.

The impossibility of writing is the subject of *Cabot Wright Begins*, and Purdy's techniques dramatize his theme. Language techniques dominate this novel. Purdy parodies the inadequacies of the styles of various forms of writing, each of which lays some claim to the truth.[5] When Cynthia, Cabot's wife, breaks down in a supermarket, Purdy reports it as if writing for a newspaper. As in "63: Dream Palace" and *Malcolm* he shows us the relative insignificance of knowing the facts: "She began throwing cans on the floor . . . After too many repetitions of this sort of thing the manager, Harry R. Cowan, had rung a bell by which he summoned extra help. . . . The ice-cream hostess, Miss Glenna de Loomis, attempted to salvage as many of their Dairy Maid frozen products as possible, but Cynthia then began to throw the articles at the fluorescent lighting fixtures. Just before the police and rescue squad came, she had managed to throw in the air nearly all the pomegranates, persimmons, apples, peaches and Jerusalem artichokes she could get her hands on" (p. 123).

In this novel, which is closest in tone to Heller's and Barth's novels, Purdy makes much use of that disparity between tone and subject they employ. An incongruous or ridiculous action is often mentioned obliquely in a sentence in which the main emphasis lies elsewhere. "It is doubtful if Mrs. Bickle would ever have been able to meet Cabot Wright or get one word or fact from him had she not, during a three-alarm fire, fallen through the skylight directly above his quarters" (p. 73), Purdy tells us, and then goes on to describe Zoe Bickle's life before she came to Brooklyn. When we are eventually given the details of Mrs. Bickle's descent into Cabot Wright's apartment, the objectivity of the description and the introduction of such irrelevant facts as the kind of sofa she landed on cut against the violence of the action and render it absurd. This discrepancy between what and how events are described suggests, of course, the impossibility of language's capturing reality.

For the first time in any of his novels, Purdy makes significant use of coincidence to suggest the futility of human action. Since there is no reason why things happen as they do, it is possible for characters to appear suddenly in unexpected places, for Bernie Gladhart, for example, to find that he is living in the same apartment building as the man he has been hunting throughout Brooklyn. Princeton Keith, the publisher, appears as the friend of almost everyone. He first appears as Zoe Bickle's employer, then as a friend of Gilda Warburton, finally as ghost writer for Zenda Stuyvesant. As Keith points out to Bernie, "Coincidence of this sort . . . you two chaps in the same establishment, well, I mean, coincidence . . . isn't tolerated by many publishing people" (p. 48). In novels we do not expect coincidence; we expect events to be related to one another and to progress to a conclusion. Purdy's novels end where they began or, if they move at all, move backwards towards nothingness.

Another way of saying this is to say that the novel unmakes itself. In his later novels Purdy has employed those techniques of self-conscious art used by Barth in *The Sot-Weed Factor* and *Giles Goat-Boy*. He casts doubt on the validity of Cabot Wright's story by constantly reminding us that it is a version invented by Bernie, a novel within a novel: "The reader, in this case the listener (Cabot Wright eavesdropping on his own story as novelized by Bernie Gladhart and revised by Zoe Bickle), has already met Dr. Bugleford, when he was Dr. Bigelow-Martin" (p. 153). Barth begins *Giles Goat-Boy* and Purdy ends *Cabot Wright Begins* with contradictory readers' reports on their own novels suggesting that art is as impossible to evaluate as it is to produce. There is no "true" version of the Cabot Wright story and, if there were, language could not describe it. Mrs. Bickle's final words seem to be Purdy's: "I won't be a writer in a place and time like the present" (p. 237).

But there is obligation as well as impossibility, and Purdy has written a fourth novel, *Eustace Chisholm and the Works*. It bears little resemblance to *Cabot Wright* in tone, is full of the agony of "63: Dream Palace" and *Malcolm*, but is concerned, like *Cabot Wright* with the dual failure of communication between lovers and between writers and their audience. It is the story of two men. The first, Eustace Chisholm, a poet, is scribbling a narrative poem on old newspaper. If the newspaper is our only version of reality, then how can one write a poem? But Eustace has second sight, knows in advance what will take place. Purdy appears to be hypothesizing: Supposing one could know the truth, he asks, would art be possible then? The answer is no. Eustace Chisholm burns his poem and says to his wife, "I'm not a writer, that's my news, never was, and never will be" (p. 241).

The second character is Daniel Haws who cannot face his homosexuality and communicate directly with the boy he loves. Instead he visits him in his sleep. Reenlisting in the service he finally communicates with another human being, Captain Stadger, in a savage, sado-masochistic act that kills them both. Daniel's story is the story of all the minor characters in the novel. Each is in love with someone who does not return his love: Maureen with Daniel, Amos with Daniel, Masterson with Amos, Carla with Eustace. They are all, in a sense, sleepwalkers, an image Purdy picks up in his next novel, unable to touch each other. Amos says to Masterson, "You've been asleep all your life, snoozing in the gray maw of money and when you're awake, you're in partial anaesthetic" (p. 162).

Amos Ratcliffe functions as the dream of illusion in which all the characters invest their lives. He greatly resembles the young man in Albee's play *The American Dream.* (Purdy's novel is dedicated to Albee).[6] There is a suggestion through metaphor that he functions as a symbolic representation of a debased deity, as Mr. Cox perhaps does in *Malcolm.* The important thing, though, is that Amos is not real to anyone. "Well, I'll never be ready. I don't belong anywhere," he says. "I'm just real enough for a sleepwalker to love I guess" (p. 122).

The stories of Amos and Daniel become the material for Eustace Chisholm's writing as for Purdy's novel, and Chisholm's failure is, of course, Purdy's own. The characters steadily disintegrate, though Purdy tries to pin them to the page with labels: "Clayton Harms, the electric-sign salesman"; "Daniel Haws, the boy's landlord." Eustace feels he is losing his intelligence; Daniel that "the scaffolding of his life was falling" (p. 82). Communication becomes worse among the characters as the novel progresses until, in the final section, people communicate only through letters, "those scraps of paper disfigured by the juices of plants and insects which tell us of fate, love, and destruction, change the circulation of the blood and configuration of the brain as we read" (p. 228), as Daniel writes in a letter.

This is a minor example of the technique of self-conscious art which is Purdy's main way of unmaking this novel. Eustace talks of the life of Amos as chapters in a novel. "If anybody had asked Eustace which of the chapters in the life of young Rat he liked the best . . . he would have had to reply, 'The Make-Believe Dance Hall' " (p. 157), says Purdy, and then proceeds to write the chapter. As Eustace waits to hear from Daniel, he is "as anxious to know the end of the Daniel-Amos story as a depraved inveterate novel-reader" (p. 238). Purdy's increasing interest in the mutual incompatibility of various versions of one story is indicated in the titles given to the three main parts of *Eustace Chisholm*: "the sun at noon," "in distortion-free mirrors," and "under earth's deepest stream." It is an interest revealed in the title of his next novel, *Jeremy's Version.*

It is difficult to know Purdy's intent in this novel which is longer, closer to realism, and at the same time less interesting than his previous ones. The reader is informed on the jacket that it is the first of three independent works collectively titled *Sleepers in Moon-Crowned Valleys.* The image of uncommunicating people as sleepwalkers is only one of Purdy's major themes to appear here. An old man, Matt Lacey, employs a young boy, Jeremy Cready, a newspaper carrier, to write down at his dictation a story from his past. Once again Purdy links fiction with newspaper reporting. The story—the material—concerns two families, the Summerlads and the Ferguses, and the effect of their destructive relationship upon a subsequent generation. For the first time Purdy deals directly with the agony of family relationships. A possessive mother, Elvira, an absent father, Wilders, a domineering aunt, Winifred, succeed in alienating two boys, Rick and Jethro. Jethro finally reaches some sort of temporary communication with his father, but only, like Daniel Haws, through violence. After watching his father fight another man, Jethro feels that his father is known to him for the first time. Similarly, Garner, a boarder at Elvira's, can only reach Vickie by raping her.

Jethro Fergus is Jeremy's double; when he first sees Jeremy, Matt tells him he is an exact replica of Jethro. Jethro, a boy badly injured in his youth, writes down in a journal everything that happens in his family as an indictment of his parents. Jethro's journal is a form of self-conscious art, for Matt Lacey wants the same story recorded for destructive purposes also: Jeremy comments that he is really writing about the provincial town of Boutflour which Matt hated bitterly and wished, on his own admission, to destroy.

Art is seen to be necessary in this novel: Matt must record the story to free himself of it; Jeremy sees it as liberation of the imagination and does in fact leave town when it is over. But is it seen to be impossible? *Jeremy's Version* does not unmake itself in quite the same way as the earlier novels. Purdy suggests, however, that he is once again interested in the incompatibility of the versions of one story. Sister Della claims she knows more about the story than Matt Lacey; Jeremy recognizes that Matt's story was about Elvira, Rick, Jethro, and himself, and their love for one another; while Della saw it as a gigantic struggle between two women. Mrs. Bainbridge writes a "letter within a letter" to Elvira in which she gives a shortened version of her own story and that of the Summerlads of Hittisleigh. We are not given any details of the other versions though I suspect they may form the basis for the subsequent novels. In that event Purdy may well unmake *Jeremy's Version* by means of the novels which follow it. The series, if not this part, will form then a novel of number.

Purdy's work to date has been, with the possible exceptions of *The Nephew* and *Jeremy's Version*, a dramatization, primarily through language and action techniques and through self-conscious art, of the Post-existential dilemma. Art has been seen to fail many times. But the detached tone of Barth and Heller characterizes only some of Purdy's novels; his concern for human suffering tends to make itself known despite his intellectual assent to the notion of the futility of human action. It may be that the realism of *Jeremy's Version* indicates Purdy's intention to deal in the future in a more realistic way with the agonies of human experience in the Post-existential world.

Chapter Four

Kurt Vonnegut, Jr.:
The Sirens of Satire

Many critics of Kurt Vonnegut's novels[1] discuss them, rather loosely, as satires and make comparisons with *Gulliver's Travels, Candide*, and *Rasselas*.[2] Warning us against treating Vonnegut as a realistic writer, Robert Scholes suggests that Vonnegut is hardly a novelist at all: "it is surely better to think of Voltaire and Swift when reading Vonnegut . . . than to think of Hemingway and Fitzgerald."[3] It is certainly true that Vonnegut appears to attack, with the familiar methods of satire, many aspects of contemporary society.

But almost all the commentators on Vonnegut betray a certain uneasiness in talking about him as a satirist; he does not quite fit the mold. C. D. Bryan complains about the simplicity of Vonnegut's satirical targets;[4] Jerry Bryant realizes that it is difficult to pinpoint the moral values the satire serves. In Vonnegut's novels, he says, "For every value there is an anti-value."[5] Scholes, himself, is anxious to distinguish Vonnegut from earlier satirists. In an interview with Vonnegut, he links him to "Writers that often get treated as if they were trying to be satirists, as if they were trying to reform the world when really they're not trying to do that at all."[6] Unlike earlier satirists, Vonnegut, he says, is among those writers who "reject all ethical absolutes."[7]

The difficulty lies in the definition of satire. Is it possible to have a satirist who rejects all ethical absolutes? Surely the methods of satire inevitably imply a standard from which the satirist operates. Distinguishing between irony and satire, Northrop Frye claims that "satire is militant irony: its moral norms are relatively clear, and it assumes standards against which the grotesque and the absurd are measured. . . . whenever a reader is not sure what the author's attitude is or what his own is supposed to be, we have irony with relatively little satire."[8] Can one satirize the cold inhumanity of the scientist, for example, without investing value in human warmth? Satire, surely, cannot exist in a world of relative values. It implies absolute values which transcend the individual; it says not merely "I choose to" but "you should." What does it really mean to talk, as Scholes does, of a type of satire that is "less certain ethically but more certain aesthetically than traditional satire"?[9]

Scholes has, however, pinpointed the problem of talking about Vonnegut as a satirist. Vonnegut's basic world view is Post-existential. He does reject all ethical absolutes. Vonnegut stresses the futility of man's search for meaning in a world where everything is "a nightmare of meaninglessness without end,"[10] where we are all the victims of a series of accidents,[11] "trapped in the amber of this moment. . . . Because this moment simply is."[12] In *Cat's Cradle* he shows how man's "nostalgia for unity," to use Camus' phrase, forces him to interpret mere chance as purposeful, leads him to create the meaning he wants to find and makes him believe in his own insubstantial structure, his own cat's cradle. Each of Vonnegut's novels shows us that there is no relation between human actions and the events that take place in human lives. All success—and, one supposes, failure—is the result of luck, just as it is for Malachi Constant in *The Sirens of Titan*. Man, like Billy Pilgrim in *Slaughterhouse-Five*, finds that among the things he cannot change are past, present and future. His actions serve no purpose he can hope to comprehend. Vonnegut also has his own version of Sartre's theory of human identity. He talks about the desire of Being-For-Itself to become Being-In-Itself as the Universal Will to Become and claims that the moral of *Mother Night* is "We are what we pretend to be."

If Vonnegut denies the possibility of absolute values, then how can he be a satirist? The answer is that he is not. He has the look of the satirist, but has no answer to give us. He is not, as Dan Wakefield says, "the prophetic type," though he has been "adopted as a kind of prophet by so many people, in so many places."[13] In the interview with Scholes, Vonnegut expresses pleasure in a description of himself that claims he finds "in laughter an analgesic for the temporary relief of existential pain."[14] Scholes agrees that Vonnegut is basically "trying to make some sort of comic structure out of things which can be pretty bad."[15]

In order to do this, he employs the methods of satire as an attack upon satire itself, or rather upon the idea of a world in which the definite answers satire implies are possible. Vonnegut deliberately uses the expectations that satire arouses to tempt the reader into easy moral answers he subsequently undermines either by later attacking the acquired moral answer or by setting it in a Post-existential philosophic framework where no value is absolute. So in *Cat's Cradle* he attacks the inhumanity of science through the character of Dr. Asa Breed and arouses our sympathy for his apparently mystified but very human assistant Miss Pefko. He follows this immediately with an attack upon the ignorance of Miss Pefko.

Vonnegut's major methods appear to be satirical, then, but he is actually just adding another technique to that repertoire of absurd techniques employed by Barth, Heller, and Purdy. Like them, Vonnegut frustrates the reader's expectations in order to bring about in him an experience of the absurd. He allows the reader the temporary illusion that he has the answer and then disillusions him. This is not just a question, as perhaps it is in the case of such other pessimistic satirists as Swift or Johnson, of not believing man likely to adopt the alternative to the vices under attack. Vonnegut does not merely disbelieve that man will become benevolent, that Gulliver will ever recognize the virtues of the Portugese sea-captain, but attacks the very idea of the workability of benevolence.[16]

In his earlier novels, Vonnegut works chiefly against the expectations aroused by satire but more recently, particuarly in his sixth novel, *Slaughterhouse-Five*, he has been making increasing use of those techniques of action, language, and characterization that work against the expectations of realism. In an interesting article on Vonnegut's methods, James Mellard discusses even as early a novel as *Player Piano* as an attack on Jamesian methods, an attempt to "break out of the single dimension of linear plot, continuous explanation, explicit characterization."[17]

In a similar way, Vonnegut uses the form of the fable against the objectives of the fable. By suggesting, through obvious patterning of characters and contrasts between our own world and those of other planets, that he is arguing to a conclusion, he arouses our expectation for revelation. The pattern will work out; the final piece of the jigsaw puzzle will make the picture clear; the fable will reveal its moral. But Vonnegut's fables do not have morals, at least none which can stand as solutions to the Post existential dilemma, just as his apparently satirical methods do not operate from any consistent ethical scheme. Again he is deliberately working to disillusion the reader. He is a novelist of number, then, primarily in the sense that he parodies himself; his novels gradually unmake themselves.

Vonnegut's first novel, *Player Piano*, initially appears to be highly derivative, particularly of Orwell's *1984* but also of Huxley's *Brave New World*. The setting is the standard future world, our own become completely mechanized; it is run by the managers and the engineers. The managers and engineers are selected early in life for their intelligence, and live in one part of the town called Ilium (a name occurring in almost all Vonnegut's novels). In another part of town, known as Homestead, live the less intelligent, long since deprived of "meaningful" work by machines, and yet somehow, we appear to be asked to believe, more "human" than the managers and engineers.

The central figure of the novel, Paul Proteus, is a familiar figure also. He is vaguely dissatisfied with the mechanized world where he is always competing for new and better jobs, has routinized sex with Anita, his wife, and goes to highly organized company vacation resorts like The Meadows. His vague dissatisfaction is triggered into open rebellion by the reappearance of an old friend, Ed Finnerty, a sort of McMurphy from Kesey's *One Flew Over the Cuckoo's Nest*, who introduces Paul to Homestead. Paul feels "love—particularly for the little people, the common people, God bless them. All his life they had been hidden from him by the walls of his ivory tower. . . . This was *real*, this side of the river, and Paul loved these common people, and wanted to help, and let them know they were loved and understood, and he wanted them to love him too" (pp. 102-103).

If we accept, as most critics have, that this novel is a satire directed against technology, then the values expressed by Paul here are those Vonnegut expects us to accept also. But even this early in the novel a careful reader would surely have to be suspicious of the tone of this passage. Vonnegut is too conscious of language to use such phrases as "the common people," "the little people," "ivory tower," "this was real," without recognizing them as clichés. He is giving us an easy answer—charity, fellow feeling, remorse— to the problems of mechanization and inhumanity, and is indicating that the answer is simplistic by his use of clichés.

Nevertheless, it is easy to miss these early clues, and the novel does for a long time seem to be a satire. Vonnegut's targets are standard ones: daytime soap operas designed to keep everyone satisfied with the status quo; the big business aspects of college football now no longer related to academic life at all; ambitious wives who feign affection. Each of these targets is attacked through the usual satirical method of slightly exaggerating a situation already present to a lesser extent in our society. Each of these targets also is an aspect of the apparently chief target of Vonnegut's novel, the mechanization of human lives. The great example of its opposite, human feeling and eccentricity, is Ed Finnerty, and Vonnegut sees to it that our sympathies lie with Finnerty and his friend Lasher throughout the novel. Who can resist the temptation to support man and human feeling against machines?

So far the novel is conventional. The methods are basically realistic, except for the use of a future world. Even the visitor from another country, the Shah of Bratpuhr, functions as travellers from other countries do in *Gulliver's Travels* or *Rasselas*, as a naive observer, not as he would in later Vonnegut novels as a creature with more knowledge from a totally different world. The action is causally related, not a series of apparently unrelated anecdotes as in later Vonnegut novels, though there is a hint of the exaggeration of action to absurdity in the riot scene at the end of the novel.

The language is so full of adverbs, transitions, and complex clauses that if you come to this novel after *Cat's Cradle* it does not read like Vonnegut at all. There is only one hint of the beginnings of the "punchline technique" that gives the later books such power:

And Paul didn't want either of those things to happen. She was what fate had given him to love, and he did his best to love her. He knew her too well for her conceits to be offensive most of the time, to be anything but pathetic.

She was also more of a source of courage than he cared to admit.

She also had a sexual genius that gave Paul his one un-qualified enthusiasm in life.

And Anita had also made possible, by her dogged attention to details, the luxury of his detached, variously amused or cynical outlook on life.

She was also all he had. (pp. 133-134)

The "punchline technique" is a technique of the novel of number because it invalidates with a final, usually brief, comment several previous statements. It contributes to the novel's self-destruction; the end of the paragraph cancels its beginning.

But *Player Piano* does not end conventionally. The values established by the satirical methods at the beginning of the novel are finally completely undercut. This is not to deny, of course, that Vonnegut prefers human warmth to mechanization; but he does not, in his novel, appear to see it as a viable solution. Those represen-tatives of human feeling against mechanization, Finnerty and Lasher, treat Paul as an object. " 'You don't matter,' said Finnerty. 'You belong to History now' " (p. 276). They are prepared to kill him if it is necessary. The Ghost Shirt Society that Paul had believed "promised a change for the better" was actually formed because it "promised some excitement for a change" (p. 278). For Lasher the revolution was a symbol, for Von Neumann an experi-ment, for Finnerty revenge. Worst of all, when the machines are destroyed, the very workers whose jobs they replace start to repair them. Man, Vonnegut says, will inevitably rebuild his mechanized society. He also appears to imply that man, unable to learn from his experience, is little more than a machine himself. In this, of course, Vonnegut is more pessimistic than Sartre or Camus, who stress man's freedom to make himself anything he wishes.

In *Player Piano* the easy answers of the initial satirical attacks are not refuted by placing them in a Post-existential framework and there are only the earliest hints of absurd techniques. But nevertheless Vonnegut does use here the basic method of all his novels; he tempts the reader into easy answers through satirical methods and later disillusions him.

The subject of man as machine is far more imaginatively treated in Vonnegut's second novel, his first attempt at science fiction, *The Sirens of Titan*. In this novel Vonnegut takes the old sophomoric debate about first cause—if God created the world, then who created God—and gives it some new turns. He is concerned with the absurdity of man's "appetite for the absolute," with his inescapable tendency to attribute meaning to his existence on earth. As Robert Scholes says, "we attribute purpose or meaning that suits us to things which are either accidental or possessed of purpose and meaning quite different from those we would supply. And it doesn't matter which of these mistakes we make."[18]

This, of course, is the Existentialist world view. Vonnegut illustrates it not only in the main plot of the novel but even in such minor episodes as Ransom K. Fern's giving Noel Constant's letter to his son Malachi Constant. When he tells him where the letter is to be found, Fern asks Malachi "for one small favor. . . . If the letter seems to cast the vaguest light on what life might be about, I would appreciate your telephoning me" (p. 85). Noel Constant's letter says, "I kept my eyes open for some kind of signal that would tell me what it was all about but there wasn't any signal. . . . The only thing I ever learned was that some people are lucky and other people aren't" (pp. 91-92).

The main plot begins with the periodic materializations of the late (in earth's terms) Winston Niles Rumfoord at his former house. Crowds come to watch the materializations, which they never see, but which they consider miracles. Religious belief, says Vonnegut, is based on no evidence at all. Rumfoord believes he knows the meaning of certain earthlings' lives, since they are part of his plan to establish the Church of God the Utterly Indifferent on earth by leading an attack from Mars. Malachi Constant, later Unk, is used by Rumfoord. What Rumfoord doesn't know is that he is part of a more complicated plan, the ultimate aim of which is to transport a replacement part for a space ship stranded on Titan. So the meaning of human life is reduced to an absurdity. Rumfoord says to Chrono, who has the replacement part in his pocket, "In your pocket is the culmination of all Earthling history. In your pocket is the mysterious something that every Earthling was trying so desperately, so earnestly, so gropingly, so exhaustingly to produce and deliver" (p. 297). The space ship belongs to Salo, who is a Tralfamadorian carrying a message he hasn't seen throughout the universe. The message has no significance either. It simply reads, "Greetings."

If human life has a pattern, a scheme, it is not a merciful one. An explosion on the sun separates Winston Rumfoord from his dog Kazak; "A Universe schemed in mercy would have kept man and dog together" (p. 295). If the plan of the universe is not merciful, suggests Vonnegut, it might just as well not have one. Our religious fantasies of all truth being revealed to us in another world might well turn out to be the truth revealed to us through the other worlds of Vonnegut's novel. At all events there is no possible way of our finding the truth. Each man is doomed to his own subjective version of it. There is really no such thing as a chromo-synclastic infundibula "where all the different kinds of truth fit together" (p. 14). The kindest action we can perform for another is to create for him an illusion of meaning, as Salo does for Malachi at the end of the novel.

Since we have no information upon which to make meaningful choices, human action is futile. We are all like Boaz, "a real commander" in the Martian army. Boaz never receives any orders, does not know who is in command of "the real commanders" and bases his actions "on what could be best described as conversational tidbits" (p. 121). All events come about through luck, though like Malachi Constant we choose to believe that "somebody up there" likes us. Noel Constant's fortune comes from his absurd scheme of dividing the first sentence of the Bible into pairs of letters—I.N. T.H. E.B. E.G.—and investing money in companies with those initials. No one believes this, because, as Vonnegut points out, "people have to believe, for their own peace of mind, that tremendous wealth can be produced only by tremendous cleverness" (p.73).

Salo's ship is powered by UWTB, The Universal Will to Become: "UWTB is what makes universes out of nothingness—that makes nothingness insist on becoming somethingness" (p. 138). UWTB is, in other words, the driving force that makes Being-For-Itself try to become Being-In-Itself, that makes us want objective identity and meaning for ourselves. In our desperation to find this meaning we do indeed create illusions as incredible as Salo's spaceship.

Vonnegut's characters treat each other as objects. When Unk tries to remember who he is, he does so by labeling other people. Each man is seen to be both a suffering victim or an agent of another's suffering. When Boaz searches for a place where he will do no harm, he ends up buried in The Caves of Mercury. Even the only apparently innocent creatures in the novel, the Harmoniums in Boaz's caves, are used by Rumfoord to spell out for Unk and Boaz "a new message of hope or veiled derision every fourteen Earthling days—for three years" (p. 197).

The Sirens of Titan invites us to read it as a satire just as *Player Piano* does. The many early targets of the book—posted bulletins about someone's health that reveal nothing; man's need to feel superior to his fellows by remembering his own achievements— suggest a satire operating from some base of consistent values. A favorite target is one that epitomizes the theme of the book: man's belief in image without substance. "The Rumfoord mansion was an hilariously impressive expression of the concept: People of substance . . . the density and permanence of the mansion were, of course, at ironic variance with the fact that the quondam master of the house, except for one hour every fifty-nine days, was no more substantial than a moonbeam" (p. 18). The dog's skeleton chained to a wall in the Rumford house is, we are told, symbolic. But symbolic of what? No dog had died there. A spy, Miss Fenstermaker, is not regarded as suspect because she has the right piece of paper, a teaching certificate from the State of Minnesota.

The major satirical method is a traditional one, to be found in *Gulliver's Travels*, for example; Vonnegut ridicules the target by making the abstract concrete. Thus the support religion has historically given to big business in the U.S.A. becomes in the novel the literal making of money by using initials from the first sentence of the Bible; the handicaps of life become actual weights carried around by some people to make the race of life fair; psychological brainwashing becomes an actual clearing out of the mind on Mars. Bee says of Rumfoord, "He wired us like robots, trained us, aimed us" (p. 242). Vonnegut tempts us into believing this using of people is bad. Surely one should have choice? Surely Vonnegut believes brainwashing is wrong? But it is not as simple as that. "Could we have done any better if he'd left us in charge of our own lives?" continues Bee. "Would we have become any more—or any less? I guess I'm glad he used me" (p. 242). As she points out later in the book, in answer to all Vonnegut's earlier criticisms of the way we use each other, "The worst thing that could possibly happen to anybody would be to not be used for anything by anybody" (p. 310).

There are some positive images of human experience in this novel, as Beatrice's comment indicates. Beatrice, Malachi, and their son, Chrono, together on Titan towards the end of the novel, can be seen as an illustration of the truth that Constant believes he has found: that one of the purposes of human life is to love "whoever is around to be loved." In this novel Vonnegut, like Barth in *The Floating Opera*, does appear to see human emotion as a value, even if a relative one. Perhaps, too, Chrono's return to nature and a more primitive way of life is, as Jerry Bryant suggests, an affirmation. It is significant, however, that neither of these events takes place on earth, and that Vonnegut's picture of Constant is of an old, lonely man accepting a comforting myth as the truth. Vonnegut, then, as in *Player Piano*, tempts the reader into accepting easy answers and then invalidates them. He also sets the assumed values in a Post-existential framework which makes them all relative.

For the first time, in *The Sirens of Titan*, Vonnegut works with some of the fantasy techniques I have described in the novels of Heller, Barth, and Purdy. He employs disguise, as does Barth in *Sot-Weed*, to illustrate Sartre's premise that we are nothingness and can thus take on entirely different roles. The difference between Barth and Vonnegut is that in Vonnegut's novels people are forced into new roles by others. The fact that people treat others as objects is illustrated by having the characters literally turn into machines— Malachi Constant becomes mechanized as Unk—much in the way Beckett's characters often do. In this way, of course, Vonnegut is working against the expectations of the reader for "human," rounded characters. He, then, undercuts his own method deliberately: Salo, a machine, is more humane than the earthlings.

The action of this novel is designed to dramatize its theme for the reader. Some of the characters have foreknowledge of events and they are used by Vonnegut to foreshadow the plot for both the other characters and the reader. We are continually in the position of believing we understand what lies behind events, only to have that solution supplanted by a new one. When we learn, for example, that Rumfoord has organized the Martian army to establish his new religion on earth, we think this explains what has happened so far. Later, of course, we learn Rumfoord himself is merely a tool of the Tralfamadorians. We are trapped into believing everything has a cause, but it is never the cause we think it has. As in all novels of number, each event in the action tends to cancel what has gone before.

The process of attempting to discover significance, a process that inevitably takes place when reading a novel as in life, involves our reason in much the same way as Unk's is involved when he tries to learn from a letter what happened to him before he was brainwashed: "All the things that the writer knew for sure were numbered, as though to emphasize the painful, step-by-step nature of the game of finding things out for sure. There were one hundred and fifty-eight things the writer knew for sure. There had once been one hundred and eighty-five, but seventeen had been crossed off" (p. 124). Subjectivity and thus the futility of any search for meaning is revealed at the end of the letter when the signature is seen to be Unk's own.

The letter is subdivided into the forms of knowledge we are accustomed to think of as leading to truth: history, astronomy, biology, theology. Similarly the language of the novel parodies the styles of the various books we are accustomed to believe lead to truth. Vonnegut parodies the methods of characterization of the realistic novel, introducing Malachi Constant with a physical description and a series of facts: "He was a well-made man—a light heavyweight, dark skinned, with poet's lips, with soft brown eyes in the shaded caves of a Cro-Magnon brow-ridge. He was thirty-one" (p. 17). He parodies the uselessness of most information in biographies, even telling us the names of those who played German batball with Rumfoord as a child; the style of travel guides: "Titan, of course, is an extremely pleasant moon of Saturn" (p. 138); the entries in Encyclopedias: "Harmonium— the only known form of life on the planet Mercury" (p. 184); the numerical emphasis of history books, typified here by Rumfoord's *Pocket History of Mars*: "In the first wave came the army reserves, the last of the trained troops—26,119 men in 721 ships" (p. 171). Each of these apparent excerpts from books of knowledge is used by Vonnegut to interrupt the main action. They suggest helpful information, but provide none. Similarly Vonnegut's basic narrative style, which is characterized by direct statements and a noticeable absence of transitions and adverbial clauses, echoes the Post-existential view that there are no causal relations in life. Sentences that provide them must therefore be lies.

The Sirens of Titan is the first Vonnegut novel to display an interest in the techniques of self-conscious art—in Vonnegut self-parody—that are so important in the later novels. His concern with the whole subject of the nature of fictional reality is revealed in the dedication: "All persons, places, and events in the book are real," reminding us of Ionesco's comment that fantasy is more real than realism. Throughout the novel Vonnegut draws our attention from what we are reading to the process of reading, by introducing other novels and stories which comment on the themes of his novel. Mrs. Rumfoord, for example, has published a collection of poems called *Between Timid and Timbuktu*, so-called because all the words in the dictionary between *timid* and *Timbuktu* relate to time. "Between Timid and Timbuktu" is the title of Vonnegut's own first chapter. Later in the novel Salo tells a Tralfamadorian legend which is a synopsis of the entire novel. It stresses particularly the relationship between the Post-existential world view and the impossibility of moral action. A group of creatures, who need to have a purpose, build machines to tell them what that purpose is; the machines report that the creatures have no purpose at all.

Superficially, at least, Vonnegut's third novel, *Mother Night*, is concerned with the converse of this proposition, the ways men use and destroy each other in the name of purpose. Given Vonnegut's concern with atrocities and his basic method of working against the expectations of the reader, it is not surprising that he should take as his subject the Nazis' treatment of the Jews. We all tend to believe World War II provided the worst atrocities in living memory and gave us a clear-cut case of right and wrong. The Nazis were the villains, the Jews the suffering victims. The apparently absolute nature of the morality involved in this situation has tempted other recent novelists to explore its opposite. *Mother Night* belongs to a subgenre of the contemporary novel which includes Robert Shaw's *The Man in the Glass Booth* and Romaine Gary's *The Dance of Genghis Cohn*. Vonnegut's novel is related by Howard Campbell, an American about to be tried by Israel for broadcasting anti-Semitic speeches for Germany in World War II. As Campbell describes his postwar escape to New York and subsequent capture, the moral certainties become less clear.

Mother Night is more like *Player Piano* than *The Sirens of Titan* in that it works primarily by reversing the easy answers provided by initial satirical attacks. Like *Player Piano*, too, it works against attitudes that Vonnegut can be reasonably certain are preestablished in the reader's head. It is not a science-fiction novel, does not present us with a future world. It is, in fact, hardly fantasy at all except in so far as its action becomes exaggerated, improbable rather than impossible, in a way that is characteristic of the novels of J. P. Donleavy and Bruce Jay Friedman.

It is, however, more overtly Post-existentialist than *Player Piano*. Vonnegut begins by reminding us how little truth we can hope to establish about history in a scene between Howard Campbell and his Israeli guard Arnold. Campbell's lack of knowledge about Hebrew history is matched by Arnold's ignorance of Goebbels. How can we know the truth about history, when we forget the past so rapidly and when each man's view of what constitutes history is different? Later in the novel Campbell even fails to recognize a play he himself has written.

In *Mother Night* Vonnegut is primarily interested in two concepts. The first is the impossibility of absolute truth. We can only have absolute answers by blocking our minds to some obvious facts: "The dismaying thing about the classic totalitarian mind is that any given gear, though mutilated, will have at its circumference unbroken sequences of teeth that are immaculately maintained. . . . The missing teeth, of course, are simple, obvious truths" (p. 162). All absolutes lead inevitably to tyranny, as Camus has pointed out. "Say what you will about the sweet miracle of unquestioning faith, I consider the capacity for it terrifying and absolutely vile" (p. 120). There are no absolute reasons for action as Campbell discovers when he finds himself paralyzed, like Horner in Barth's *End of the Road*, because he has "absolutely no reason to move in any direction" (p. 167).

The second concept is Sartre's theory of human identity: "We are what we pretend to be." We cannot pretend to be evil, as Campbell does, and remain good secretly. We can choose our roles, but we are what we choose. Man, Vonnegut shows, has an infinite capacity for living in bad faith. Campbell can sustain a lovenest— a "nation of two"—while he helps destroy thousands. Stalin can love a romantic play about the Holy Grail and yet be Stalin. This play, one of Campbell's, functions as a comment on the novel itself for, in spite of its romantic treatment, its subject is the tyranny of Christianity, which, like the absolutes in *Mother Night*, has destroyed human lives.

The basic technique of *Mother Night* is that of *Player Piano*: to play against our preconceived attitudes and the expectations which the initial satirical attacks have aroused in us. As a former hate-monger for the Germans Campbell must be the villain, but, it turns out, he was also working for Americans. Eichmann's ability to translate atrocity into journalistic profit—"Do you think a literary agent is absolutely necessary?" (p. 125) is his first question to Campbell—is equalled only by Campbell's—"My photograph was taken while I looked up at the gallows. . . . The picture was on the cover of *Life*, and came close to winning a Pulitzer Prize" (p.33). The American who captured Campbell and resents his escape, Bernard O'Hare, is as vengeful as any Nazi. The negro, whose attitudes about his race the liberal reader is likely to share, is prejudiced against Jews and doesn't consider the Chinese colored. Dr. Lionel J. D. Jones, editor of *The White Christian Minuteman*, whose right-wing extremism is heavily satirized in the early part of the novel, turns out to be the only honest friend Campbell has. All absolutes, all preconceived notions, are undercut in this novel. The reader is left, as Campbell is, without any values to cling to. Campbell hangs himself.

Cat's Cradle is perhaps Vonnegut's most successful novel. The use of the methods of satire to attack satire is at its sharpest; the techniques of science fiction are turned upon science itself. But the novel works primarily because of the quality of the two central images, ice-nine and cat's cradle, and because of a fundamental irony underlying Vonnegut's conception of the narrator.

Felix Hoenikker, inventor of the atom bomb, created just before he died a substance called ice-nine, an even more terrible weapon that turns all water it touches very rapidly to ice. His three children all have pieces of ice-nine; they and their pieces are literally "chips off the old block." This using of clichés in new ways, which Vonnegut has occasionally employed before, becomes a major technique in the novel. He takes this cliché, reverses the traditionally benign associations of it, and shows how our inheritance from the past is not necessarily benign at all. Evil, cold like ice, spreads like water and is inevitably passed, like the ice-nine, from one generation to the next. The narrator, Jonah, is about to write a book about the day the atom bomb was dropped, to be entitled *The Day The World Ended*. In the course of his research he tracks the three Hoenikker children to San Lorenzo where he in fact witnesses the destruction of the world by ice-nine.

Ice-nine is part of Vonnegut's attack on science in *Cat's Cradle*. The opening sections of the novel tempt the reader into believing that this is a satire on the inhumanity of scientists. Asa Breed, who helped to create the atom bomb, tells with apparent horror of a man who murdered twenty-six people. Felix Hoenikker is so detached from human emotion that his children are unknown to him, and on one occasion he tips his wife at breakfast. We are obviously intended to shudder at the irony implicit in the plaque in Hoenikker's laboratory. It reads, "In this room, Dr. Felix Hoenikker, Nobel Laureate in physics, spent the last twenty-eight years of his life. 'Where he was, there was the frontier of knowledge.' The importance of this one man in the history of mankind is incalculable" (p. 45). Newton Hoenikker's letter to Jonah recounts a conversation between his father and another scientist on the day the atom bomb was first tested: ". . . a scientist turned to Father and said, 'Science has now known sin.' And do you know what Father said? He said, 'What is sin?'" (p. 21).

Throughout the early scenes of the novel there is much ironic juxtaposing of Christianity with inhuman technology. Christmas Eve is the night Angela Hoenikker divides up the ice-nine among the children. We are tempted into believing Vonnegut offers Christian compassion as the answer. Yet Christianity is associated with destruction too. There is a Fort Jesus on San Lorenzo to remind us of all the wars fought over that faith. The most overt Christian in the book, Hazel Crosby, happily advocates capital punishment, is only interested in family connections, and has a husband whose exploitation of his workers she apparently supports. Perhaps, then, if capitalistic Christianity is no answer, communism is? Vonnegut undercuts that solution also. When San Lorenzo was reorganized, it was announced that the country's total income would be divided among the inhabitants. Each share came to between six and seven dollars. Once again Vonnegut has used the methods of satire only to refuse us a solution.

There can be no absolute solution, of course, because there is no meaning to human existence. The second important image of the novel is the image of the child's game cat's cradle. The significance of this is explained by Newt Hoenikker: " 'No wonder kids grow up crazy. A cat's cradle is nothing but a bunch of X's between somebody's hands, and little kids look and look and look at all those X's.' 'And?' '*No damn cat, and no damn cradle*' " (p. 114). Cat's cradle is a structure without substance or the meaning ascribed to it. Cat's cradle is a concrete example of the religious and philosophic structures man seems driven to build to explain his existence.

The Post-existentialist world view of *Cat's Cradle* is that of *The Sirens of Titan*. Vonnegut has invented a religion called Bokononism,[19] which most critics have described as Existentialism and take as Vonnegut's own philosophy. Certainly Bokononism recognizes that life has no purpose, as an interview with God in the First Book of Bokonon reveals: " 'Everything must have a purpose?' asked God. 'Certainly,' said man. 'Then I leave you to think of one for all this,' said God. And he went away" (p. 177).[19] It is equally true that "Man got to tell himself he understand" (p. 124). Bokonon recognizes that even his own cosmogony is a "pack of foma," all lies. Here, surely, is the point. As Von Koenigswald replies to the narrator when he asks whether or not he is a Bokononist, "I agree with one Bokononist idea. I agree that all religions, including Bokononism, are nothing but lies" (p. 148). Von Koenigswald realizes you cannot believe in Bokononism as absolute truth, any more than in other religions, without living in bad faith. The narrator has missed the point, calls himself a Bokononist, just as he used to call himself a Christian, and thus is in the ironic position of believing in lies as his truth. Of course, Vonnegut claims, so are we all. Man does invest meaning in mere chance, does tend to think that other people have a purpose in relation to himself, are part of his "karass," and is willing to believe that everything happens "as it was meant to happen."

Vonnegut recognizes that we cannot live without "foma"; he does not insist like Sartre and Camus on our keeping the knowledge of absurdity always before us. Nevertheless the vision of the novel is very pessimistic: "Maturity is a bitter disappointment for which no remedy exists, unless laughter can be said to remedy anything" (p. 134). Vonnegut, in fact, ends the novel on the same laugh of ironic detachment with which Purdy ends *Cabot Wright Begins*; it is the cosmic laugh characteristic of the novel of number. Vonnegut's final words are Bokonon's final gesture, "I would make a statue of myself, lying on my back, grinning horribly, and thumbing my nose at You Know Who" (p. 191).[20]

Vonnegut brings the reader to that laugh of ironic detachment by many of the same means as Purdy, by undermining his expectations of realism. The characters of *Cat's Cradle* are caricatures, often defined, as in Heller's *Catch-22*, by their particular obsessions. Hazel Crosby, for example, is concerned only with Hoosier family connections. This obsession grows as the book continues until we realize that she considers everyone a Hoosier. Several of the characters are grotesques and, like Purdy, Vonnegut springs the facts of their grotesqueness upon the reader some pages after the characters' introduction. Newt Hoenikker, we learn from a post-post-script to a letter, is a midget.

The action of the novel works similarly to that of *The Sirens of Titan*, by a series of surprises which reverse what we had previously taken as fact. So we discover that although Bokononism is out-lawed, everyone is a Bokonist. Angela Hoenikker's marriage which had appeared happy is an unhappy one: " 'From the way she talked,' I said, 'I thought it was a very happy marriage.' Little Newt held his hands six inches apart and he spread his fingers. 'See the cat? See the cradle?' " (p. 122). The action is full of such absurd coincidences as Jonah's chance meeting with Marvin Breed just after leaving his brother Asa, and the discovery of a pedestal on which his own name is engraved. There is little causal relation between the scenes; each is a short anecdote, often complete in itself. In many of these anecdotes action is exaggerated to the point of absurdity, such as the account of San Lorenzo's history, characterized by each conqueror's willingness to give up his new territory.

The technique Vonnegut uses to best advantage in this novel, however, is that discrepancy between tone and subject Heller used so successfully in *Catch-22* to disorient the reader. Vonnegut's comic anecdotes turn very swiftly to horror. The one entitled,

"When Automobiles Had Cut-glass Vases," lures the reader into laughing about Felix Hoenikker's car, a Marmon, with little cut-glass vases full of flowers on the doorposts, which he abandoned in downtown traffic one day. Emily, his wife, came to pick it up. " 'Do you think anybody would object if I used the story about the Marmon in my book?' I asked. 'As long as you don't use the end of it.' 'The *end* of it?' 'Emily wasn't used to driving the Marmon. She got into a bad wreck on the way home. It did something to her pelvis. . . . And that was why she died when little Newt was born' " (p. 30).

The lack of substance behind the image, a recurring theme of *Cat's Cradle*, is dramatized in two ways by Vonnegut's language techniques. Several times in the novel he tempts the reader into believing the San Lorenzan language needs translating for his understanding. But there is no actual difference behind the apparent one. San Lorenzan is simply a phonetic variation of English: "Tsvent-kiul, tsvent-kiul, lett-pool store" reads "Twinkle, twinkle little star." Similarly Vonnegut shows us the lack of substance behind the labels and definitions of any religious or philosophic sect. "If you find your life tangled up with somebody else's life for no very logical reasons," writes Bokonon, "that person may be a member of your karass" (p. 12). But, of course, *karass* is simply a label for chance encounter. Everyone one meets is a member of one's karass.

As in all his novels since *Player Piano*, Vonnegut's style is characterized by the deliberate omission of adverbial clauses, transitions, and unified paragraph structure which suggest through causally related sentences a causally related universe. Typical of all the novels is this passage about Julian Castle:

> Castle's hospital was called The House of Hope and Mercy in the Jungle. Its jungle was on San Lorenzo, among the wild coffee trees on the northern slope of Mount McCabe.
>
> When I flew to San Lorenzo, Julian Castle was sixty years old.
>
> He had been absolutely unselfish for twenty years.
>
> In his selfish days he had been as familiar to tabloid readers as Tommy Manville, Adolf Hitler, Benito Mussolini and Barbara Hutton. His fame rested on lechery, alcoholism, reckless driving and draft evasion. (p. 63)

Where did Castle change? Why did Castle change? Why did he choose San Lorenzo? Only in meaningful universe is cause related to event. Vonnegut does not presume to tell us.

Vonnegut's interest in the technique of self-conscious art is apparent in *Cat's Cradle* on two occasions. The novel *2000 A.D.* which is sent by its author to Felix Hoenikker is about the end of the world. So, of course, is the book the narrator Jonah is planning to write, and Vonnegut's own. It becomes clear as the novel progresses that the Books of Bokonon are also a metaphor for *Cat's Cradle* itself. The final words of Bokonon and of *Cat's Cradle* are the same and Vonnegut, like Bokonon, tells us not to believe a word he says. "Nothing in this book is true," reads the epigraph.

Eliot Rosewater, alcoholic millionaire hero of Vonnegut's fifth novel, *God Bless You, Mr. Rosewater*, addresses a writer's convention in Milford:

> And it occurred to him that a really good science-fiction book had never been written about money. "Just think of the wild ways money is passed around on Earth!" he said. "You don't have to go to the Planet Tralfamadore in Anti-matter Galaxy 508G to find weird creatures with unbelievable powers . . . Look at me! . . . *There's* fantasy for you. . . . I leave it to you, friends and neighbors, and especially to the immortal Kilgore Trout think about the silly ways money gets passed around now, and then think up better ways." (pp. 21 22)

The book Eliot Rosewater imagines is the book in which he appears, *God Bless You, Mr. Rosewater*, and it is indeed fantastic only in so far as the action is improbable. There is no travelling to other planets.

It is Vonnegut's most optimistic book. It appears to be an attack upon human greed and upon the notion that there is a relation between hard work and wealth. Most of the people with money in America are like Stewart Buntline, whose father left him fourteen million dollars and who sleeps all day. What you own depends primarily upon how near the banks of the money river you were born, and the only way to make money is to flatter or trick the rich into giving it to you. Free enterprise is not by any means always a desirable thing. Lila Buntline has made a business from being able to recognize pornography in the local drugstore, buying it, and selling it to her friends at a massive profit. We buy and sell love as we do all commodities in our society, says Vonnegut.

In opposition to this materialism Vonnegut offers the actions of Eliot Rosewater, a Christ figure who attempts to love everyone. He settles in Rosewater and uses his extensive fortune running a telephone help service and being a member of the local fire department. He is pursued by a greedy young lawyer, Norman Mushari, who has devised a scheme for making money by proving Eliot insane. It seems clear that Vonnegut is writing a sanity-in-madness novel like Kesey's *One Flew Over The Cuckoo's Nest* and that we are supposed to take Eliot Rosewater's humanitarianism as a model. But is this really Vonnegut's final comment? The subtitle of the novel is *Pearls Before Swine* and certainly all those Rosewater helps are ungrateful. Fifty-seven of the women end up suing him in paternity suits in order to obtain his money. Eliot has a split personality himself on occasions; he yells at one of his clients Mary Moody when she calls him on the fire department telephone by mistake. As Senator Rosewater points out to him, when he explains he is motivated by love, "Love . . . you certainly loved me, didn't you? Loved me so much you smashed up every hope or ideal I ever had. And you certainly loved Sylvia, didn't you?" (p. 160). It is impossible, as Boaz discovered in *The Sirens of Titan*, to do good without harming someone.

The key to understanding Vonnegut's attitude to Rosewater lies in interpreting the ending. Eliot Rosewater accepts the paternity of all the children of Rosewater; the money will be divided among them. (One should remember this was tried unsuccessfully on San Lorenzo in *Cat's Cradle*.) But Eliot's final words are "Tell them to be fruitful and multiply" (p. 190). If one reads this as one would realistic novel, Eliot's God-complex is a clear indication that he really is insane. If Vonnegut means us to read it symbolically, then it merely emphasizes Eliot's God-like function in the novel. But what sort of God is he? His father tells him that now he has left Rosewater the people " 'run around like chickens with their heads cut off, just as though you really were God, and one day walked out.' Eliot felt his soul cringe, knew he could never stand to return to Rosewater County again" (p. 186).

If Eliot is God, he is Vonnegut's usual absent God. Kilgore Trout says the example of Eliot Rosewater showed that a man was able to give [uncritical] love over a long period of time. If one man can do it, perhaps others can do it, too. It means that our hatred of useless human beings and the cruelties we inflict upon them for their own good need not be parts of human nature. Thanks to the example of Eliot Rosewater, millions upon millions of people may learn to love and help whomever they see. (pp. 186-187).

Vonnegut cannot be unaware that mankind has had an example of this kind before and failed to do anything. Kilgore Trout's words must be meant ironically. We are left at the end of the novel wondering about Eliot Rosewater's actions. Is this really one of the better ways for money to get passed around or has Vonnegut once again tempted us with the methods of satire into believing it is? To love other human beings is perhaps a good in this novel as in *The Sirens of Titan*, but to act upon that love seems to cause insoluble problems.

We are separated from any possibility of identification with Eliot Rosewater in this novel by Vonnegut's very skillful use of the technique of self-conscious art. He introduces two writers into the novel, both parodies of himself. The first is Arthur Garvey Ulm who sends Eliot a manuscript and a love letter describing the helpful advice he believed he had received from him. "They [his pages of prose] could not have been created by me without you, and I do not mean your money. (Money is shit, which is one of the things I have tried to say in the book.) I mean your insistence that the truth be told about this sick, sick society of ours, and that the words for the telling could be found on the walls of restrooms" (p. 69). This description, slightly exaggerated, of Vonnegut's own theory of writing, has produced in Arthur Garvey Ulm's case eight hundred pages of pornography.

The second writer is Kilgore Trout, a science-fiction novelist much like Vonnegut himself. Eliot's words to science-fiction writers, one imagines, express Vonnegut's own views: "You're the only ones with guts enough to *really* care about the future, who *really* notice what machines do to us, what cities do to us, what big, simple ideas do to us, what tremendous misunderstandings, mistakes, accidents and catastrophes do to us" (p. 18). Kilgore Trout's novels have plots and themes very similar to Vonnegut's own: *2BR02B,* in which all work is done by machines, is obviously *Player Piano*. Science fiction and pornography have something in common, Vonnegut explains: they are both "fantasies of an impossibly hospitable world" (p. 20). This is also a fairly accurate description of *God Bless You, Mr. Rosewater*.

Slaughterhouse-Five, Vonnegut's sixth novel, comes to terms with the question that has in one way or another been central to all his novels: What is the significance of human suffering? Is it possible for human beings to be other than cruel to one another in an Existentialist world where "There is no why" (p. 66), and where everything happens "if the accident will" (p. 2). Rosewater, who appears in this novel too, finds life meaningless because he shot a fourteen year old fireman thinking he was a German soldier; Billy Pilgrim has seen what Vonnegut considers the greatest massacre in European history, the firebombing of Dresden. For Vonnegut the firebombing of Dresden, which he refers to both in *God Bless You, Mr. Rosewater* and in his 1966 introduction to *Mother Night*, is the ultimate symbol of purposeless human cruelty. This explains the symbolic value of fire departments and firemen in so many Vonnegut novels. They suggest the possibility of salvation from human cruelty. Vonnegut, like Billy Pilgrim, hero of *Slaughter-house-Five*, has witnessed the suffering in Dresden. How, asks Vonnegut, can the knowledge of such suffering, the memory of it, be made bearable? Can anything make sense of it?

In our own world we are like Billy's mother, who tried "to construct a life that made sense from things she found in giftshops" (p.33), or like Billy whose limited "earthling" perception is described as looking through a pipe: "whatever poor Billy saw through the pipe, he had no choice but to say to himself, 'That's life' " (p. 100). Only in another, imaginary world, represented here by Tralfamadore, would a solution be possible. Vonnegut says Billy and Rosewater "were trying to re-invent themselves and their universe. Science fiction was a big help" (p. 87). Billy's solution is "to come unstuck in time" and to have the capacity to travel backwards and forwards in his own life. He learns from the Tralfamodorians that all time is eternally present, "all moments, past, present, and future always have existed, always will exist" (p. 23), and that though this means one cannot change past present and future, it also means that "when a person dies he only appears to die. He is still very much alive in the past, so it is very silly for people to cry at his funeral (p. 23). If one can believe this, death can indeed be made bearable, even the deaths at Dresden, and one need say only what the Tralfamadorians say about death, "So it goes."

The action of the novel is a series of events in Billy's life, but they are not revealed chronologically. As Billy moves backwards and forwards in time he continually comes up against death, and each time Vonnegut adds, "So it goes." There are at least twenty-seven "so it goes" in the novel, four of these on the last two pages. Vonnegut dramatizes for the reader that whatever scheme one may devise to handle the idea of death, nothing can minimize the fact of it. "So it goes" comes at us with increasing momentum. The final image is the image of Dresden, a wagon shaped like a coffin and a meaningless question from a bird, "Poo-tee-weet?" "Everything is supposed to be very quiet after a massacre, and it always is, except for the birds. And what do the birds say? All there is to say about a massacre, things like 'Poo-tee-weet?' " (p. 17).

One of the effects of the "so it goes" on the reader is the effect produced by the disjunction of tone and subject. We expect death to be treated with more apparent concern. It is a technique used elsewhere in the novel by Vonnegut. One of the few human moments of *Slaughterhouse-Five* is the banquet set out by the British prisoners for the arriving Americans. At each place they have laid a razor, chocolate, cigars, a bar of soap, a pencil, and a candle: "Only the candles and the soap were of German origin. They had a ghostly, opalescent similarity. The British had no way of knowing it, but the candles and soap were made from the fat of rendered Jews and Gypsies and fairies and communists, and other enemies of the state" (p. 83).

The temptations of the methods of satire function in this novel as in all the others. Not only does Vonnegut tempt us into supporting the value of human life and then undercut us by means of his Post-existential world view, but he also reverses the targets within the space of one section:

> Robert Kennedy, whose summer house is eight miles from the home I live in all year round, was shot two nights ago. He died last night. So it goes.

> Martin Luther King was shot a month ago. He died, too. So it goes.
> And every day my Government gives me a count of corpses created by military science in Vietnam. So it goes.
> My father died many years ago now of natural causes. So it goes. He was a sweet man. He was a gun nut, too. (p. 182)

The reference to recent political figures in this last quotation is an illustration of the major technique of *Slaughterhouse-Five*, self-conscious art. Vonnegut constantly moves the reader between real life and fiction, mentioning the Kennedys, Martin Luther King, Harry Truman. As in Barth's *Chimera*, there are numerous references also to characters from his own earlier novels: to Bernard O'Hare and Howard Campbell from *Mother Night*, to Eliot Rosewater, to the Rumfoord family from *The Sirens of Titan*, and, of course, to Kilgore Trout, who has written a book called *The Big Board* that bears a striking resemblance to *Slaughterhouse-Five*. In this way he reminds us of the fictional nature of all experience. We read of "Lance Rumfoord, of Newport, Rhode Island, and his bride, the former Cynthia Landy, who had been a childhood sweetheart of John F. Kennedy in Hyannis Port, Massachusetts" (p. 104). Is there any real difference in our awareness of Kennedy, who actually lived, and the Rumfoords who are characters in Vonnegut novels? All remembered experience, actual or imagined, takes on the same quality in memory.

Through other self-conscious art techniques, Vonnegut draws our attention to the fact that we are reading. He introduces himself as author to the reader and places himself in Billy Pilgrim's experience: "An American near Billy wailed that he had excreted everything but his brains. . . . That was I. That was me. That was the author of this book" (p. 109). He comments on the techniques of the book himself, telling the reader "There are almost no characters in this story, and almost no dramatic confrontations" (p. 140). More or less everything, he announces at the beginning of the novel, is true, not just metaphorically true, but actually true. Billy Pilgrim's attempt to come to terms with the horrors of Dresden is Vonnegut's own attempt. Billy Pilgrim creates an imaginary world, Tralfamadore; Vonnegut creates an imaginary world, *Slaughterhouse-Five*. In fiction, of course, as on Tralfamadore, all time is eternal, the past can be recaptured, the dead returned to life. Art is apparently a way of dealing with death, but the novelist of number is not Zeus and must ultimately fail.

Vonnegut's description of the method of *Slaughterhouse-Five* is as accurate a description of all his novels as one is likely to find. He says it is "a novel somewhat in the telegraphic schizophrenic manner of tales of the planet Tralfamadore." Billy is told by the Tralfamadorians that their novels are clumps of symbols: "each clump of symbols is a brief, urgent message—describing a situation, a scene. We Tralfamadorians read them all at once, not one after the other. There isn't any particular relationship between all the messages, except that the author has chosen them carefully. . . . There is no beginning, no middle, no end, no suspense, no moral, no causes, no effects" (p. 76).

Vonnegut is, indeed, a writer of brief messages. The image of the message bearer, particularly that of Jonah who is the narrator of *Cat's Cradle* and who is associated also with Malachi Constant and his spaceship, "The Whale," in *The Sirens of Titan*, appears to haunt him. He is sending us telegrams but what do they say? It is hard to tell for the telegrams are schizophrenic, reversing themselves, always self-destructing, refusing us a grip on a moral world. As J. Michael Crichton says of Vonnegut, "One begins snuggly, enjoying the sharp wit of a compatriot as he carves up Common Foes. But the sharp wit does not stop, and sooner or later it is directed against The Wrong Targets. Finally it is directed against oneself. It is this switch in mid-stream, this change in affiliation, which is so disturbing. He becomes an offensive writer, because he will not choose sides, ascribing blame and penalty, identifying good guys and bad."[22]

Crichton's comments remain true, I think, even of Vonnegut's most recent novel, *Breakfast of Champions*, which, for all its Post-existential world view, appears to argue that there are ways of living with the absurd dilemma: "It is hard to adapt to chaos, but it can be done" (p. 210). It may still be "exhausting, having to reason all the time in a universe which wasn't meant to be reasonable" (p. 253), but we may be able to improve the human situation.

The three chief characters in this novel are Vonnegut himself, Kilgore Trout, Vonnegut's alter ego, a science-fiction writer from the earlier novels, and an incipiently crazy Pontiac dealer called

Dwayne Hoover. The action leads these three towards a moment of revelation at an Arts Festival in Midland City. Each of the characters in the novel is dependent on someone else: Wayne Hoobler, a black ex-convict, depends on Hoover to give him a job; Francine Pefko upon Hoover's need for her; Kilgore Trout upon Vonnegut, his creator. It is a world of interdependent people; we have the power to be each other's saviour rather than his slavemaster, but we are unaware of that fact, Vonnegut seems to be arguing.

The solution, apparently, is to set each other free. What is valuable, Vonnegut learns from minimal painter Karabekian at the Arts Festival, is the core of awareness in each one of us, an awareness which appears to be identical with Sartre's concept of Being-for-itself: "It is the immaterial core of every animal—the 'I am' to which all messages are sent. It is all that is alive in any of us. . . . Everything else about us is dead machinery" (p. 221). It is not enough to adopt the Kilgore Trout view, perhaps intended to represent Vonnegut's in his earlier novels, that everyone is a machine except oneself. Dwayne Hoover reads this message in Trout's new novel, *Now It Can Be Told*,[23] at the Arts Festival: "You are the only one who has to figure out what to do next— and why. Everybody else is a robot, a machine" (p. 253). Since everyone is a machine, nobody suffers, argues Dwayne and, justifying his actions on the basis of Trout's philosophy, goes on a rampage injuring everyone he meets. What Hoover and Trout have overlooked is that we all have a core of awareness: "At the core of each person who reads this book is a band of unwavering light" (p. 225).

It seems to me, though, that Vonnegut, here as in all the other novels, undercuts this proposed solution which may remain an ideal but is seen in the novel as unworkable. Vonnegut decides to give Trout and all his other characters their freedom, to respect, in fact, their band of light. Having unmade his characters, Vonnegut retreats to what he calls "the void" (p. 294). But Trout becomes once again Vonnegut's father, the man upon whom the character was modelled, and what he wants is not freedom but further control from his creator; "Here was what Kilgore Trout cried out to me in my father's voice: 'Make me young, make me young, make me young!'" (p. 296).

Has Vonnegut become an optimist? Hardly. Even if one does not read the ending of *Breakfast of Champions* as ironic, recognition of each other's value is not a solution to the Post-existential dilemma; it is at best, what it is with Barth, a way of making bearable the absurdity of the human condition. Vonnegut is ultimately a pessimist. "Everything, he confessed in 1970 to the graduating class at Bennington, "is going to become unimaginably worse and never get better again. . . . I beg you to believe in the most ridiculous superstition of all; that humanity is at the center of the universe, the fulfiller or the frustrator of the grandest dreams of God Almighty. If you can believe that and make others believe it, human beings might stop treating each other like garbage."[24] Vonnegut does not hold out much hope that we can believe it. What is more, he keeps reminding us that it is not true.

Technically, as well as philosophically, Vonnegut's most recent novel resembles Barth's, despite the fact that the language of *Chimera* appears designed for the well educated and Vonnegut's audience is a child from some future world. Here once more are the typically Vonnegut characteristics: anecdotes which end in a punchline, directed in *Breakfast of Champions* at such targets as the Vietnam war, air pollution, overpopulation, and racism; deliberate attacks on our preestablished language responses as in his frequent use of the word "nigger"; the introduction of such specific and irrelevant details as the length of characters' penes. This last is, of course, as Vonnegut explains, a parody of old fashioned storytellers who made "people believe that life had leading characters, minor characters, significant details, insignificant details, that it had lessons to be learned, tests to be passed, and a beginning, a middle, and an end" (p. 209).

As this quotation suggests, Vonnegut's attacks upon realism are even more vigorous in this novel. He claims he agrees with Kilgore Trout "about realistic novels and their accumulation of nit-picking details" (p. 278). He comes close to suggesting Barth's theory of a literature of exhaustion: "The proper ending for any story about people it seems to me, since life is now a polymer in which the earth is wrapped so tightly, should be that same abbreviation, which I now write large because I feel like it, which is this one: E T C. And it is in order to acknowledge the continuity of this polymer that I begin so many sentences with 'And' and 'S,' and end so many paragraphs with 'and so on.' And so on" (p. 228).

Vonnegut's commentary on his own methods here, again reminiscent of *Chimera*, is typical of the self-conscious art techniques in *Breakfast of Champions*. He gradually unmakes his novel not only by constant reference to characters from his other novels—Trout, Eliot Rosewater, Miss Pefko—but by gradually dominating the novel with comments on the act of creating it, as Barth does in the Bellerophoniad: " 'This is a very bad book you are writing,' I said to myself behind my leaks. 'I know,' I said" (p. 193). At the end, Vonnegut has unmade his entire novel, taken his reader to the void and left him with chaos. *Breakfast of Champions*, like all Vonnegut's fiction, is a novel of number, but it is unique in providing the reader with a direct statement of Vonnegut's intent:

> Let others bring order to chaos. I would bring chaos to order, instead, which I think I have done.
> If all writers would do that, then perhaps citizens not in the literary trades will understand that there is no order in the world around us, that we must adapt ourselves to the requirements of chaos instead. (p. 210)

Part Two

Nightmare

Chapter Five

Anthony Burgess:
Double Vision

Heller, Barth, Purdy, and Vonnegut appear to believe with Beckett that "the supreme obligation of art is to its own impossibility," "that art is a 'fidelity to failure.' "[1] Their novels, therefore, gradually self-destruct, leaving the reader alienated from the work, capable only of an ironic laugh of detachment from the human condition. "Laughing at our existence," says Hassan, "we exhaust its final possibilities."[2] Each of these four authors writes novels of number.

For Anthony Burgess, on the other hand, as for Joyce, "The artist is a Promethean figure who ends by usurping the place of Zeus."[3] Burgess writes in *Re Joyce*: "The fundamental purpose of any work of art is to impose order on the chaos of life as it comes to us; in imparting a vision of order the artist is doing what the religious teacher also does (this is one of the senses in which truth and beauty are the same thing)."[4] It is not surprising that of twentieth-century fantasy writers Burgess most admires Nabokov and Joyce, because his use of fantasy is for their purposes rather than for the purposes of the Post-existential novelists of number. Burgess, like Joyce, is "a free-thinking fabulist."[5] He needs his reader to be detached and observing, and so he needs fantasy rather than the techniques of realism, but he does not finally alienate his reader.

Burgess, like Joyce, wishes to manipulate "the commonplaces of language into a new medium that should shock the reader into a new awareness."[6] His language has infinite reverberations. The important thing for Burgess is to keep the reader observing the pattern, yet involved, willing to fit the pieces of the jigsaw puzzle together, and then to believe in the picture. He does not take the reader towards nothingness, but towards an image of all-inclusiveness, where "everything is there at once." His purpose, like Joyce's, is the "atonement, at-one-ment, of contradictions."[7] Burgess writes novels of nightmare.

Burgess, one of the most prolific of postwar British writers, is the author of sixteen novels published under his own name,[8] of two published under the pseudonym Joseph Kell,[9] and of a prodigious amount of criticism, among the best of which is his work on Joyce: *Re Joyce* and *A Shorter Finnegan's Wake*. Although almost all of Burgess's fiction illustrates the same basic philosophic stance, the kinds of fantasy he employs vary considerably. Since it would be impossible in a chapter of some thirty pages to discuss each book in detail, I have chosen the five novels that illustrate most clearly both Burgess's answer to the Post-existential dilemma and his basic method of conveying it: *A Clockwork Orange*, *The Wanting Seed*, *Tremor of Intent*, *Enderby*, and *MF*.

Burgess's novels deal with the same metaphysical questions as those of Heller, Barth, Purdy, and Vonnegut: the purpose of human existence, the nature of identity, the value and significance of language; but his answers—and he, unlike the previous novelists I have discussed, has answers—are not the Post-existential ones. As comments in various interviews and many of his novels indicate, Burgess is directly answering Sartre's and Camus' notion that there is no essential pattern in the universe and that the relationship between man and his universe is therefore irrational.

MF, perhaps, demonstrates most clearly that Burgess is answering the Post-existential view. The protagonist, Miles Faber, believes he can define himself through acts of will, create his own identity in the way Sartre suggests. He imagines he is completely free and seeks for the poems of a little-known writer in whose work he hopes to find "Words and colors totally free because totally meaningless" (p. 11). He learns, however, that "Nobody's free. . . . choice is limited by inbuilt structures" (p. 10). Burgess reveals his interest in Existenialism also in his comments about his novels. For example, in an interview with Thomas Churchill, Burgess has stated that the central theme of *A Clockwork Orange* is "the idea of free will. This is not just half-baked existentialism, it's an old Catholic theme."[10]

If Burgess's answer is the Catholic one—and he says himself that he "will not allow Catholicism to go over to the converts" nor "allow the Protestants to attack it," that what he writes looks like Catholic writing"[11]—it is certain only some Catholic doctrines interest him. Like Hillier, the hero of his novel *Tremor of Intent*, Burgess seems to have an Augustinian belief in the existence of evil and a sense of "what a bloody Manichean mess life is" (p. 28). Duality is the key to Burgess's view of reality; the essence of reality for him—and there are essences in Burgess's scheme as opposed to Sartre's—is its double nature. "Ultimate reality," says Hillier,"is a dualism or a game for two players" (p. 113). In religious terms this means that good and evil cannot exist without one another, "There is truly evil lying coiled in the good."[12] But as Burgess realizes,"we don't believe in good and evil any more";[13] we need new terms. Each of the five Burgess novels illustrates this duality in new terms: *A Clockwork Orange* in psychological terms; *The Wanting Seed* in historical/sociological terms; *Tremor of Intent* in political terms; *Enderby* in aesthetic terms; *MF* in terms of the relationship between society's structures and those of language.

The basic method of each Burgess novel is to present the reader with two visions, sometimes two antithetical world views, sometimes two apparently opposed aspects of one personality, and to invite him to make a choice. The choice often proves to be a false one; the two visions are a double vision, a dualism, inseparable parts of the one reality. The true choice lies elsewhere, between this duality and another negative value. The great evil in Burgess's view is to see life as unstructured and therefore capable of being completely controlled by man. The world is not neutral, not simply there. Burgess's use of the double vision is reminiscent of Vonnegut's, but there is an important difference between them. Vonnegut, a novelist of number, allows each vision to undercut the other, leaving the reader with nothing; Burgess, a novelist of nightmare, shows how the two visions are really one, leaving the reader with unity.

In *A Clockwork Orange* Burgess presents a concept of human nature quite different from the Sartrean view that there is no essential human nature and that man is free to create his own identity. His view, like the Catholic one, is that there is a permanent and universal essence to man. Free will for Burgess, as for all Catholics, is the choice of "whether or not to realize a given essential nature. Sartrean man invents his own essence."[14]

The narrator of *A Clockwork Orange* is a fifteen-year-old named Alex who enjoys violence and whom the state selects for a brain-washing experiment aimed at making delinquents socially adjusted human beings. He tells his story in a teenage slang, Nadsat, a language invented by Burgess from Russian and from English cockney slang. The novel is set sometime in a future England and is the kind of science fiction which is fantasy only to the extent that it exaggerates certain tendencies found in the present world.[15] Alex and his friends drink in milkbars that serve "milk plus something else" (p. 9); drugs are widely used by the young. Juvenile crime, particularly of the violent kind, muggings, rapes, burglaries, has increased alarmingly; the old cry out for law and order. Everyone watches world TV.

It is a dreary world which appears to have been socialized, perhaps communised. The equation of socialism, which he claims in later novels springs from a mistaken view that man is perfectible, with a depressing sameness and loss of identity is typical of Burgess. The Russian influence apparent in the teenage slang Alex speaks has affected other aspects of life also. The municipal apartment building where Alex's family lives has a painting on the hallway wall of the dignity of labor; his mother shops in a statemart. God has been reduced to an "Old Bog"; the state is in control.

Burgess maintains a careful balance between the fantasy world he has created and our own. He begins the novel with Alex's long and detailed descriptions of his acts of violence, shocking the reader by the discrepancy between tone and subject: "at one place I ran over something big with a snarling toothy rot in the head-lamps, then it screamed and squelched under and Old Dim at the back near laughed his gulliver off—'Ho ho ho'—at that" (p.25). This, of course, seems at first like fantasy, partly because of the language. But Burgess keeps us constantly aware of the similarities between the horrors of the fantasy and those of our own world. His aim is not the alienation of the reader, but acceptance of this violence as an innate part of human nature.

The first vision we are given is of a free Alex. Alex runs a gang of boys who beat up an old man coming home from a library and enjoy killing the wife of an author whose house they gain admittance to, an incident based on Burgess's own life. After several initial descriptions of the violence, Burgess tells us about Alex's passion for classical music, when he is not out with his gang he spends his time listening to Beethoven, Mozart, Bach on his stereo equipment. The reader is slightly uneasy. Violent criminals are not supposed to enjoy classical music. What is worse, Alex fantasizes about his violent assaults to the Brandenburg Concerto. Either our responses to violence or our associations with classical music must be in question here. Alex describes an article he once read: "Great music, it said, and Great Poetry would like quieten Modern Youth down and make Modern Youth more civilized. Civilized my syphilised yarbles. Music always sort of sharpened me up, O my brothers" (p. 26).

The second vision Burgess gives us is of a conditioned Alex. Caught by the police, Alex is in prison, the object of an experiment called the Ludovico technique. This technique involves injecting Alex with a substance which will make him nauseated and then forcing him to watch films of violence. The theory is that he will associate sickness with violence and be unable to act violently again. It works. But Burgess, whose vision of the free Alex horrified us, makes it clear that he considers a conditioned Alex worse. He is now merely a thing.

At first, the reason for Burgess's disapproval of the conditioning seems clear enough. Alex has been deprived of the capacity for moral choice. In his interview with Churchill Burgess said, "Choice, choice is all that matters, and to impose the good is evil, to *act* evil is better than to have good imposed."[16] In the novel it is the Chaplain who expresses this point of view: "He has no real choice, has he? He ceases to be a wrong-doer. He ceases also to be a creature capable of moral choice" (pp. 125-126). But are we to believe this Chaplain who is a far from admirable character, smelling of liquor as he preaches about divine suffering? He is capable of rationalizing any scruple he may have about the Ludovico technique, saying to Alex, "And yet, in a sense, in choosing to be deprived of the ability to make an ethical choice, you have in a sense really chosen the good. So I shall like to think" (p. 96). Ironically, he has always treated Alex as a thing anyway, calling him 6655321, his prison number.

A further question is raised about the significance of moral choice to this novel, when Burgess makes it clear that not only has Alex never exercised his power of moral choice, but is not likely to do so after he is returned to his former state. The novel ends with Alex signing a piece of paper for the government, "not knowing what I was signing and not, O my brothers, caring either" (p. 174).

If it is wrong to condition someone like Alex out of his antisocial behavior, then it is wrong for a reason that goes beyond the question of moral choice. The clue lies perhaps in the passage from a book called *A Clockwork Orange* which Alex reads when he invades the author's home and kills his wife: "The attempt to impose upon man, a creature of growth and capable of sweetness, laws and conditions appropriate to a mechanical creation, against this I raise my sword-pen" (p. 27). Man may be capable of sweetness but as the following pages describing the gang' attack on the wife show us he is also capable of violence. The author of *A Clockwork Orange* in the novel is called F. Alexander; he is Burgess himself but also, as Alex realizes, "he is another Alex" (p. 156), a fact he amply demonstrates at the end of the novel in his desire for violent revenge on the person who killed his wife. The implication is, of course, that we are all violent by nature: Alex gets pleasure from reading the violent parts of the Bible; the police are as brutal as the criminals; the old men in the library want their revenge; and how about the filmmakers who photographed the violence Alex is forced to watch? "You couldn't imagine them being allowed to take these films without like interfering with what was going on" (p. 104).

What we think of as good and bad are both equally parts of human nature, a passion for violence and a passion for classical music. Human nature is composed of opposites, is a duality. As Alex explains: "More, badness is of the self . . . they of the government and the judges and the schools cannot allow the bad because they cannot allow the self" (p. 43). Man may find violence socially inconvenient but cannot claim it needs explanation: "They don't go into what is the cause of goodness, so why of the other shop?" (p. 43). When man is made a thing he is inevitably deprived of all aspects of his humanness, his love of classical music as well as his tendency towards violence. Dr. Brodsky, practitioner of the Ludovico technique, explains: "Delimitation is always difficult. The world is one, life is one. The sweetest and most heavenly of activities partake in some measure of violence—the act of love, for instance; music for instance" (p. 116).

Finally Alex is returned to his natural state and the reader is left knowing he will commit more acts of violence. Burgess has presented us with two unattractive visions, but has made us see that the choice is not between "goodness" and "badness" but between a dual reality composed of good and bad and the neutrality of "thingness." Given these alternatives, the choice of life, and hence of the violence, seems inevitable.

Burgess's fable is constructed on a series of doubles: there are two characters called Alex; two visits to the old men in the library; two visits to the house of the author; two views of Alex's friends, as criminals and as policemen. The clarity of the pattern forces us to make comparisons. But Burgess's aim is our involvement. His use of the title of his own novel as the title of the author's book, which in a novel of number might have served to alienate us by means of the self-conscious art technique, is employed here to suggest that Burgess is F. Alexander, "another Alex," and therefore partakes equally of the violence. Throughout the novel Alex addresses his readers as "O my brothers," a phrase with obvious implications of complicity. Finally the teenage slang, Nadsat, that Burgess invented for the novel, serves to include us also. Initially strange, the words of the language are learned by the reader as he learns any language by being constantly exposed to them. He is, in fact, conditioned as Alex was; the effect of Nadsat on the reader functions as an ironic comment on the novel itself.

The Wanting Seed, written before but published after *A Clockwork Orange*, is a fantasy in exactly the same sense as the other novel. It posits a future England where overpopulation has reached mammoth proportions and drastic measures have been taken to combat the problem. Just as in *A Clockwork Orange*, the reader is initially shocked by being presented with a world in which all the accepted values are reversed. Heterosexuality is discouraged, homosexuality the norm; no one is allowed to have more than two children; the dead are used to fertilize the ground. Again the subject and the casual tone in which it is described are at variance: "Beatrice-Joanna Foxe snuffled a bereaved mother's grief as the little corpse, in its yellow plastic casket, was handed over to the two men from the Ministry of Agriculture (Phosphorus Reclamation Department). They were cheerful creatures, coal-faced and with shining dentures, and one of them sang a song which had recently become popular" (p. 5).

Once more Burgess keeps the reader midway between his own world and the fantasy world of his creation, though the recent stress on the problems of population and the campaign to limit families to two children have brought the fantasy nearer our world than Burgess perhaps intended. In the novel overcrowding has made it necessary for children to go to school in shifts, some at night, and for London to spread as far as Brighton. The place names anchor the fantasy in an actual England, however, as does the description of cricket as the sacred game.

In the interview with Thomas Churchill, Burgess stated that *The Wanting Seed* is a Catholic book: " . . . it's a very Catholic book. It's a total vindication of the encyclical. You know, of course, what the encyclical leaves out of account is the acceptance of natural checks, you know, is fact Malthusianism. Malthus has always been condemned by the church, yet the church will now accept Malthusianism, at least tacitly. What's going to happen to our excess population? 'Well, Nature will take care of it,' As Malthus said, in other words, wars and pestilence, earthquakes."[17]

If the novel functions as a defense of the encyclical on birth control, it is also a defense of Burgess's own view of reality as duality. In the book Burgess expresses his view as a defense of the Augustinian against the Pelagian doctrine, this time in terms of history rather than those of psychology. History is seen as a cycle of alternating and opposed attitudes, the Pelagian and the Augustinian. Tristram, hero of the novel, explains that the Pelagian view is liberal. The name is that of the monk Pelagius, who "denied the doctrine of Original Sin and said that man was capable of working out his own salvation" (p. 10). If man is perfectible then society by regulation and state control can be made perfect. Thus Pelagianism leads to socialism and communism. It is the disappointment at the failure of this society, Burgess claims, which leads to an interphase and then gradually back to Augustinianism.

The Augustinian is the opposed thesis, that man is inherently sinful and needs redemption through divine grace. This view, Tristram explains, leads to "conservatism and other laissez-faire and non-progressive political beliefs" (p. 11). When human nature turns out to be better than any pessimistic Augustinian could have expected, the interphase begins again and eventually Pelagianism is returned. Burgess stresses the cyclical and inevitable nature of history in *The Wanting Seed*, and in spite of his comment that he is concerned with choice and free will in this novel,[18] none of the characters, except possibly Beatrice, exercises it, anymore than Alex does in *A Clockwork Orange*. Burgess gives the impression of a deterministic universe.

The first vision of *The Wanting Seed* is the end of a Pelagian phase. Man is in control, has turned God into a comic cartoon character for children to laugh at, Mr. Livedog. Man's efforts to control the problems of overpopulation, which have led to synthetic foods, the encouragement of homosexuality, the use of the dead as fertilizer, have been attempts to stabilize the society. Heterosexuality, the joining of the yin and the yang, a duality, is discouraged because it inevitably brings change, not stability. Beatrice and Tristram, husband and wife, are separated in this section of the novel. As a result of these denials of life, comes famine. Emma, Tristram's sister, writes that the rice crops have failed in Fukien Province in China; at Shonny's farm, where Beatrice goes to have her illegal twins, the hens won't lay and the pigs die. By the Fall the earth is afflicted with an unknown blight: "fruit fell off the trees and the hedges, stricken with a sort of gangrene.   And then there was the animal world. worms, coccidiosis, scaly leg, marble bone disease" (p. 87). Burgess uses the unpleasantness of such descriptions as this to emphasize that the Pelagian philosophy is wrong. It is that life-denying neutrality which is evil in Burgess's scheme.

The second vision of the novel is of a world becoming Augustinian once more. Everywhere Tristram travels he comes across heterosexual orgies. Life is returning; "all life was one. That blight had been man's refusal to breed" (p. 139). But with the return of life comes a return of the natural checks the Pelagian government had removed: war and cannibalism, the opposite of breeding. "It was reported . . . that a vast communal nocturnal gorge of man-flesh had been followed by a heterosexual orgy in the ruddy light of the fat-spitting fires and that, the morning after, the root known as salsify was seen sprouting from the pressed earth" (p. 104). The acceptance of life involves the acceptance of both the good and bad composing the duality of reality. The recognition that there is innate evil, an Augustinian attitude, brings back the necessity for

God. "In Him we become one with all things, and He is one with all things and with us" (p. 159). Nevertheless, Burgess shows that the return to Pelagianism is inevitable in spite of the reconciliation of Beatrice and Tristram at the end of the novel.

The Wanting Seed, like A Clockwork Orange, is constructed on obvious doubles: the day versus the night, "Pelagian day, Augustinian night" (p. 31); twin brothers Derek and Tristram, the Pelagian and the Augustinian, later repeated in Beatrice's twins also called Derek and Tristram; "The human dichotomy. The division. Contradictions. Instincts tell us one thing and reason tells us another" (p. 36). The structure of the novel forces us to compare the separate journeys of Beatrice and Tristram. At the beginning alternate chapters are devoted to each, the link between them being a word or phrase carried over from the final sentence of one chapter to the first of the next. Chapter Four ends: " 'What, sir,' asked Bellingham, 'is the cold-water treatment?' " Chapter Five opens: "Beatrice-Joanna, the waste of life-giving cold-water behind her, entered the open mouth of the Ministry" (p. 18). Just as in A Clockwork Orange, Burgess has presented us with two unattractive visions and through the relentless logic of the fable method forced us to prefer his view of a dual reality over neutrality.

Tremor of Intent is not a fantasy novel in the same sense as A Clockwork Orange and The Wanting Seed. It is not science fiction, but takes place in a world very definitely that of the cold war period of postwar Europe. It is a spy-thriller, of the kind practiced by Ian Fleming and E. Howard Hunt,[19] fantasy only to the extent that Burgess has deliberately exaggerated some of the characteristics of the form. As Geoffrey Aggeler says, "The typical Bond feats of appetite are duplicated and surpassed, sometimes to a well-nigh ridiculous extent."[20] Indeed the gastronomic and sexual excesses of someone like James Bond pale beside those of Burgess's hero, Hillier. He becomes involved in a shipboard eating competition with Mr. Theodorescu and in a scene of sexual acrobatics with Miss Devi, Theodorescu's assistant, who has learned to give pleasure from Indian sex manuals.

But Burgess explodes the spy-thriller form by relating its essential characteristic, sensationalism, to the evil of the book, Mr. Theodorescu. Hillier, who describes himself as subject to satyriasis and gluttony, a duality he claims tends to cancel itself out, sacrifices both at the end of the novel. The novel, with its surface story of spy intrigue, is actually the account of Hillier's spiritual regeneration after a mock death; "He had been discharged dead, after all. Only after death, he had once said, was regeneration possible" (p. 216). Burgess has turned a superficial form into a metaphysical fable. There is, he appears to believe, some natural connection between metaphysics and spying. Wriste, the steward on board, says, "Perhaps all of us who are engaged in this sort of work—international intrigue, espionage, scarlet pimpernellianism, hired assassination—seek something deeper than what most people term life, meaning a pattern of simple gratifications" (p. 151).

Tremor of Intent recounts Hillier's last spy mission before his retirement, a mission which involves a journey to Russia to return to England a scientist who has defected. The scientist, Roper, is an old school fellow of Hillier's. The choice Burgess is offering us is apparently once again a choice between the Pelagian and Augustinian views of the universe. When we first see Roper at school, he attacks his Catholic teachers with rational arguments and believes that the world is ultimately knowable through science. Hillier writes to his superiors about Roper: "If he's a heretic at all it's your heresy he subscribes to—the belief that life can be better and man nobler. It's not up to me, of course, to say what a load of bloody nonsense that is" (p. 10). Hillier associates this Pelagian view of human perfectibility with state control, with a tendency towards loss of full humanity: Roper "was turning into a thing, growing out of boyhood into thinghood, not manhood" (p. 20). We expect the usual Burgess condemnation of this attitude, particularly since Hillier is associated with St. Augustine and shares with Burgess an Augustinian pessimism and a belief in the fundamental sinfulness of human beings.

On board ship, however, Burgess's second vision of Hillier reveals that Hillier's true enemy is not communism or Pelagianism but those qualities represented by Mr. Theodorescu. Mr. Theodorescu is a neutral "in the pay of no power, major or minor" (p. 91). He is homosexual, and homosexuality here, as elsewhere in Burgess's novels, is used to suggest a denial of life, a denial of the great duality. Like Hillier, Theodorescu has used gluttony and self-indulgence as a way of avoiding real commitment. For Hillier, who describes himself as "nothing more than a superior technician" (p. 10), is, he discovers, a neutral too. Alan, a boy he meets on the ship, finally accuses him: "Bloody neutrals. That bitch with the grief-stricken headache and filthy Theodorescu and grinning Wriste and *you*" (p. 193).

This neutrality, as in *A Clockwork Orange* and *The Wanting Seed*, is the real evil. The choice is between a reality which includes both capitalism and communism, Catholicism and Protestantism, Pelagianism and Augustinianism, and neutrality. Roper, foolishly running from one faith to another, is at least committed and therefore preferable to the Theodorescus. Finally able to form an intention of his own, Hillier kills Theodorescu and becomes a priest in order to fight in the war between God and Not god, "The two sides of the coin of ultimate reality," "the war of which temporal wars are just a mere copy" (p. 218).

The concept of the game is important to this novel and Hillier's progress is marked by a change in his attitude to the significance of the war he is fighting. Early in the novel, he tells Theodorescu that spying is a game, "a great childish game on the floor of the world" (p. 95); he explains that we play it because we don't believe in good and evil anymore. "If we don't play it, what else are we going to play? We're too insignificant to be attacked by either the forces of light or the forces of darkness" (p. 114). Alan tells him that games are all right for children but not for adults, and aligns Hillier's game-playing with the idea of neutrality. Hillier's final realization is that "The big war can be planned here as well as anywhere" (p. 218); the game on the floor of the world is a copy of the big war and as such must be taken seriously.

As in *A Clockwork Orange*, Burgess sets up a false choice and then reveals the true one. The pattern is again made obvious through the striking use of doubles: death must be compensated for by the other half of the duality, procreation. When Hillier's father dies, he is afflicted with spermatorrhea, and is told it is "an unconscious assertion of the progenitive impulse" (p. 107). Miss Devi, the dark assistant of Mr. Theodorescu, is balanced by Clara, a fair-haired sixteen year old. The structure of the novel is a series of double scenes: the first visit to Miss Devi is balanced by the second; the sexual experience with Miss Devi is balanced by that with Clara; Hillier's letter with Roper's confession; the great eating scene with the scene of Hillier's destruction of Theodorescu in which he literally stuffs the villain with information. Burgess forces upon us the necessary degree of detachment so that we can perceive the metaphysical fable underneath the spy thriller. Form echoes theme brilliantly for the spy-thriller form here is an imposture, a game version of a metaphysical fable, just as the war between good and evil on earth imitates that in Heaven.

Part of *Enderby* was originally published as *Inside Mr. Enderby* under the pseudonym, Joseph Kell. The novel *Enderby* as it now stands in the edition published in the United States presents two visions of a poet. In the first and last parts, posterity, through a fantasy visit of a schoolmaster and a group of unappreciative school children, is watching the sleeping Enderby. Only in this way does the reader learn that Enderby has become a major poet, whose poems are assigned as set books for national examinations. Ironically, in becoming important Enderby has become an object; the children have to be reminded that he is "not a thing to be prodded; he is a great poet sleeping" (p. 5). "Thingness" is what Enderby, whose life is seen from his own point of view in the rest of the novel, has been avoiding all his life. While living he is a minor poet, not included in the anthologies, hardly known, with only the slightest intimation of the fantasy visit of posterity which he apprehends as a dream.

The part of the novel concerning Enderby's life seen from his point of view is fantasy only in the sense that the action is exaggerated, possible but improbable. Nevertheless, in spite of the fact that the exaggeration serves primarily to make this a very comic book, similar in many ways to Joyce Cary's *The Horse's Mouth*, and the fact that the skeleton of Burgess's fable is much more fleshed than in the earlier novels, the same basic theme is here. Art depends on a choice of the duality of life over the neutrality of non-life.

In the first part of the novel Enderby is living in a furnished apartment in a seaside town in England in total disorder, eating badly, mostly on scraps given him by the local bartender, sleeping in his clothes, rarely bathing, using the bathtub to hold notes, books, ink bottles, cigarette-packets, and scraps of left over food. Masturbation has taken the place of sexual activity with women, and he is obsessed by his late stepmother, whose loathsome personal habits he hated as a child.

The ambiguity of Enderby's relationship to his stepmother,

whose life-style he has in part imitated, whose strong tea is always a comfort to him, continues throughout the book. In one sense she is the ugliness and vitality of the reality he needs in order to write, his sexual feelings for her the guilt which is "creation's true dynamo" (p.427). In another she is the false mother. About to have sexual relations with Vesta, he thinks "that it was a mother he had always wanted, not a stepmother, and he had made that mother himself in his bedroom, made her out of the past, history, myth, the craft of verse. When she was made, she became slimmer, younger, more like a mistress; she became the Muse" (p. 159). Every real woman is a stepmother to Enderby, and he is prevented by the Muse, his true mother, from having sexual relations with her. Enderby is, therefore, impotent; true sexual consummation for him is the creation of a poem. Burgess echoes the Joycean statement in *Portrait of the Artist* of the essential identity of the aesthetic, sexual, and spiritual impulses.

The dual nature of Enderby's life in this first part of the novel, composed of dirt and beauty, is summed up in the image of the lavatory, Enderby's "poetic seat." His poetry is written here, partly to suggest the function of art as time's cleanser and cathartiser, partly to suggest "a cell, smallest unit of life" (p. 393) which is all that is necessary for art. Most of all, though, it conveys that duality which to Burgess is the essential nature of reality. The reader's associations with excrement and poetry are obviously in opposition to one another.

In the second part of the novel, Vesta Bainbridge, who works for a woman's magazine called *Fem* attempts to separate the poet in Enderby from the disorder of his antisocial life. She marries him and turns him into a clean, neat, well-ordered man, younger looking and better socialized. But this life is a non-life, artificial like its creator; like Vesta, whose upper-class accent becomes working class when she is excited, it is a mere veneer. When Enderby leaves Vesta, he has realized the necessary connection between the disorder of his old life and the creative impulse: "And as for poetry; that's a job for anarchs. Poetry's made by rebels and exiles and outsiders, it's made by people on their own, not by sheep baaing bravo to the Pope. Poets don't need religion and they don't need bloody little cocktail-party gossip either; it's they who make language and make myths. Poets don't need anybody except themselves" (pp. 164-165). Order, in other words, is something poets make through intercourse with reality; prepackaged order, like women, like religion,[21] is a step-mother and merely in the way.

Once he returns to England from Rome, where he leaves Vesta during the honeymoon, Enderby finds his poetic gift has deserted him. He no longer feels the guilt, which, as he illustrates in his long narrative poem "The Pet Beast", is necessary for civilization. "The Pet Beast," as he explains to fellow-poet Rawcliffe, is the story of the story of the Minotaur, original sin, destroyed by "The Pelagian liberator, the man who had never known sin, the guilt-killer" (p. 13). Without original sin, in a Protestant world where there is "nothing sure and nothing mysterious" (p. 61), there is no art. Enderby attempts suicide and the state takes over his life, in the form of a state psychiatrist who makes him take his mother's name, Hogg—makes him become his mother not seduce her—and forget poetry. He becomes a bartender, the seller of wine not a consumer, once again in the wrong relationship for a poet to the life juices. Enderby/Hogg is prepared to join the Church of England. He is an ex-poet, an unfrocked priest, and as a neuter thing is evil, just as a conditioned Alex was in *A Clockwork Orange*. Rawcliffe, talking of his own loss of inspiration, explains: "The unfrocked priest does not become a mere neuter harmless being; he becomes evil. He has to be used by something, for super-nature abhors a supervacuum, so he becomes evil" (p. 172).

The linking of spiritual and artistic experience apparent in Rawcliffe's comments occurs again in the figures of Yod Crewsy and his Fixers, a group of pop-singers, who represent for Burgess degenerate religion and degenerate art. It is Hogg's resentment of Yod's plagiarizing of Enderby's poems that causes his violent attack upon Yod and subsequent regeneration as Enderby. Like Vesta from whom he obtains Enderby's poems, Yod Crewsy is mere veneer, a copy. He has a double in the novel in Rawcliffe, the homosexual poet, who has one poem in all the anthologies and who has also plagiarized from Enderby, taking his idea for "The Pet Beast" and turning it into a bad film. Enderby says of Crewsy to Rawcliffe: "He deserved to be shot. Plagiarism. A travesty of art. He stole my poems. The same as you" (p. 376).

Although the end of the novel doubles the beginning—Rawcliffe in his dirt and excrement dying of cancer can finally write again briefly—there is less emphasis in *Enderby* on the duality of reality, which this doubling has dramatized in other Burgess novels. It is implied, however, in Enderby's need for disorder to create order. Although *Enderby* offers the usual Burgess choice between life and no-life of the earlier novels, three important themes here—incest, the mysteriousness of reality, and the nature of bad art—point towards his next novel, *MF*.

At the time of the Churchill interview, Burgess was working on *MF*. He described the novel in this way: "I want to write a structuralist novel. The first of the structuralist novels, I hope, based on the Lévi-Strauss theatre of the correlation between language and social forms. So that I want to exploit the Algonquin legend, the boy who was bound to commit incest because he could answer all the riddles correctly, which is a direct tie-up with Oedipus."[22] Burgess's myth is the story of Miles Faber whose search for the works of a little-known poet, Sib Legeru, leads him to answering riddles set by monsters and birds, and ultimately to incest. As the double connotation of his initials suggests, the two implications are interwoven from the beginning. The initials stand for Miles Faber, Latin for "a soldier in the service of the craftsman," which is perhaps a way of describing a riddle-solver, and also, of course, they stand for mother-fucker.

MF is an incredibly difficult book; Burgess has more than fulfilled the prophecy he made to Jim Hicks in 1968: "The sort of things I write will be more and more involuted, more and more difficult, less and less saleable. This just has to be. You get fed up with existing technique. You have to do something more daring."[23] Burgess has dared to put the reader in the position of solving a whole series of riddles, not just those which Miles has to solve, but the riddles of the book itself. The reader is obviously intended to be placed in a position parallel to that of Miles, just as in *A Clockwork Orange* Nadsat conditioned the reader much as Alex was conditioned. *MF* is full of scraps of foreign languages—Sanskrit, Welsh, Italian, Indonesian—of conundrums, some of which Burgess has invented and some of which belong in folklore, of palinlogues, of every possible kind of word game.

To understand what Burgess is attempting here it is helpful to refer to two comments in his book on Joyce, who, after all, practiced many of these games before he did. The first concerns the significance of riddles and talks of the relationship between the mysteries of the cosmos and those of language. To Burgess, as to Joyce, there is more than a metaphorical connection between them: "The difficulties of *Ulysses* and, very much more, of *Finnegans Wake* are not so many tricks and puzzles and deliberate obscurities to be hacked at like jungle lianas: they represent those elements which surround the immediate simplicities of human society; they stand for history, myth, and the cosmos. Thus we have not merely to accept them but to regard them as integral."[24]

The second is a comment about himself and the relationship between languages:

> Waking literature (that is literature that bows to time and space) is the exploitation of a single language. Dream-literature, breaking down all boundaries, may be more concerned with the phenomenon of language in general. Living in the West, I have little occasion to use Malay, a tongue I know at least as well as I know French. In dreams, I am no longer in the West; with the collapse of space, compass-points have no meaning. Hence English and Malay frequently dance together, merging, becoming not two languages conjoined but an emblem of language in general."[25]

In *MF* Burgess uses many languages as an indication of a fundamental structure basic to all languages. The fact that the reader does not need a translation is itself an illustration of Burgess's point.

The relationship between apparently dissimilar languages, like the relationship between linguistic and social structures, is explained by Burgess in terms of the Lévi-Strauss theory that the mind of man has been operating in the same pattern since the beginning of time. This theory is obviously in opposition to the Sartrean denial of inherent structure in man or the universe and can very easily include the possibility of, though does not necessarily imply, what Burgess calls in *The Wanting Seed*, "a pattern-making demiurge." Merleau-Ponty points out in his article "From Mauss to Claude Lévi-Strauss": "Society itself is a structure of structures: how could there be absolutely no relationship between the linguistic system, the economic system, and the kinship system it employs?"[26]

In the novel Burgess indicates the link between language and social forms by the similarity of the pronunciation of Keteki, name of the professor whose riddle Miles solves and who sends him on his journey, and Kitty Kee, nickname of Miles's sister whom he is forced to marry. Hence a parallelism is established between solving riddles and sleeping with one's sister. Throughout the novel Burgess draws the two concepts, "postures and language" (p. 3), together. Pardaleos explains: "We condemn incest because it's the negation of social communion. It's like writing a book in which every sentence is a tautology" (p. 48). Man's drive to reproduce himself is described as one of the "great structural machines throbbing away, those messages in code" (p. 37). As Burgess explains at the end of the novel: "Communication has been the whatness of the communication" (p. 241).

That the structure of two myths can be the same in two very separate cultures is in itself a confirmation of the structuralist theory. The significance of the myth used by Burgess here, a combination of the Algonquin legend and the Oedipus myth, is described by Lévi-Strauss in *Structural Anthropology*:

> The myth has to do with the inability, for a culture which holds the belief that mankind is autochthonous, to find a satisfactory transition between this theory and the knowledge that human beings are actually born from the union of man and woman. Although the problem obviously cannot be solved, the Oedipus myth provides a kind of logical tool which relates the original problem—born from one or born from two?—to the derivative problem: born from different or born from same? By a correlation of this type, the overrating of blood relations is to the underrating of blood relations as the attempt to escape autochthony is to the impossibility to succeed in it. Although experience contradicts theory, social life validates cosmology by its similarity of structure. Hence cosmology is true.[27]

The myth cannot determine whether man is free, sprung from the earth itself, or whether he is bound by the structures that parental inheritance imply. Myths do not solve a problem, but by creating a balance between the opposing forces of the dilemma, they do provide a way of dealing with it.

Although Burgess's own comments on *MF* are a convenient way into any discussion of the novel, they are not necessary in order to understand his purpose. Clues lead back to the myths throughout the novel, but are particularly numerous in the first few chapters. Three epigraphs begin the novel. The first, "In his *Linguistic Atlas of the United States and Canada* Hans Karath recognizes no isogloss coincident with the political border along Latitude 49° N.—Simon Potter," links the ideas of language and culture together and, as we learn some pages into the novel, is also a comment on the fact that the Iroquois and Algonquin tribes recognized no such border. It is also a reference to a central theme of the novel, that there is an evil in divisions; all life is one. The second is a French quotation about the impossibility of God's ever being understood without the French, which is probably a reference to Lévi-Strauss: "C'est embêtant, dit Dieu. Quand il n'y aura plus ces Français / Il y a des choses que je fais, il n'y aura plus personne pour les comprendre.— Charles Péguy." The third is a stage direction from *Much Ado About Nothing*: "Enter Prince, Leonato, Claudio, and Jacke Wilson—*Much Ado About Nothing*, First Folio," which is reference to Burgess's real name, John Anthony Burgess Wilson, and presumably a comic reference to this novel.

There are many references to the Algonquin myth. When the novel opens Miles is staying at the Algonquin Hotel; on TV he hears an Indian talking about the Weskerini and Nipissing tribes which he remembers "are members of the great Algonquin family" (p. 14); he dreams of a toothless squaw surrounded by owls; he drinks a new soft drink called a Coco-Coho, meaning owl, in an owl-shaped bottle; Kitty, his sister, keeps her money in a little china owl; the name of Aderyn, who has a bird act in the circus, means owl in Welsh; her birds, who ask riddles, are named after contemporary novelists: Iris, Angus, Charles, Pamela, John, Penelope, Brigid, Anthony, Muriel, Mary, Norman, Saul, Philip, Ivy, presumably all askers of riddles.

There are an equally large number of references to the Oedipus myth: Loewe talks of a cocktail called a Clubfoot; Mr. Pardaleos refers to cultural taboos on incest, "Oedipus, Electra, all that" (p. 45), "This house of Atreus nonsense" (p. 50); Llew tells Miles about the time Aderyn had a man from the audience answering the birds' questions "and if he got the answer wrong they'd all fly on to him like to peck his fucking jellies out" (p. 112); Miles smokes Dji Sam Soe cigarettes which actually exist in Indonesia and have "2, 3, 4" on their package, a translation of Dji Sam Soe; Aspinwall drinks Azzopardis' White Cane Rum, a reference to both lameness and blindness; and if the reader has missed all this, Burgess has Miles at the end of the novel refer to Swellfoot the Tyrant, "a man with a clubfoot" who "had once answered the unanswerable and moved on to sleep with his mother" (p. 213). To suggest to the reader that the connection between the myths confirms structural anthropological theory, there are various references to people called Strauss, to Richard and Johann through titles of their compositions, and later to "Strauss and the Romantic School" (p. 219).

Burgess trains the reader to solve the riddles by demonstrating how. "Up, I am a rolling river; Down a scent—and—color giver" (p. 10) gives flower, we are told. As the novel progresses Burgess expects the reader to solve them himself, but invariably gives the answer obliquely in the following sentence. For example, three riddles, the answers to which are Breath, Mouth, and Heart, are followed by the sentence, "The breath grew sour in my mouth, and my heart pumped hard" (p. 76). This is one of Burgess's methods of keeping the reader parallel to Miles, in the same relation to the experience of the novel.

In a conversation with the monstrous Gonzi halfway through the novel, Miles learns the purpose of myths: "Only by entry into myth can reconciliation be effected" (p. 85). *MF* is the story of Miles's entry into myth and of his reconciliation with the structural pattern of the great duality. In order to suggest the idea of resurrection this implies, Burgess employs yet another myth, the Christian one. Miles was born on Christmas Eve; his twin's name is Llew or Noel. The miracle of Senta Euphorbia, which involves the emission of blood from the penis of the statue of Jesus, is foreshadowed when Miles earlier suffers the same problem on board the plane. The dead body of Llew mysteriously disappears from its hiding place. The final section of the novel contains an image of the hanged man, which relates Christ to Oedipus, "That poor Greek kid hanging from a tree by a twig thrust through his foot" (p. 241).

Miles's entry into reality is defined primarily, however, in terms of freedom versus structure. The first vision of the novel is of Miles in New York. He has just taken part in a protest demonstration which included having sexual intercourse in the open air with a fellow student called Carlotta Tukang. He views this as a gesture of freedom and in a conversation with his lawyer, Loewe, the first of many lions in the novel, expresses in Existentialist terms his belief in his own freedom. "I'm a free man" (p. 10), he says to Loewe; later to himself, "I could, like the imagined work of Sib Legeru, be wholly free" (p. 55).

He wants "the death of form and the shipwreck of order" (p. 64) and expects to find it in the work of Sib Legeru, poet of free verse. The works of Sib Legeru are supposedly in Castita where they have been placed by Sir James Pismire. Miles is also trying to avoid a marriage with a Miss Ang, arranged by his father whose own incestuous background has led him to believe in creative miscegenation. What to his father is a way of avoiding incestuous bondage is a restriction to Miles. The careful reader is suspicious of Miles's search for reality and meaning in Sib Legeru (Sibyl Guru), from the beginning. The name Pismire and the name of Miles's substitute mother, Miss Emmett, are names of ants, those models of social organization, who, in a Burgess novel, must be trusted.

Nevertheless, at the beginning of the novel, Miles believes he can create his own world; at this point he invents the riddles, creating word puzzles on the names of Loewe and Pardaleos. He does not appear to notice the synthetic nature of the world where man is in control, where the soup is instant, where no one enjoys violence, gets "no kicks from mugging" (p. 20), where emotions are "not to be engaged," and we must "school ourselves to new modes of feeling, unfeeling rather" (p. 21). Here the sexual impulse is perverted, as in the scene with the impotent Chester and his girl Irma. This world is an Electronic Village where the link between people is artificial; it is the lifeless neutral one which Burgess wished us to reject in *A Clockwork Orange*, *The Wanting Seed*, and *Tremor of Intent*.

The second vision of *MF* is the world of Grencjita (Green City) in Castita (Chastity), the world of doubles, paradoxes, and riddles where Miles learns the truth. It is undoubtedly significant that there are so many references to Shakespeare in the novel, for this second world functions much as the world of Shakespeare's romances, as a place where all is put right. Miles travels to this country on a "Pluribus" run by "Unum" airlines, *ex pluribus unum* being a way of expressing Burgess's view of reality, and on a boat belonging to two homosexuals, Pine Chandeleur and Aspinwall. They seem to be examples of the two worlds, New York and Castita; as homosexuals in a Burgess novel they belong to the neutral world, yet they also represent the world of paradox. Burgess makes a point of stressing how different the two men are, says they "were free, though in desperate sexual bondage to each other" (p. 55), and has Pine Chandeleur wear a shirt upon which are printed such religious paradoxes as "The more God is in all things, the more He is outside them" (p. 58).

Castita is more obviously a fantasy world. Here a religious procession turns into a circus, monsters ask riddles, men meet their doubles. Hints, clues, and the fact of the fantasy itself keep the reader in position of riddle solver. The most important doubles in Castita are the two men, Z. Fonanta and Mr. Gonzi, who ask Miles riddles at the end of an open-air meeting soon after his arrival in the city. The answers to the riddles they ask are the male and female sex organs, the yin/yang of reality, and these two men are representatives of the opposing halves of the duality. Zoon Fonanta, we learn, means the talking animal, man. In the novel he is Miles's grandfather, the boss who is in control of everything: "Dr. Fonanta sets the pattern like" (p. 220).[28] The pattern of the mind of man, in Lévi-Strauss terms, is universal and is the origin of all. Mr. Gonzi, Italian for *fool*, is the representative of darkness, Mr. Dunkel in the novel. Leonine and deformed, he is obviously intended to take the place of the sphinx in the myth. The riddle which Miles is finally forced to answer is his own name, "Gonzi," perhaps suggesting the complete self-absorption, that inward turning incest partly represents.

The other important set of doubles Miles meets are his own brother and sister, Llew and Kitty. Miss Emmett calls Llew "The bad Miles" (p. 168). Like Alex in *A Clockwork Orange*, Miles has both good and bad within him. Llew, another Lion, is identical to Miles in appearance, different only in voice and background. Miles dislikes the similarity because of Llew's violence and vulgarity and welcomes the minor differences: "To me his voice . . . was the hateful blessed key to a return to the total variousness of life against which he and I were blaspheming" (p. 102). Ironically, Llew shares Miles's philosophy of life, is son of Aderyn, the bird woman in the circus, and does an escape act for which he is billed "Llew the Free." Miles and Llew become interchangeable after Miles has murdered Llew for attempting to rape his sister and thus is forced to sleep with his sister himself. According to the myth the underrating of blood relations, the murder of kin, is balanced by the overrating of blood relations, incest: " 'You,' Aderyn said, 'are Miles Faber. That girl is your sister. You have committed the worst deadly sin, and it must be only to cover up the twin of that sin which is murder' " (p. 220).[29]

Meanwhile Miles has discovered the works of Sib Legeru, coincidentally concealed by Sir James Pismire in the house where his sister is staying. Coincidence in *MF* is indicative of a patterned universe, not of a universe ruled by chance. The poems of Sib Legeru appear to Miles to illustrate complete freedom, as he had expected them to. But, as Fonanta explains later to Miles, they are in fact structured "on the meanest and most irrelevant of taxonomies, they derive their structure from the alphabetic arrangements of encyclopedias and dictionaries" (p. 234). They are also creations of Fonanta. The very name Sib Legeru means in Anglo Saxon to sleep with one's kin or incest, so Miles in search of freedom had been also in search of incest. Incest as taboo breaking is a false freedom, just as the works of Sib Legeru are pseudo-literary works. "It is man's job to impose manifest order on the universe, not to yearn for Chapter Zero of the Book of Genesis" (p. 235).[30]

Miles learns also that Tukang means craftsman, as does Faber, so that his initial act of protest with Carlotta Tukang was in a sense incestuous too. "The whole of the stupid past is our father" (p. 57), and so in a sense exogamy is incest. Miles finally recognizes that "nobody's free" (p. 10). He accepts marriage with Miss Ang, who is presumably the Ethel of the final chapter of the novel, and the reader learns, to his surprise, that Miles is black. Their marriage, then, is an example of "creative miscegenation."

The statement of the book is a statement about the duality and mystery of the structure of the universe. The nature of a paradox is its unanswerability: "For order has both to be and not to be challenged, this being the anomalous condition of the sustention of the cosmos. Rebel becomes hero; witch becomes saint. Exogamy means disruption and also stability; incest means stability and also disruption. You've got to have it both ways" (p. 214). The universe is not irrational but ordered; man in search of total liberty will only find prison.

Burgess says, "the story I've told is more true than plausible" (p. 240), and he reverses the self-conscious art technique to ask us to believe in the fantasy. "Believe that I said what follows" (p. 3), says Miles at the beginning, later adding, "I recognize the difficulty my reader is now going to experience in accepting what I wish to be accepted as a phenomenon of real life and not as a mere property of fiction" (p. 100). Burgess, like Joyce, has used his novel to show that the disparate parts of human experience are one. All is "a seamless unity." There are no borders among language, behavior, geography, anatomy. There are also hints that *MF*, like Joyce's *Portrait*, follows other structural schemes. There is a suspiciously large number of trees referred to. There is a suggestion of the life cycle: we start with figs (the big-bosomed lady, F. Carica) and progress to milk producers (Euphorbia). And what of all the lions? The parts of the body? Some riddles, as Burgess warns, must be left unanswered.

Like all novelists of nightmare, Burgess takes us towards the mystery of infinity not the nothingness of the void. He answers the Post-existential premise that the world is irrational by a leap of faith that what we see is mystery not muddle. Each novel is constructed on a pattern of doubles to suggest a patterned, and therefore meaningful universe. His technique forces the reader to reconstruct the pattern, to fit the pieces together in an all-inclusive picture. The act of reading a novel of nightmare, like the act of writing it is, then, itself a way of transcending the Post-existential dilemma.

Chapter Six

Iris Murdoch:
The Revelation of Reality

The wealth of critical material on Iris Murdoch's novels[1] is strangely contradictory. It is not just a question of evaluating the later fiction, though there is a sharp division between those critics who, somewhere between *The Italian Girl* and *The Nice and the Good*, came to the conclusion that she was merely repeating herself and those who didn't. Even among the commentators on her first five novels there are widely different opinions both about her philosophy and the novels themselves. Critics seem unable to agree not only on the quality of her work but even about what she is trying to say. Bernard Dick, for example, says that she "warns against any absolute norms for truth."[2] This view is supported by Peter Wolfe, who claims she thinks that "nothing is given in logic or experience to justify our going beyond the constituents of matter to ratify the supremacy of a single point of view at the expense of another."[3] It is, however, flatly contradicted by G. S. Fraser's opinion that there is "a feeling in Miss Murdoch that the ordinary current and texture of life is . . . more bound to some large pattern of order than we usually are ready to recognize."[4] There is similar disagreement over her techniques: George Whiteside starts an article with the statement that she is a realist,[5] while many other critics, Walter Allen among them, appear to believe that, whatever her stated preferences for realism in the novel, she nevertheless writes some form of fantasy.

It is precisely this difficulty in reconciling her philosophical and critical statements—she is a practising philosopher and has written widely on philosophical subjects and on the novel—with her practice in her own novels which has caused problems with the criticism. It is an obvious temptation either to damn her for not living up to her own intentions or to assume, without detailed study of the novels, that she is the kind of novelist she praises. The latter approach is typified by an article by Richard Wasson in *Partisan Review*.[6] He uses Iris Murdoch's comments against myth-making in the novel to identify her with John Barth and Thomas Pynchon, who both write novels of number which have far more in common with each other's than they do with hers. It is a clear instance of a failure to trust the tale rather than the teller. The former approach, that of such critics as Linda Kuehl, who compare her novels with her ideas and find the novels wanting, makes the questionable assumption that the kind of novel she admires is necessarily the best illustration of her philosophy. Both groups of critics are equally guilty of failing to look carefully at what she has actually achieved in her novels.

Iris Murdoch's book on Sartre, *Sartre, Romantic Rationalist*, and the frequent references to Existentialism in her articles make Existentialism an understandable, and probably necessary, starting point for any consideration of her ideas. Again, however, critics are divided. Frederick J. Hoffman claims that "she is preoccupied with a set of human conditions that serve well to adorn a Sartrean text";[7] William Van O'Conner that "she finds existentialist theories a necessary supplement, although she is not committed to any particular existentialist school."[8] On the other hand, Cyrena Norman Pondrom in an article entitled "Iris Murdoch: An Existentialist?"[9] suggests that she is not an Existentialist, as does A.S. Byatt in *Degrees of Freedom*.[10] A careful reading of the novels and the criticism clearly demonstrates that, although she is writing within the framework of Existentialist terminology,[11] she differs fundamentally from Sartre and Camus and from the Post-existential novelists of number. In "The Sublime and the Beautiful Revisited" she explains that for her purposes "There are two important philosophies, existentialism . . . and linguistic empiricism."[12] She connects both of these with "symptoms of decline in our literature,"[13] since both make the individual the center of the universe and "neither pictures virtue as concerned with anything real outside ourselves."[14]

Nevertheless the starting points of her philosophical system are the Sartrean premises that the world is contingent, unfathomable by man's reason, and that man is a creature driven to seek meaning. Sartre and Murdoch would probably agree that man is like Dave's students in *Under the Net*: "To Dave's pupils the world is a mystery; a mystery to which it should be reasonably possible to discover a key. The key would be something of the sort that could be contained in a book of some eight hundred pages" (p. 27). The problem for man, as Iris Murdoch sees it, is "that we must have theories about human nature, no theory explains everything, yet it is just the desire to explain everything which is the spur of theory."[15] The contemporary world is the time of the angels. Carel explains in the Murdoch novel of this title that God is dead and that all we have now are the thoughts of God, his angels, but no generally accepted truth which links them together. Hannah in *The Unicorn* explains that the angels, the illusions contemporary man constructs in order to survive, are false Gods and that the "false God is a tyrant. Or rather he is a tyrannical dream" (p. 248). Every Murdoch novel is filled with characters who live in fantasy worlds of their own making, but the greatest fools are seen to be those who make a profession of system-building, those, like Marcus in *The Time of the Angels* and Rupert in *A Fairly Honourable Defeat*, who write philosophical treatises.

Although Iris Murdoch agrees with Sartre that "What *does* exist is brute and nameless, it escapes from the scheme of relations in which we imagine it to be rigidly enclosed,"[16] she does not draw the same conclusions he does. For her this apparent contingency is itself a value, a reality which includes other people and must be respected for its otherness. That the true nature of this reality must always remain mysterious to man—"Nor is there any social totality within which we can come to comprehend differences as placed and reconciled. We have only a segment of the circle"[17]— does not mean to her that there is no circle. She does not stress the possibility of a divine scheme, but her position is closer to Burgess's than it is to Sartre's.[18] There is for her a truth beyond our subjective consciousness; good faith, sincerity is not enough. She sets against the Sartrean idea of good faith "the hard idea of truth,"[19] the idea of a reality which transcends us even if we can never perceive it. Everything is ultimately one for her as for Burgess; she is, like him, a novelist of nightmare. In *A Severed Head* she sets the American psychiatrist Palmer, the representative of sincerity, in opposition to his twin sister Honor, who is a believer in truth. It is Palmer among others who causes the complications of the novel; Honor who unravels them.

The primary value that we must create in this contingent world is love, and many of Iris Murdoch's novels can be read as attempts to define love. Love is the essence of both art and morality, she explains in "The Sublime and The Good": "Love is the perception of individuals. Love is the extremely difficult realisation that something other than oneself is real. Love, and so art and morals, is the discovery of reality."[20] "To find a person inexhaustible is simply the definition of love" (p. 31), explains Dave in *Under the Net*. Demoyte criticizes Mor in *The Sandcastle* for his lack of perception of his lover's reality. "I just wonder whether you can really *see* her" (p. 120), he says. Bledyard criticizes Mor for the same fault: "There is such a thing as respect for reality. You are living on dreams now, dreams of happiness, dreams of freedom. But in all this you consider only yourself. You do not truly apprehend the distinct being of either your wife or Miss Carter" (p. 216).

It is significant that Bledyard is an artist, for it is the artist in Murdoch's novels who usually comes closest to the accurate perception necessary for love. Like all novelists of nightmare, Iris Murdoch elevates the position of the artist. Dora Greenfield's experience in the National Gallery in *The Bell* is an example of this:

> It occurred to her that here at last was something real and something perfect. . . . Here was something which her consciousness could not wretchedly devour; and by making it part of her fantasy make it worthless. . . . the pictures were something real outside herself, which spoke to her kindly and yet in sovereign tones, something superior and good whose presence destroyed the dreary trance-like solipsism of her earlier mood. When the world had seemed to be subjective it had seemed to

be without interest or value. But now there was something else in it after all.   (pp. 191-192)

This view of the uniqueness of the individual is in direct opposition to Sartre's view of identity as nothingness. The recognition of the reality, the essence of other people is impaired in Existentialist thought by Sartre's stress on the preeminence of the subjective consciousness which, as Dora realizes, "wretchedly devours" the outside world and make it part of one's own fantasy. Iris Murdoch's novels are full of characters who turn other people into objects in their own fantasy world. Muriel in *The Time of the Angels* has created an Elizabeth, whom she thinks of as her cousin, who does not exist. She even plans a future for her, envisaging her with a husband whom they would manage between them. Similarly, Michael in *The Bell* tries to neutralize and yet prolong his homosexual infatuations by treating Nick as a son: "Vaguely Michael had visions of himself as the boy's spiritual guardian, his passion slowly transformed into a lofty and more selfless attachment. He would watch Nick grow to manhood" (p. 106). In *The Unicorn* the unreality of Effingham's feeling for Hannah is exposed every time he meets her after an absence: "When he was absent from her he felt almost perfectly serene about their relationship. Only when he approached her again the real, breathing, existing Hannah, did he realize how large a part of the fabric was contributed by his own imagination" (p. 88).

George Whiteside contends that the two kinds of false love in Iris Murdoch's novels can be categorized as Platonic love, which he describes as the love of a parent for a child, and courtly love, the love of a child for a parent, abject love. "Both kinds are romantic," he explains, "illusory idealizations, because the loved one is not your parent or your child, does not have the personality, fit the role you have endowed him or her with."[21] If Effingham is the supreme example of the courtly lover, the character who best represents the Platonic lover is Antonia in *A Severed Head*. Antonia has "a sharp appetite for personal relations" (p. 18), believes in "a spiritual interlocking where nothing is withheld and nothing hidden" (p. 18), has a mystique about people whose names begin with *A* like her own, holds everyone in "a loving net," and calls him child. She combines all the main qualities of false love: she attempts to turn others into herself which denies their otherness; she wishes nothing to be hidden, and so denies their mysteriousness; she tries to possess them, and so denies their freedom.

Iris Murdoch differs from Sartre strongly in her view of freedom. "Freedom is not choosing,"[22] she says; "We need to be enabled to think in terms of degrees of freedom."[23] Our freedom is limited by several aspects of our lives beyond our control. The situation we are born into may force us to become "unloved machine-minders" like the Lusiewicz brothers in *The Flight from the Enchanter*. We may be born the wrong side of a political line like Rosa in the same novel. " 'It would be a sad thing for a man,' said Hunter, 'to have his fate decided by where he was born. He didn't choose where he was born.' " Rainborough replies, "life is full of that sort of injustice. We have to be things that we didn't choose" (p. 106). Freedom is restricted, too, by chance events and by the actions of other people. Towards the end of *A Fairly Honourable Defeat*, Hilda says to Rupert, "don't you see that these things are completely automatic? My will can do nothing here. I can't undo this change any more than I can make the sun turn back. You and Morgan have simply altered the world" (pp. 367-68).

The other great enemies of freedom are those we bring upon ourselves; these we are capable of overcoming. Some degree of freedom at least is possible for the human being in Iris Murdoch's scheme. The two enemies of freedom are neurosis, which she associates with Sartrean Existentialism, and convention, which she connects with empiricism: "One might say that whereas Ordinary Language Man represents the surrender to convention, the Totalitarian Man of Sartre represents the surrender to neurosis: convention and neurosis, the two enemies of understanding, one might say the enemies of love."[24] What she means by neurosis and convention is made clearer in "The Sublime and the Good":

> The enemies of art and morals, the enemies that is of love, are the same: social convention and neurosis. One may fail to see the individual because of Hegel's totality, because we are ourselves sunk in a social whole which we allow uncritically to determine our reactions, or because we see each other exclusively so determined. Or we may fail to see the individual because we are completely enclosed in a fantasy world of our own into

which we try to draw things from outside, not grasping their reality and independence, making them into dream objects of our own.[25]

It becomes apparent that the enemies of freedom and the enemies of love are one. Love and freedom are in Iris Murdoch's terms the same thing, the imaginative apprehension that other people exist. Just as Michael's fantasy world in *The Bell* prevents his really loving Nick or Toby, it also prevents his freedom. Michael is a good example of neurosis in the sense Iris Murdoch uses it. His sermon on the bell is developed entirely in terms of self. " 'The chief requirement of the good life,' said Michael, 'is that one should have some conception of one's capacities. One must know oneself sufficiently to know what is the next thing.' " (p. 201).

In the same novel another sermon on the bell is given by James, who begins, "The chief requirement of the good life is to live without any image of oneself. . . . We should consider not what delights us or what disgusts us, morally speaking, but what is enjoined and what is forbidden" (pp. 132-133). James is the conventional man living too rigidly by rules imposed upon him from outside. The error in this is that all rules are necessarily generalizations and must ignore the particularities of a situation. All theorizing falls into this category. Annandine, a character in Jake's book *The Silencer* in *Under the Net*, is made to say: "When you've been most warmly involved in life, when you've most felt yourself to be a man, has a theory helped you when you were in doubt about what to do?" (p. 66). Pattie in *The Time of the Angels* comes across a philosophical text on Carel's desk and reads the open pages. She thinks, "The words sounded senseless and awful, like the distant boom of some big catastrophe. Was this what the world was like when people were intellectual and clever enough to see it in its reality? Was this, underneath everything that appeared, what it was really like?" (p. 158). Pattie's instincts are more to be trusted than Carel's theorizing.

Iris Murdoch returns not only to the particular for value, but also to what Fraser calls the normal. Pattie's reaction is to be preferred in part because it is normal. Although convention in the sense of theorizing is an impediment to love and freedom, ordinary morality appears to be necessary in Murdoch's scheme. Since the ordinary world is the one we have agreed upon, it is the only "real" world we know and hence the only place we can really "see" other people as different from ourselves. She criticizes Sartre for his impatience with "the stuff of human life"[26] and for his failure "to emphasise the power of our inherited collective view of the world."[27] Martin in *A Severed Head* tells his brother, " 'You have a technique for discovering more about what is real,' 'So have you,' said Alexander. 'It is called morality' " (p. 49). Similarly, Norah in *The Time of the Angels*: "but I don't see any point in either affirming or denying that the Good is One. I still ought to pay my bills. Ordinary morality goes on and always will go on, whatever the philosophers and theologians have to say" (p. 201).

Ordinary morality is very much a matter of paying one's bills. Honor Klein, the great truth-teller of *A Severed Head*, believes in "not letting people off"; people have to pay their emotional and moral debts in her world as in Iris Murdoch's. In the novels truth telling and paying one's debts are both related to a respect for the particular, the contingent. Georgie, who lives in a room "whose effects were always a little ramshackle" (p. 3), where everything is contingent, hates lies. She explains to her lover, Martin, when all has been revealed: "I had to do something of my own. I feel twice as real now. I was just stopping being free. And for me that's stopping existing. I was getting to be no good to either myself or to you. You've got to *see* me, Martin" (p. 125). Freedom, here as elsewhere, is equated with reality, with accurate perception and with telling the truth.

The progress for one or more characters in an Iris Murdoch novel is from enchantment with an illusion to a recognition of reality. But reality itself is mysterious and unfathomable, so it would be fair to say the characters progress from a false enchantment to a true one, to the wonder of the real world. So Jake in *Under the Net*, who is always trying to put his universe in order and wants everything in his life to have reason, ends by admiring the infinitely varied litter of kittens in Mrs. Tinckham's shop. "It's just one of the wonders of the world" (p. 286), he says. The illusory worlds of the characters are frequently broken by violence of one sort or another. "Shocks, threats, violences, deprivations, however distressing, lead to leaps forward in self-knowledge,"[28] explains Fraser. In *A Fairly Honourable Defeat* Simon regains his freedom from the fabric of lies woven about him by pushing Julius in the swimming pool; Nick's suicide in *The Bell* awakens Michael from his fantasy; in

The Unicorn, Alice Lejour's infatuation with Effingham Cooper disappears after a violent sexual episode between them.

The changed perception that leads the characters to recognize the enchantment of the real frequently comes about through love. Love teaches the real is primitive, mysterious, instinctive rather than rational. Dogs and children are often closer to it than adults. In *The Bell* the dog's reality and Toby's innocence are part of the same substance. Those characters who respect the primitive world are, for some reason, often Eastern Europeans. Julius King in *A Fairly Honourable Defeat* turns out to be Julius Kahn; Jan and Stefan Lusiewicz are refugees from Poland. The best example of this type is Honor Klein who is described as savage, primitive, the daughter of a German Jew. She is an anthropologist, interested in primitive tribes, who talks of dark gods and says she believes in people.

Honor Klein is Martin's means of liberation in *A Severed Head* and his development is typical of the progress towards freedom in a Murdoch novel. Martin, symbolically surrounded by fog in the early part of the novel, is enslaved by a love affair with Georgie, which he lies about, and by a continued relationship with both his wife Antonia and her lover Palmer who treat him in a civilized manner but like a child. He has not paid for his affair with Georgie and in turn "lets off" Antonio and Palmer. Honor Klein, Palmer's sister, explains to him that "you cannot have both truth and what you call civilization. . . . You cannot cheat the dark gods. . . . By gentleness you only spare yourself and prolong this enchantment of untruth which they have woven about themselves and about you too. Sooner or later you will have to become a centaur and kick your way out" (pp. 75-76). Martin is involved in various violent scenes, including a fight with Honor in a basement, and after punching Palmer in the jaw, is free of Antonia's "loving net." Finally Martin's observation of Honor's incestuous relationship with her brother frees her to act as a "real" person towards him.

As many of the passages I have quoted indicate, Iris Murdoch believes that the function of art is the same as that of morals and love, to bring about a perception of what is real. The novelist, then, must devise techniques to awaken his reader from his preconceptions about the novel and bring him to a revelation of the enchantment of the real world.

Iris Murdoch's comments about the modern novel indicate that she does not think that most contemporary novelists succeed in doing this. The trouble, she believes, is form. "Form is the temptation of love and its peril, whether in art or life: to round off a situation, to sum up a character."[29] She dislikes what she calls the "crystalline" novel, a dry, tightly patterned, over-formal piece of fiction which rounds everything off and does not allow for contingency. She obviously wishes to write novels which do not exclude, but give the impression of including everything at once. Her aim is, then, the novel of nightmare.

She admires the nineteenth-century realistic novelists, particularly George Eliot, for what she calls their tolerance: "There is in these novels a plurality of real persons more or less naturalistically presented in a large social scene, and representing mutually independent centers of significance which are those of real individuals. What we have here may be called a display of tolerance."[30] The duty of the of the novelist and his greatest difficulty is the creation of people different from himself: "How soon one discovers that, however much one is in the ordinary sense 'interested in other people,' this interest has left one far short of possessing the knowledge required to create a real character who is not oneself. It is impossible, it seems to me, not to see one's failure here as a sort of spiritual failure."[31]

It is precisely this failure to create "real" characters that the critics accuse her of, as indeed she accuses herself. Ann Culley praises her for being her own best critic and quotes interviews in which she admitted that "some of her characters fail to emerge as independent individuals."[32] Similarly Linda Kuehl claims that "measured by her own standards," *The Flight from the Enchanter*, *A Severed Head*, and *The Unicorn* fail because the tight structure kills all hope of "free and independent characters."[33] Ms. Kuehl also points out that the recurrence of certain predetermined types in Iris Murdoch's novels, enchanter, enchantress, and observer, indicates that she is unable to create free characters.

What none of the critics has pointed out is a fundamental conflict between two of Iris Murdoch's aims in the novel. The appearance of "real" characters is created in the nineteenth-century realistic novel and elsewhere primarily through the establishment of a clear connection between motivation, decision, and result. Characters appear to be free if they are seen to exercise their choices successfully.

Iris Murdoch, however, wishes to show the restrictions on man's freedom imposed both from without and by himself. Her method is to invent a series of constantly surprising events, surprising to the characters and to the reader. Her novels are full of characters whose motives are often unclear and who decide upon one course of action only to perform another. In *A Fairly Honourable Defeat* Hilda swears she will not look through Rupert's desk but does so; in *A Severed Head* Martin swears he will hit Palmer if he asks him to behave in a civilized manner but doesn't. If she wishes situations to surprise the characters, there is no way that events can be shown as arising out of character motivation. It is primarily for this reason that we have the impression that the characters are trapped in a predetermined pattern and are hence not free.

This method of characterization deliberately withholds a full sense of a character's motives and is obviously an attempt to suggest that mysteriousness of other people which is one of Iris Murdoch's beliefs. But it has led to some misunderstandings. Pondrom points out that "the mystery is deliberate, a part of her art which itself suggests something of her view of man,"[34] but connects this with the idea of an ambiguous moral scheme: "The 'moral' to her novels is neither explicit nor immediately implicit."[35] This is simply not true. When Harold Hobson interviewed Iris Murdoch, he asked her, "People sometimes say you tend to leave 'moral' questions unresolved in your novels. Do you agree?" She replied. "In *The Bell* I offer three extremely clear types of moral reaction to a certain situation and I indicate to the reader which is the right one. I don't know what more he wants."[36]

Another reason for the "failure" to create free and independent characters may be that she is more interested in the idea of the uniqueness of people than in people themselves. There is some justification in Fraser's comment that "she offers in her fiction a world imaginatively constructed from her thinking about life rather than a world imitated, in the Aristotelian sense, from her observations of it .... She presents us with characters ... have a coherence and simplicity, in the philosophical sense an essence, which the opacity of ordinary life, and the contrariness of ordinary character, does not as a rule expose to us."[37] Her comment to Harold Hobson about *The Bell* makes it fairly clear that the characters are designed to illustrate philosophical responses to a moral problem.

It is an admission that she writes fables, designs each novel to illustrate a conclusion which preceded its conception. Like Anthony Burgess, she has "an answer" and argues it in fiction. A.S. Byatt says that the novels "presented themselves, it seemed to me, like puzzles out of which a plan of ideas, a scheme of references could be extracted for examination, with some effort."[38] Like Burgess, she takes the infinitely varied world of reality and imposes pattern upon it, leading the reader by means of clearly defined contrasts and parallels to realize he has a puzzle to solve and to solve it. Like all novelists of nightmare, she plays the role of God creating a unified world. There are clues to the pattern everywhere in an Iris Murdoch novel: characters who are opposites of one another such as James and Michael in *The Bell*; scenes that repeat each other with variations such as Antonia's confessions of her love for Palmer and her love for Alexander; words that are repeated, as are the words *slave* and *secret* in *The Flight from the Enchanter*, to show their significance to the moral scheme. However much she may admire the realistic novel and argue against myth-making, she writes fantasy fables and creates myths.

I do not mean to suggest in any way that this is a failure on Iris Murdoch's part. For all her advocacy of realism, there is no way in which realistic techniques could be adequate to her vision.[39] The chief characteristic of realistic methods is that they are transparent, are so accepted as fictional convention that they allow for the complete involvement of the reader with the experiences they describe. Although, as Booth and others point out, the author can never truly disappear in fiction, the creator of realistic fiction does not deliberately draw attention to his own artifice. Iris Murdoch, however, wishes to suggest the mysteriousness, the enchantment of reality, wishes it to be a revelation to the reader. What she needs— and what she writes—is a form of fantasy, not fantasy that undermines the reader's expectations of realism as in the novels of Barth, Heller, Purdy, and Vonnegut, but a sort of supra-realism. Iris Murdoch exaggerates certain aspects of realistic techniques until they draw attention to themselves. This serves a double function: it draws the reader's notice to the pattern of the book by separating him from the experience of the characters; it suggests that the real world is stranger than he had thought.

The characteristic realistic novel, such as George Eliot's *Middle-*

march, which concerns a group of characters all of whom know each other because they live in the same town, is exaggerated in Iris Murdoch's repeated use of a very isolated setting where relationships either are or become an intricate web of connection. *The Unicorn* concerns two houses of characters, one surrounding Hannah, a sort of prisoner, and the other living with Max Lejour. The setting is a completely isolated coastal area in a remote part of what seems to be Ireland. *The Bell's* setting is a lay religious community called Imber, inhabited by a group of people who have deliberately chosen seclusion from the outside world. In *The Time of the Angels*, Carel's household is isolated in what is probably an ordinary London parsonage by a bad siege of fog. The isolated setting suggests that we are meant to take these groups of characters as a microcosm of the larger world, but it also makes the intricacy of relationships in some way more plausible. It is true, though, that even in novels without an isolated setting the characters all seem to know each other. *Under the Net* treats this comically. "So Sammy was a friend of Sadie's, was he? I knew instinctively that the two of them were up to no good" (p. 129), says Jake; and later when Jake and Hugo meet Lefty: " 'I didn't know you knew Lefty,' said Hugo. 'I didn't know *you* knew Lefty,' I said" (p. 166).

The movement in the novels is away from the intricate web of connection out into a "real" world. The connected web is an image of a fantasy world where everything is spun from one consciousness, in Iris Murdoch's terms an image of neurosis. The separation of the characters suggests a perception of the particularity, the uniqueness of individuals. An interesting example of this is the separation of brothers and sisters, particularly of twins. The closeness and sense of sameness felt by twins—there is, for example, a strong bond between Catherine and Nick Fawley in *The Bell*—seems to be in Iris Murdoch's scheme a denial of the uniqueness of the individual, a form of illusion. Jan and Stefan Lusiewicz in *The Flight from the Enchanter*, who share everything including their women at the beginning of the novel, finally deceive each other. In the same novel Annette's brother Nicholas fails her at her moment of greatest need. Nigel and Will, the twins in *Bruno's Dream*, are held together by a sado-masochistic bond which finally snaps at the end of the novel.

The web of connection may preexist the beginning of the novel or be formed during it, but it is always broken at the end. In *The*

Bell Michael's former homosexual attachment to Nick Fawley, Catherine Fawley's love for Michael, preexist the story; Dora and Michael both weave fantasies linking them with Toby. A series of secrets exists which can only be broken by confession. The liberation of Michael and Dora comes about because Toby confesses verbally, Nick through suicide and Catherine through attempted suicide. The novel ends with the disbanding of the community. In *A Fairly Honourable Defeat* the web of secrecy is deliberately spun by Julius King, who plays on the human tendency to lie, in order to bring about the separation of two married couples—one homosexual, Alex and Simon; the other heterosexual, Rupert and Hilda. Simon saves his marriage by a violent act and by telling the truth. The novel ends with the other characters scattered.

Julius is one of Iris Murdoch's "enchanter" figures, people at the center of the web around whom the others revolve. Frequently, though, she makes it clear that the enchanter is simply the creation of other people. Hannah, the prisoner in *The Unicorn*, explains to Marian: "I have lived on my audience, on my worshippers, I have lived by their thoughts, by your thoughts . . . You all attributed your own feelings to me. But I had no feelings, I was empty. I lived by your belief in my suffering" (pp. 248-249). The best example of an "enchanter" is Mischa Fox in *The Flight from the Enchanter*. Mischa Fox is the focus of everyone's attention; he is, in fact, their creation. When Annette meets him she says, "I believe you are famous for something or other . . . but I'm afraid I can't remember what it is" " 'I am not surprised that you do not remember,' said Mischa Fox, 'for in fact I am not famous for anything in particular. I am just famous' " (p. 87). In *Bruno's Dream* the central figure is a dying old man, Bruno, a symbol of the past linking everyone together. Both his son Miles and son-in-law Darby are trapped by neurosis in past fantasy worlds with wives whom they idealized and who died. The extreme difficulty of clearing one's perception of the past, the theme of this novel, is solved by the introduction of Lisa around whom both Miles and Darby weave new webs. Finally the web is broken by a flood; water, an obvious image of fluidity, is always an image of contingency in Murdoch's novels.

As the characters weave fantasy worlds around themselves, their self-enchantment is usually described to us in passages which make much use of words suggesting magic, spells, and mystery. In *Under the Net*, Jake finds Anna working in a mime theater. He is about to incorporate her into some plan he has for his future in which he has given her a starring role. The strangeness of the actors in the theater is a description of Jake's mental state: "The actors meanwhile were continuing to execute their movements in the extraordinary silence which seemed to keep the whole house spellbound. . . . I observed something of that queer expressiveness of neck and shoulder in which Indian dancers excel . . . the effect was hypnotic" (p. 40). The same use of words suggesting mystery and strangeness characterizes Pattie's first meeting with Carel in *The Time of the Angels*: "She entered into Carel's presence as into the presence of God and, like the souls of the blessed, realized her felicity not through anything which she distinctly saw but by a sense of her own body as glorified. . . . Indeed Pattie's dazed senses could scarcely have distinguished these things from each other" (p. 25). What is significant about these passages is the lack of any distinct image conveyed by the language. False enchantment in Iris Murdoch's novels is always told to us, described for us, never shown.

The "true" enchantment of reality is given to us in language as transparent as prose can be so that we have the impression that it is given to us in action and not in words at all. In her book on Sartre, Iris Murdoch distinguishes between literary prose language, "deliberately disposed so as to conjure up before us some steady and internally coherent thought or image," and "ordinary discourse," which "may be thought of as transparent not only in the sense of not drawing attention to its particular wordy properties, but also in the sense of being useful. It very often does what shouts or gestures or pictures might equally well achieve, when what matters is the achievement. It directs attention to things in the world, it alters courses of action, it arouses feelings and conveys information."[40]

She uses ordinary discourse, at least a discoure far more ordinary than that of the passages from *Under the Net* and *The Time of the Angels*, to convey those events which break the net of fantasy. Iris Murdoch is a master of the surprise event, and her novels are perhaps characterized most clearly by the sensational scenes at their climax. These scenes come as a surprise to characters and reader alike and are, of course, not mere sensationalism. They are an attempt to suggest that reality, what actually happens, is other and more amazing than our expectations. Paradoxical as it may sound, the extraordinary events are a form of supra-realism. They always transcend our expectations, yet have the quality of appearing to reveal to us what we half suspected, that darker and more mysterious world which our own sexual fantasies long since taught us was there. They do not bring us to nothingness by undermining our expectations, but substitute for our expectations a nightmare world in which everything is there at once.

Perhaps the most memorable of these revelations is the scene in *A Severed Head* when Martin, who has recently realized his love for Honor Klein, follows her to Cambridge and discovers her in bed with her brother:

> I saw opposite me a large double divan bed. The room was brightly lit. Sitting up in this bed and staring straight at me was Honor. She was sitting sideways with the sheet over her legs. Upwards she was as tawny and as naked as a ship's figurehead. I took in her pointed breasts, her black shaggy head of hair, her face stiff and expressionless as carved wood. She was not alone. Beside the bed a naked man was hastily engaged in pulling on a dressing gown. It was immediately and indubitably apparent that I had interupted a scene of lovers. The man was Palmer   (p. 155).

The characteristics of this episode, the clarity of the image, the simplicity of the prose in both sentence structure and vocabulary also mark a similar scene in *The Time of the Angels*. Here Muriel, through a peephole, discovers Elizabeth in bed with her father:

> She twitched herself awake, trying to recompose the fragile image, which was quivering now like water disturbed. She concentrated her vision at last into a small circle of perfect clarity. She saw the end of the chaise longue close up against its mirror double. Beyond it in the mirror she saw the heaped and tousled bed. She began to see Elizabeth, who was on the bed. She saw, clear and yet unlocated like an apparition, Elizabeth's bare shoulder. Then there were other movements, other forms, an entwining suddenly of too many arms. And she saw, slowly rising from the embrace, beyond the closed eyes

and the streaming hair, white and dreadful, the head and naked
torso of her father   (p. 170).

In these episodes there is the suggestion of an image gradually
coming into focus like the image on a photograph, an idea Iris
Murdoch uses literally in *The Flight from the Enchanter* when
Calvin Blick forces Hunter to watch the developing of a film showing
his sister Rosa in the arms of the Lusiewicz brothers. By means of
this technique Iris Murdoch forces her reader, with her characters,
into that clarity of perception she says is necessary for art, love,
and morality.

I do not mean to suggest that these scenes of revelation are
always sexual in nature, though they frequently are since sex is
part of that darker world Iris Murdoch believes is more real than
the civilized one we usually inhabit. The darker world is equally
concerned with violence and with death. The revelation of Nick's
suicide in *The Bell* has many of the same characteristics as the
scenes from *A Severed Head* and *The Time of the Angels*: an
observer who enters a room; a sudden and very clear image; short,
often simple, sentences; a plain vocabulary with few adjectives.
"He was almost at the lodge now. The door was open. Michael
called Nick's name. There was no reply. Just outside the door he
stopped. Something was lying in the doorway. He looked more
closely and saw it was an out-stretched hand. He stepped over the
threshold.

"Nick had shot himself. He had emptied the shotgun into his
head. To make quite sure he had evidently put the barrel into his
mouth. There was no doubt that he had finished the job" (pp. 300-
301).

Almost all the critics writing about Iris Murdoch have commented
on the long, detailed, technical descriptions in her novels. In *Under
the Net* she describes how Finn and Jake attempt to rescue Mars,
the aging film dog, from a barred cage in which they find him. The
description lasts for some ten pages of the novel. Similarly in *The
Bell* she tells the reader exactly what engineering manuevers were
necessary for Toby to extricate the medieval bell from the lake at
Imber. In *The Sandcastle* there are two such episodes, one describing
how Rain Carter's car becomes marooned in the river, the other
relating Mor's rescue of his son Donald from the school tower.

Although these descriptions are more characteristic of the early novels, in *The Nice and the Good* there is an account of Ducane's pursuit of Pierce into the cave under the sea and, in *A Fairly Honourable Defeat*, Hilda's struggles with her broken telephone:

> But something seemed to have gone wrong. The telephone was an old-fashioned one with a projecting dial. As Hilda put her finger into the hole to spin the dial she realized that something or other must be broken. The outer part of the dial moved easily, too easily and unresistingly, while the inner part with the circle of numbers appeared to be shifting too . . . She looked at the machine and tried to think. In a second the telephone had been transformed from a natural means of communication, an extension of herself, into a grotesque senseless object, useless and even sinister. (pp. 405-406)

This quotation gives support to Gindin's theory that these descriptions illustrate man's failure to execute his designs[41] and to Fraser's that they "create a sense of intractability in things, sometimes ingeniously conquered, sometimes farcically and wretchedly triumphant."[42]

The function of these episodes goes beyond this, it seems to me. In the exhaustive, yet very simple detail in which they are described, in their clarity of image, they are related to those revelatory episodes of action. In the same way these technical descriptions force us to look at operations in a new way, they change our perception. The use of detail is, according to Ian Watt, characteristic of realism. Iris Murdoch shows us, however, that realistic novelists rarely do more than refer to or suggest substantive action; they do not make us see it. This technique is another form of supra-realism.

The progress in Iris Murdoch's attempt to make individual objects, "things," more extraordinary than we normally think of them as being can be documented from two novels, an early one, *The Flight from the Enchanter*, and a later one, *The Time of the Angels*. In *The Flight from the Enchanter* she has the characters comment on the miraculous quality of certain objects:

> " 'Hello there!" said Hunter, with his mouth full. "What's that heavenly cake you've got in the kitchen?"
> "A neighbor brought it," said Rosa.

"It's got a most extraordinary and marvellous taste," said
Hunter.

"Yes," said Rosa, "it's cider, from Tiverton. Give Annette a
piece."   (p. 165)

Later in the same novel Annette asks Mischa about two ivory figures
she sees on his mantelpiece:

> "They're called netsuke," said Mischa. "They were made in
> Japan in the eighteenth century. People used to wear them on
> their clothes."
> "Was it magic?" asked Annette.
> "No," said Mischa, "or only in the way in which magic can
> be part of ordinary life.   (pp. 207-208)

By the time she writes *The Time of the Angels* she has found a way
of communicating the richness, the density of "things" to us without
finding it necessary to comment upon their miraculousness. Marcus
has afternoon tea with Norah Shadox-Brown at the very beginning
of the novel:

> Huge as a cheese, a segmented cherry cake revealed its creamy
> interior, studded with juicy cherries, Marcus noted approvingly,
> all the way up to the top. Toasted scones fainted limply under
> their load of melting butter. Greengage jam, called by its maker
> "greengage chutney" in order to indicate that it was very special
> and to excuse its being very expensive, formed an oleaginous
> mountain in a dish of Waterford glass. The teapot had just been
> filled and a sharp, clear smell of hot water and Indian tea
> welcomed Marcus to the table. He sat down.   (pp. 9-10)

If one understands Iris Murdoch's theory of the novel, then her
attitude to symbolism is what one would expect. She sees symbols
as limitations, artificially restricting the contingency of reality. They
are one of the ways in which form is a temptation. She writes in "The
Sublime and The Beautiful Revisited": "One might say of the Symbol
that it is an analogon of an individual, but not a real individual. It
has the uniqueness and separateness of an individual, but whereas
the real individual is boundless and not totally definable, the symbol

is known intuitively to be self-contained: it is a making sensible of the idea of individuality under the form of necessity, its contingency purged away."[43] What seems inconsistent with this view is the fact that her novels are apparently so heavily symbolic. Many are even given the title of their central symbol: *The Sandcastle*, *The Bell*, *A Severed Head*, *The Unicorn*.

However, the symbols in Iris Murdoch's novels are either themselves images of inexhaustibility, such as the sandcastle Rain keeps attempting to build with dry sand, or the symbolic pattern is handled in such a way that it is seen to be endless. As the reader attempts to work out the patterns of symbolism in the novel he is led outwards in so many different directions that he has the impression they are infinite. The patterns all turn out to be like the snowflake Pattie watches in *The Time of the Angels* which composed "a huge rotating pattern too complex for the eye," and gave the impression that "The whole world was very quietly spiralling and shifting" (p. 90).

The images of *The Bell* do indeed form "a huge rotating pattern too complex for the eye." There are images of flight, of music and of water, but they interrelate in such a way as to make an exact description of the pattern impossible. As soon as one attempts to limit the significance of one symbol, as both Michael and James do in their sermons on the bell, one sets artificial limits. The bell is part of a pattern connected with sound which includes the nuns' singing in their chapel, the music of Mozart and Bach which is played at Imber, the jazz records in Noel's apartment, the various birds which Dora hears, the blackbird on the phone and the sedgewarbler she hears with Toby, and the night jars Toby and Michael hear. Peter Topglass's artificial bird songs are held to be less desirable than those of a living bird because of the "natural attractiveness of truth" (p. 129). Catherine sings a madrigal of "slightly absurd precision" (p. 130) immediately echoed in the precision of the jet fighters overhead, apparently not absurd. In one instance artificiality is undesirable, as in bird songs; in the other, that of the jet fighters, acceptable.

The jet fighters are part of the flight pattern of the novel picked up again, of course, in all the birds, in the butterfly Dora finds and sets free in the train, and in the flights of the medieval bell, of the guilty nun, and of Catherine into the lake. To swim, that is to function in water, an image of contingency, appears to be the talent of the innocent, of Toby, of the dog Murphy, of Mother Clare who rescues Dora and Catherine at the end of the novel. The water, music, and flight patterns all come together in the christening ceremony for the new bell, for even without the legend of the old bell's disappearance in the lake, the idea of christening links the bell with water.

Iris Murdoch's handling of symbolism in *The Bell* is in many ways similar to Joyce's handling of it in *Portrait of the Artist*. Like him, she uses the images of water, of flight, and of sound, perhaps for the same reasons, because they are in themselves formless but capable of having form imposed upon them. They suggest, therefore, that balance between form and no-form, between the crystalline and the journalistic documentary, she thinks the novel should aim for. Like Joyce, too, Iris Murdoch's aim is the impossible one, to incorporate everything, she shows that the fact that man cannot circumscribe and fully comprehend his universe is not a condition for regret, as the novelists of number would have us believe, but for wonder. Through her supra-realistic techniques she forces the reader to recognize and respect the mystery of reality. Like Burgess and Golding, she is a novelist of nightmare.

Chapter Seven

William Golding:
Islands

Critics vary almost as much about William Golding's philosophy as they do about Iris Murdoch's. They are agreed that each of his six novels[1]*—with the possible exception of *The Pyramid*—has basic metaphysical concerns, that Golding is concerned with the human condition rather than with the condition of contemporary man, but they differ considerably over what his metaphysics are. Many believe him to be an orthodox Christian, some taking him as Catholic, others as Calvinist; and one cannot deny that he writes primarily in terms of Christian mythology. James Baker, however, thinks that this is the great error of Golding criticism, that because critics have concentrated on Golding's debts to Christian sources "he is now popularly regarded as a rigid Christian moralist."[2]

Bernard Dick is one of several critics who discuss Golding in relation to Existentialism. He claims that in *Free Fall* "Golding has abandoned myth for Existentialist soul-bearing"[3] and that "Sartre did it much better in *Nausea*."[4] Baker, too, suggests that Golding sees reality as a purely subjective pattern "which we compose according to the limitations of our own nature"[5]—an Existentialist premise—but recognizes that he considers man's creation of God in his own image as presumptuous, not heroic. In *Pincher Martin*, as Baker points out, Golding inverts "the existential formula certain of the critics wished to impose upon it."[6]

Golding denies that there is any direct Existentialist influence upon him, just as he denies any Freudian influence, but he has admitted that we are all living in an Existentialist climate: "People have done a sort of Freudian exegesis on me. Well, I don't know my Freud, but both Freud and I have been looking at ourselves and human society. There must be points at which we agree. Well, now, my generation is the existentialist generation."[7] Given his interest in metaphysical matters, Golding is, as he wisely points out, bound to be concerned in this society at this time with many of the same questions as the Existentialists. Such questions as what is human identity? does man have "a center"? how far is man free? is there a reality transcending man's subjectivity? dominate his novels.

In every instance, though, he opposes the Post-existential view and comes up with answers very similar to those of Anthony Burgess and Iris Murdoch. It is untrue that Golding's novels leave us without answers, as Mark Kinkead-Weekes and Ian Gregor suggest.[8] Golding admits that he cannot subscribe to any particular religion, but insists that he is a fundamentally religious man: "The whole thing surely *has* to *be* a unity. If there is one faith I have, it is that there *is* a unity. And it seems to me—that man hasn't seen this."[9] This faith in a pattern that transcends man is not the only difference between Golding's position and that defined in the early work of Sartre and Camus, but it is the basic one. As with Anthony Burgess and Iris Murdoch it is this belief which underlies all other aspects of his philosophy and determines the techniques of his novels.

It is because "man hasn't seen this" that he is in trouble, according to Golding. Golding sees man as trapped in himself, "islanded," a condition he appears to believe comes inevitably with consciousness of self, with the loss of Innocence. In his discussion of *Free Fall* Bernard Dick explains that to Golding "loss of freedom comes . . . with the creation of a macrocosm inhabited and orbited by the self."[10] All Golding's major characters—Sammy Mountjoy, Pincher Martin, Dean Jocelyn—are men who have created the world in their own image, who turn everything into themselves.

As one might expect, metaphors of entrapment, cellars or prisons, and of absorption by self, eating, dominate the novels. The "eating" image is, of course, associated with greed, as Bernard Oldsey and Stanley Weintraub point out, and greed is a form of pride. The passage they quote from W. Burnet Easton, Jr.'s *Basic Christian Beliefs*, is worth quoting again since it makes clear Golding's associations with greed: "The fundamental sin according to the Bible is pride, egocentricity, self-deification, and the insistence that each of us is the final arbiter of what is good for him."[11] For Golding, then, the great sin is to see everything in terms of self, a sin Iris Murdoch, opposing Sartre on the same grounds, calls neurosis.

To what extent, though, can man be held responsible for this islanding of the self which, after all, happens to him inevitably with maturity? And what, if anything, can he do to save himself? Golding suggests, most clearly in *The Inheritors*, that man in a state of innocence is an integral part of his universe. The separation of man from the rest of his world through consciousness is apparently Golding's way of defining original sin. At this point man is islanded. As Baker suggests: "The island is an important symbol in all of Golding's works. It suggests the isolation of man in a frightening and mysterious cosmos."[12] This is perhaps true, though it puts too little emphasis on man's responsibility for his own condition to be a completely accurate account of Golding's views. Baker concludes by saying the island also represents "The futility of his attempt to create an ordered preserve for himself in an otherwise patternless world."[13] This is simply not true. There are bridges to the mainland, if not for Sammy Mountjoy, at least for William Golding.[14] In one conversation Jack Biles reminds Golding of a comment in his essay on Copernicus: there is an "overriding human necessity of finding a link between separate phenomena."[15]

Golding is an antirationalist, as are Murdoch and Burgess. He does not, however, believe that salvation lies in a reacknowledgement of the primitive with its concomitant violence, as does Iris Murdoch; nor does he, like Burgess, demand our acceptance of the violence he admits is a basic part of man's nature. Golding believes man's salvation lies in a recognition of the macrocosm in which he is a microcosm; man must find a bridge off the island of himself into an outer reality. As Golding himself explains it, "I see, I think I can see, that the only kind of real progress is the progress of the individual towards some kind of—I would describe it as *ethical*—integration."[16]

Howard Babb's account of Sammy's experience in *Free Fall* introduces another element necessary for salvation: the willingness to
express one's awareness of an external reality, through a cry for
help; in other—Christian—words, man needs the grace of God.
Babb's comments are interesting also in that they could apply
equally well to so many Iris Murdoch characters: "Sammy Mountjoy—at the moment of being sunk most completely in his self—can
cry out for help, thereby acknowledging the otherness of the universe and indeed experiencing its divinity. . . . he both feels
enclosed within a guilty self yet is periodically visited, when the
demands of the self are in abeyance, by perceptions of the world
about him as miraculous."[17]

Each of Golding's novels is a fantasy fable in the sense in which
I have defined the term, except *The Pyramid*, an attempt at comic
realism which has no place in this discussion. Samuel Hynes's
general comments on the form of the other five novels are interesting primarily because they exactly describe the basic elements of
fantasy fable: "Golding so patterns his narrative actions as to make
them the images of ideas, the imaginative forms of generalizations;
the form itself, that is to say, carries meaning apart from the meanings implied by the character or those stated more or less didactical-
ly by the author. Consequently we must look for human relevance
to the patterned action itself; if we 'identify,' it must be with the
moral—with conception of man and the shape of the universe—
and not with this character or that one."[18] Even in Golding's most
realistic novel,[19] *Free Fall*, set in present time and in a familiar
England, the scenes are separated from one another, only flashes
in Sammy Mountjoy's mind, so that we are forced to search for the
pattern, the relationship between them. Kinkead-Weekes and Greg-
or write of *Free Fall*, "Page by page the scenes convince, but they
are always felt to be in the service of some governing purpose which
frames them, islands them . . . out of the complexities of living."[20] In their more general discussion of the novels in their
concluding chapter, they point out that the reader, continually
trying to piece together a pattern, is involved in a process of reading with a continuous need for translation: "Our awareness of
meaning depends on our awareness of correspondence. Nothing is
offered for its own sake. Situations, relationships, protagonists,
figures are selected; controlled for a purpose beyond themselves,
serving an analytic design or debate."[21]

In spite of this accurate observation of the effect of Golding's novels, Kinkead-Weekes and Gregor seem to have missed Golding's intention. They see this method as a dramatization—presumably ironic—of "the limitations of the pattern-maker and the tragic consequences of his vision."[22] Surely this is a distortion designed to make their account of technique fit their view of Golding's thesis. What they describe dramatizes much more obviously the necessity for microcosm to recognize macrocosm. The reader moves steadily outward, from the islands of Golding's beginning situation to the mainland of his whole pattern, until he begins to suspect, as Golding himself says to Biles, that "everything is symbolic."[23]

Each novel is a microcosm of a greater whole: in *Lord of the Flies* the innate violence of the children alone on the island is a version in miniature of the adult world represented by the officer with his cruiser; the prehistoric world of *The Inheritors* is one episode in a history repeating itself in every man, as each loses his innocence; Pincher Martin, actually centered on his own nagging tooth, is living out in miniature the story of his whole life; *Free Fall* is closely related to *The Inheritors* and again deals with each man's loss of innocence in terms of one man, Sammy Mountjoy; Dean Jocelyn's obsession with building a spire is revealed as every man's drive to find meaning. Each islanded situation is gradually seen to incorporate more significance until one has the feeling that Golding has incorporated everything. "Everything is there at once." This, of course, is the great art of myth Golding himself has described to Frank Kermode as "something which comes out from the roots of things in the ancient sense of being the key to existence, the whole meaning of life, and experience as a whole."[24]

The experience of expansion the reader goes through in Golding's novels happens with every aspect of his technique: his characters, first recognizable as individuals, are seen to function also as allegorical figures; the patterning of the plot gradually adds increasing significance to each episode as its place in the overall scheme becomes clearer; each novel is related to earlier books by other writers, as Oldsey and Weintraub demonstrate, and thus is seen to be part of a larger culture; and, perhaps most importantly, Golding's language is so densely metaphoric that the reader is constantly given the sense of one thing's relation to another. These techniques are, of course, Joycean, and in many ways serve the same ends. They are, in fact, the defining characterisitics of the novel of nightmare.

As every student knows, *Lord of the Flies* concerns a group of children who are plane-wrecked on a friendly South Seas island during World War II. After reverting to savagery, they are finally "rescued" by a naval officer with a cruiser who presumably returns them to a world as violent as that which they created for themselves on the island. This comparison is Golding's final word to the reader. As James Baker points out in his introduction to the Casebook edition of *Lord of the Flies*, the appearance of the naval officer generalizes the experience of the novel.[25] The island society is a microcosm of a larger whole.

The failure of the island society comes about because of an innate tendency towards violence in the boys. Golding is, then, in opposition to the romantic notion of noble primitives. Human beings are not innately innocent, so human progress is unlikely. Like Burgess, Golding is Augustinian rather than Pelagian. Like Burgess, too, his belief in certain predetermined tendencies in human nature and his belief in a patterned universe set him in opposition to the Post-existential world view. The violence of the boys marooned on the island is, Golding makes clear to us, only part of what is to be found in nature as a whole. The novel opens after a violent storm "that wasn't half dangerous with all them tree trunks falling" (p. 6), the forest is swept by a raging fire Golding describes in terms of wild animals; even the clouds, Simon feels, "were sitting on the land; they squeezed, produced moment by moment this close, tormenting heat" (p. 127). In this final quotation the use of the word *squeezed* in connection with heat and clouds suggests the relationship between the boys and the natural world. During the ritual dance Ralph feels the desire to "squeeze and hurt" Robert; this scene is a foreshadowing of the one where Simon is killed by the fire and his death is followed by a cloudburst

What happens to the children is in large measure seen to be inevitable, though they are at first innocent because ignorant of their own natures. In an interview with James Keating, Golding has explained:

> They don't understand their own natures and therefore, when they get to this island, they can look forward to a bright

future, because they don't understand the things that threaten it. This seems to me to be innocence; I suppose you could almost equate it with ignorance of men's basic attributes, and this is inevitable with anything which is born and begins to grow up. Obviously it doesn't understand its own nature.[26]

The decline of the children's society on the island and the gradual revelation of evil is paralleled to the boys', particularly Ralph's, increasing self-consciousness. He begins to have a recurring "strange mood of speculation that was so foreign to him" (p. 70). Self-consciousness is, of course, the separation of self from the not-self, the outside world, and it is in terms of a breaking up of an initial harmony that Golding defines evil in the novel. At first the "littl'uns" separate themselves from the older children and then from each other; then Jack's group separates from Ralph's. "Things are breaking up. I don't understand why" (p. 75), Ralph says to the meeting and then later to Piggy, "what makes things break up like they do?" (p. 129) Finally each boy is alone, an island, afraid of everyone else.

Mistakenly the children feel that the evil is outside, a beast they can hunt and kill. Only Piggy and Simon realize that they themselves contain the seed of the trouble: Piggy tentatively suggests, "What I mean is . . . maybe it's only us" (p. 82); Simon is told in a vision by the pig's head on a stick, "You knew, didn't you? I'm part of you? Close, close, close. I'm the reason why it's no go? Why things are what they are" (p. 133). The decline of their society is also marked in the novel by their gradual forgetting that rescue must come from outside. At first talking of almost nothing else but parents, home, and rescue, they make fewer and fewer references to the world of which they are a part. Percival Wemys Madison, trained by his parents to memorize his address and telephone number, his place in the world, gradually forgets them and when the officer comes at the end, finds he can remember nothing about his life outside the island. Similarly, the fire Ralph recognizes they need in order to send smoke signals to possible rescuers is neglected by the others and goes out. The scene in which Ralph discovers this is significantly followed by the first pig hunt. Jack later takes the fire to cook his pig, and it becomes associated not with rescue and the outside world, but with eating, Golding's image for self-absorption. Piggy's increasing blindness is also a parallel loss of vision in a wider sense; he, too, becomes trapped in his own body, unable to see the outer reality.

If human nature is innately violent and selfish, then what hope does Golding offer us? Not much in *Lord of the Flies*. In various interviews and essays he has suggested a possibility of curbs voluntarily imposed by individuals upon themselves, though he does not talk very optimistically about the likelihood of this. In the interview with Keating, Golding says of the children in *Lord of the Flies*:

> They're too young to look ahead and really put the curbs on their own nature and implement them, because giving way to these beasts is always a pleasure, in some ways, and so their society breaks down. Of course, on the other hand, in an adult society it is possible society will not break down. It may be that we can put sufficient curbs on our own natures to prevent it from breaking down.[27]

There is some suggestion in the novel that others act as a curb on violence, that social organization has its values in spite of the history of Western civilization. Initially Roger, the most savage of the boys, does not throw stones at the little'uns because his "arm was conditioned by a civilization that knew nothing of him and was in ruins" (p. 57). Golding obviously believes that the parliament organized by Ralph is a force for good, in spite of the fact that the boys are incapable of making the necessary allowances for others that would help it work. When Jack and Ralph work together early in their stay on the island, they find two can lift logs too heavy for one.

Although Golding suggests the harmony of an ideal society, he does not indicate any faith in its creation. If man is to be helped, he appears to need help from God, represented in this novel, not altogether successfully, by Simon, the boy Golding himself has called a saint. More sensitive, more farseeing than the others, Simon has visions and attempts to communicate them to the others, only to be murdered by mistake as the beast. Golding in a conversation with Jack Biles says that Ralph should have been weeping for Simon at the end of the novel, not Piggy.[28] James Baker agrees that

"In his martyrdom Simon meets the fate of all saints," and adds, "the truth he brings would set us free from the repetitious nightmare of history, but we are, by nature, incapable of perceiving that truth."[29] There is no way of refuting this from the evidence available in the novel. It may or may not be true. It is not clear. What is clear, however, is that Simon represents for Golding a supernatural world which does exist. As long as it exists, then, there must be hope that we can recognize it, unless to Golding's God we really are as flies to wanton boys. The later novels at least reject this concept of God.

The techniques of *Lord of the Flies* are all designed to move the reader outward to a recognition of the macrocosm of which the situation in the novel is a microcosm. On the simplest level the violence on the island is echoed by constant references to the adult world beyond, to atom bombs, naval cruisers, parents in the various services. This world is represented by the dead parachutist, whom Golding has explained to Frank Kermode, he intended to represent history, the past.[30] The reader is constantly being drawn to compare his disappointment, his horror at the boys' savagery, with the institutionalized savagery of his own world.

The action of the novel is a gradual expansion. Each event foreshadows another or, to put it another way, eventually becomes the event of which it had earlier been an imitation or representation. Everything is, then, seen to be an integral part of everything else, as in all novels of nightmare. The first page of the novel describes the plump boy, Piggy, being caught and scratched by the unfamiliar twigs and thorns on the island. This scene with its suggestion of a trapped, plump animal is echoed by the later scene in which an actual pig is trapped by the boy hunters in the undergrowth. The real significance of such hunting is revealed only in the final scene in which Ralph is hunted by the boys through the thickets. The description of Ralph at this point has overtones of all the earlier hunting scenes: "There was a shout from beyond the thicket and then Ralph was running with the swiftness of fear through the undergrowth. He came to a pig-run, followed it perhaps for a hundred yards, and then swerved off. . . . Ralph thought of the boar that had broken through them with such ease" (p. 180). Similarly, the episode in which the boys push the rock over the cliff in play gains its full significance when the rock is later dropped on Piggy and kills him; the ritual dance in which all the boys pretend Robert is the pig they have killed and Ralph feels the first desire in him to destroy living flesh culminates in the killing of Simon in a later ritual.

Samuel Hynes comments accurately that Golding's characters, "while they are usually convincing three-dimensional human beings, may also function as exemplars of facets of man's nature— of common sense or greed or will."[31] Golding's ability to create characters which function both realistically and allegorically is illustrated particularly well in *Lord of the Flies*. It is necessary for Golding to establish the boys as "real" children early in the novel —something he achieves through such small touches as Piggy's attitude to his asthma and the boys' joy in discovering Piggy's nickname—because his major thesis is, after all, about human psychology and the whole force of the fable would be lost if the characters were not first credible to us as human beings.

Increasingly, though, Golding shows the children responding differently to the same object or event and the highly patterned nature of these episodes makes it clear that the reader is intended to read them as allegory. Typical are the reactions of Jack, Ralph, and Simon to some evergreen bushes: Simon sees them as candles, associating them and himself with religious services; Ralph, the practical one, points out that they cannot be lit; Jack, concerned as always with eating, first slashes at the buds and then decides they can't be eaten. Golding associates each boy with a certain set of images. Jack is animalistic, "bent double," "dog-like," "naked," "with flared nostrils, assessing the current of warm air for infor- mation" (p. 43). Simon becomes increasingly Christlike and is seen helping to feed the "littl'uns." The strength of Golding's charac- terization lies in the fact that while the reader is led out from the reality of individuals to a wider significance, his initial sense of real people is not lost. When, for example, at the death of Piggy the reader recognizes this is the death of reason or logic, he neverthe- less retains the sense of horror at a child's being murdered by other children.

The allegorical aspects of the characterization and the action lead the reader imaginatively into other worlds of the cultural macro- cosm. There are, as so many critics have pointed out, innumerable Biblical associations with the Eden myth and many political implications in the democracy/fascism opposition represented in Ralph and Jack. Oldsey and Weintraub, among others, have shown how Golding is in fact answering Ballantyne's boys' adventure story *Coral Island* in *Lord of the Flies*;[32] James Baker relates the novel to classical Greek literature, particularly to Euripides's *The Bacchae*. These critics are, of course, illustrating the same point about Golding's work, that one of its important aspects is its relation to a cultural whole he wishes the reader to perceive.

The final and perhaps most important way in which Golding's techniques dramatize his theme is the metaphorical density of the language itself. Golding describes everything in terms of something else. This is particularly true of his descriptions of natural phenomena. Here Ralph watches the lagoon and imagines its rise and fall as the breathing of a sea creature. The passage is thus related in the reader's mind to the beast the children think is causing their problems on the island and which Ralph is at this moment hunting. It also points up the fact that the violence of nature—albeit their own —is in fact the cause of the breaking-up:

> Ralph shuddered . . . Now he saw the landsman's view of the swell and it seemed like the breathing of some stupendous creature. Slowly the waters sank among the rocks, revealing pink tables of granite, strange growths of coral, polyp, and weed. Down, down, the waters went, whispering like the wind among the heads of the forest. There was one flat rock there, spread like a table, and the waters sucking down on the four weedy sides made them seem like cliffs. Then the sleeping leviathan breathed out, the water rose, the weed streamed, and the water boiled over the table rock with a roar. (pp. 97-98)

Golding frequently uses the images of worlds or globes to illustrate his theme of the necessity for relating microcosm to macrocosm. Jack and Ralph walk along like "two continents of experience and feeling, unable to communicate" (p. 49); Ralph examines his bitten nail and watches "the little globe of blood that gathered where the quick was gnawed away" (p. 122). The ability to use metaphor and simile, to perceive relations, is an essential characteristic of the loss of innocence, as Golding makes clear in his second novel, *The Inheritors*. But even though one must perceive things as separate before one can compare them, the act of comparison, of course, is a putting together and thus a sign of hope, of possible salvation from the prison of oneself.

The Inheritors, like *Lord of the Flies*, is concerned with the fall of man and with the loss of innocence. Set in prehistoric times, it tells of the destruction of a Neanderthal tribe and particularly of one member of it, Lok, by a group of "new" men, homo sapiens, led by Tuami. But the new men are not superior to the Neanderthals in much that Golding feels matters; Golding has reversed the notion of history as progress to suggest the notion of history as spiritual decline. The notion he rejects is that represented by H. G. Wells in his *Outline of History*, that Neanderthal man was bestial, hairy, gorilla-like, with possible cannibalistic tendencies. Golding uses a quotation from Wells as an epigraph to the novel and explains it in a conversation with Frank Kermode: "Wells' *Outline* played a great part in my life because my father was a rationalist, and the *Outline* was something he took neat. It is the rationalist gospel in excelsis. . . . By and by it seemed to me not to be large enough . . . too neat and too slick. And when I reread it as an adult I came across his picture of Neanderthal man, our immediate predecessors, as being these gross brutal creatures who were possibly the basis of mythological bad men. . . . I thought to myself that this is just absurd. . . ."[33]

Like the boys in *Lord of the Flies*, at the opening of the novel Lok's people are innocent. They live in a harmonious world, in which, whatever its physical dangers and difficulties, they are one with each other. Lok takes for granted that "People understand each other" (p. 59), that "it is bad to be alone. It is very bad to be alone" (p. 178). Going away, separation, is an evil for them. On returning to familiar places they are pleased to discover that a stone "has not gone away. It has stayed by the fire until Mal came back to it" and that "the river had not gone away either or the mountains" (p. 20).

They do not need language to communicate but use a form of telepathy or shared pictures. Language apparently carries implications of the separation of name and object, of distortion, that Golding does not wish to assign to the state of innocence. The pictures they share may be less exact, in some ways less useful than language, but they undoubtedly indicate a closer communication. The early

scenes of the novel are full of such remarks as: "[Fa] did not need
to speak" (p. 2); "as so often happened with the people, there were
feelings between them" (p. 4); "without warning, all the people
shared a picture inside their heads" (p. 27). The pictures not only
transcend the barriers among people, but also those between
present and future. After they have found food by following Lok's
directions, he says, "And Lok saw a true picture. Honey for Liku
and little Oa" (p. 47). Lok's people are totally responsible for
one another and provide that sort of warmth and acceptance of
each other contemporary sensitivity groups attempt to imitate.
After searching for the "new" man, Lok is welcomed back to the
group and restored spiritually through physical means: "But the
strings that bound him to the people were still there. . . . they
drove in until they were being joined to him, body to body. They
shared a body as they shared a picture. Lok was safe" (pp. 79-80).

The loss of a log and the disappearance of one of them, Ha, leads
Lok's people to suspect the existence of others in their area. Lok's
ability to relate to another, ironically, makes him "become" a "new"
man through hunting him: "as the smell of cat would evoke in him
a cat-stealth of avoidance and a cat-snarl . . . so now the scent
turned Lok into the thing that had gone before him" (p. 64). He
learns from this that the "other" is frightened and greedy, not at
one with his world as are Lok's people. Unlike Lok's tribe, "new"
people kill and eat meat; their sexuality is a form of rape. Lok
observes that the mating of Tuami and the fat woman is a "fierce and
wolflike battle" (p. 159). Tuami's people have already lost their
innocence. They are afraid of the darkness. Golding has written in
a letter to John Peter that "God is the thing we turn away from
into life, and therefore we hate and fear him and make a darkness
of him."[34] Tuami's people, then, in their inability to see beyond
themselves, in their sense of being surrounded by a frightening
darkness, have in Golding's terms lost touch with the macrocosm
which is the unity of God.

Lok gradually takes on the characteristics of the "new" people.
Their existence forces him into self-consciousness. He discovers
metaphor. There are now two parts of Lok, inside-Lok and
outside-Lok. After drinking the new people's alcohol, he becomes
violent, snatching at the pot, hitting Fa with a stick. "He found
that when he looked at the trees they slid apart and could only

be induced to come together with a great effort that he was not disposed to make" (p. 185). He has indeed become, as he says, one of the "new" people. This connection between Tuami and Lok has already been suggested by the fact that they both have chestnut hair. The "new people with their intelligence, violence, and strength supersede the Neanderthals by literally destroying them, but it is also clear that their characteristics are dominant anyway; "Neanderthalness" is dead in Lok before Tuami destroys Lok's people.

The Inheritors is a pessimistic book in the sense that Golding does not show the way to salvation for fallen man. Does he mean hope to lie in the implications of metaphor: "Likeness could grasp the white-faced hunters with a hand, could put them into the world where they were thinkable and not a random and unrelated irruption" (p. 176)? Does he mean it to lie in the brief picture of the two children Tanakil and Liku together? In the hope of unity offered by the baby Neanderthal Tuami's people take with them? It is hard to say. Salvation must lie through the darkness, on its other side, but, like Tuami at the end of the novel, we cannot "see if the line of darkness had an ending" (p. 213).

The Inheritors is a microcosm of the whole of human history. What happens here is repeated in every child as he grows to maturity. Read this way, Golding's view is Wordsworthean in its stress on the loss of childhood vision through self-consciousness, although *The Inheritors*, less than *Lord of the Flies*, emphasizes the paradisical elements of innocence. Lok's integration with his world is, however, no different in kind from the boy Wordsworth's in *The Prelude*.

The action of the novel functions in two ways. On the simplest level it traces the separation and death of Lok's people brought about by Tuami's. Mal dies first of a fever brought about by falling in the river; he falls in the river because the "new" people have removed their log bridge. Ha disappears on a hunt for the "new" people. Liku, the little girl, and her baby brother are stolen by Tuami's tribe and Liku is eaten. Fa goes over the waterfall. Finally Lok is alone, separated from his people, and separated from the reader by a sudden shift in point of view at the end of the novel. For the reader the plot is an opening out; his view is, for much of the novel, as limited as Lok's. Golding forces the reader to leap ahead guessing at what Lok cannot see, placing him in the macrocosm of human history. At the end, when the reader suddenly sees Lok from the point of view of Tuami, "a red creature," and "it," he has passed beyond Lok and Tuami both, since he is able to compare them with each other. The novel allows the reader, then, to make the relationship necessary in Golding's view, to transcend the Fall, even if it is not possible for Lok or Tuami.

Golding's descriptions of nature follow the pattern of separation in the plot. At first nature is seen as a harmonious whole; there are numerous images of inclusiveness and expansion:

> Over the sea in a bed of cloud there was a dull orange light that expanded. The arms of the clouds turned to gold and the rim of the moon nearly at the full pushed up among them
> The light crawled down the island and made the pillars of spray full of brightness. . . . it discovered grey forms that slid and twisted from light to shadow or ran swiftly across the open spaces on the sides of the mountain. It fell on the trees of the forest so that a scatter of faint ivory patches moved over the rotting leaves and earth. (pp. 31-32)

Everything is personified. Lok's people make no distinction between animate and inanimate—flames, stones, logs are as alive as Fa and Liku—and, as the previously quoted passage indicates, neither initially does Golding. As Lok loses his innocence his world becomes one of separate objects, of contrast not similarity: "Ivy and roots, scars of earth and knobs of jagged rock—the cliff leaned over so that the top with its plume of birch was looking straight down on to the island. The rocks that had fallen were still jumbled against the cliff at the bottom and their dark shapes, always wet, contrasted with the grey gleam of the leaves and the cliff" (p. 111).

The avalanche at the end causes this world to crumble and separate even more violently but, if indeed it marks the end of the ice age, as some critics have suggested, then it is also a sign of hope, of a new world. The description of the avalanche contains the two elements; images of separation and disintegration are followed by those of expansion and inclusiveness: "The hyenas lifted their hindquarters off the earth, separated and approached the interior of the hollow from either hand. The ice crowns of the mountains were a-glitter. They welcomed the sun. There was a sudden tremendous noise that set the hyenas shivering back to the cliff. It was a noise that engulfed the water noises, rolled along the mountains, boomed from cliff to cliff and spread in a tangle of vibrations over the sunny forests and out towards the sea" (p. 202).

Golding seems to have talked more about *Pincher Martin* than about any of his other novels. This is probably because of the critical controversy that has arisen about two aspects of the novel: the so-called trick ending, a final chapter in which the reader learns that Christopher Martin, who he had thought was struggling for his life on a rock, has been dead since the first page;[35] and the response to the central character, about whom critics hold diametrically opposed views. Is *Pincher Martin* an Existentialist novel with Pincher an heroic, Promethean figure standing out against death, forging his own identity with his intelligence? Are we to take as good in a Sartrean sense Pincher's awareness that he can have no "complete identity without a mirror" (p. 116), that he has created God in his own image, or not? Certainly it is hard to believe Golding is not consciously concerned with Existentialism here. The passage in which Pincher analyzes his feeling of lost identity, his comments on the way he used mirrors to watch himself as if he were watching a stranger, his use of others to assure himself of his own existence would not be out of place in *The Myth of Sisyphus* or in *Being and Nothingness*. It is difficult, too, for the reader not to feel some respect for the tenacity and courage Pincher displays. Nevertheless, Golding does not think Pincher heroic but presumptuous; critics who judge the experience by Existentialist criteria have, as James Baker points out, "made a hero out of Golding's villain."[36]

Golding makes the significance of Pincher Martin clear in some comments in the British BBC publication *Radio Times*:

Christopher Hadley Martin had no belief in anything but the importance of his own life; no love, no God. Because he was created in the image of God he had a freedom of choice which he used to centre the world on himself. . . . The greed for life which had been the mainspring of his nature, forced him to refuse the selfless act of dying. He continued to exist in a world composed of his own murderous nature. His drowned body lies rolling in the Atlantic but the ravenous ego invents a rock for him to endure on. It is the memory of an aching tooth. . . . He is not fighting for bodily survival but for his continuing identity in the face of what will smash it and sweep it away—the black lightning, the compassion of God.[37]

"To achieve salvation, individuality—the persona—must be destroyed,"[38] Golding has written elsewhere; and it is his individuality that Pincher refuses to surrender. He is physically and spiritually islanded, clinging to his own identity as to his rock. Relieved to find his identity disc around his neck, he shouts, "Christopher Hadley Martin. Martin. Chris. I am what I always was! (p. 68); he survives by shouting, "I am! I am! I am!" (p. 129), knowing only that he "must hang on" (p. 144).

He is nothing but greed, as the flashbacks to his past life reveal; his role of Greed in the morality play is type casting. Everything and everyone is food to feed Pincher Martin and, as he realizes himself, "eating with the mouth was only the gross expression of what was a universal process. You could eat with your cock or with your fists, or with your voice" (p. 79). He is guilty of Golding's greatest sin, self-obsession; he turns everything into himself, just as he has created his own purgatory on the rock. A recurring image in the novel, that of the Chinese box, in which a fish is buried and gradually eaten by maggots who subsequently eat each other, is obviously intended to reflect Pincher's experience: "The big ones eat each other. Then there are two and then one and where there was a fish there is now one huge and successful maggot. Rare dish" (p. 120). Throughout the novel Pincher hears a sound like the knocking of a spade against a tin box.

As in *The Inheritors*, man's intelligence is not seen as a good. Frank Kermode points out that "Golding is fascinated by the evidence—in the nature of the case ubiquitous—that human consciousness is a biological asset purchased at a price."[39] It is possible to go further than this, I think and suggest that for Golding the price is too high and the extent to which it is an asset debatable. It is precisely Pincher's intelligence, as he himself recognizes, that makes the purgatorial experience possible and prevents his surrender to God. Pincher knows that man makes patterns and superimposes them on nature, that he labels objects to control his world, and he uses this talent, apparently, to survive on the rock. But if the struggle for survival is here an evil, then the means used to achieve it are a liability not an asset. Pincher's intelligence has isolated him, kept him in that dream of a dark cellar that haunted his childhood. The last few pages of the novel are dominated by Pincher's recognition of his aloneness: "I'm so alone! Christ! I'm so alone! . . . Because of what I did I am an outsider and alone. . . . Now there is no hope" (pp. 160-161). Hope, however, has already been implied for Pincher in that in his aloneness he has called out, "Christ," even if blasphemously, and in that his next comment is the name of the Christ figure in the novel, his friend Nathaniel.

The scene in Pincher's memory immediately following is one in which he recognizes that the only genuine love he ever felt was for Nat. Once again in a Golding novel salvation lies through love, a reaching out to someone else. It is, of course, too late for Pincher to reach out for Nat now, but he has come to terms with a reality other than himself through a recognition of his place in the pattern. It is important to note that there is an essential difference between recognizing the pattern and imposing it; Golding's distinction is the one made by Burgess in *MF* between creating riddles and solving them. If we can take Nat's words as Golding's, Golding really believes in Vonnegut's ironic Bokononist term "karass": "One is conscious when meeting people that they are woven in with one's secret history. Don't you think?" (p. 138). Pincher has learned how people fit into his secret history.

What is more important he knows that he is not the last maggot, but "the last maggot but one" (p. 163). He recognizes something beyond himself, that there is a God, even if up to the end he is shouting, "I shit on your heaven!" (p. 178). It is not necessary to read the ending of *Pincher Martin* pessimistically. The mouth may be blaspheming but "the centre knew what to do. It was wiser than the mouth" (p. 177). The centre, Pincher's inner core, always described as black, finally merges with the black lightning which is God "in a compassion that was timeless and without mercy" (p. 179). The gap between the island, which is Pincher, and the mainland, which is not, is finally bridged; of course in spite of, rather than with, Pincher's conscious will.

In one sense the apparent experience Pincher Martin undergoes

is the macrocosm of which he is actually experiencing the microcosm. The reader is asked to believe that he is in his own head; the
rock he imagines he is on is his own tooth. This is a dramatization
of Pincher's whole life; he is smaller, less significant than he
thinks. Although there are various clues to the fact that Pincher is
inside his own head, it is really only on a second reading that this
becomes clear. The discovery in the last chapter that Pincher was
dead all along comes as a shock, not as a confirmation of suspicions.
The clues are frequently in the form of metaphors: Pincher com-
pares his experience to lying "on a rim of teeth in the middle of the
sea" (p. 82); he feels as if "the pressure of the sky and air was right
inside his head" (p. 141). Much of the metaphoric density of the
novel lies in this set of images. But in order for the reader to see
these comments as ironic, he already has to know the truth of
Pincher's situation. Other clues come in the form of Pincher's
dawning awareness of the familiarity of the rock. He resists recognizing the truth, refuses to connect himself with a reality beyond
his illusory world, but the awareness comes to him anyway. At the
end of the novel his realization of the nature of his own character,
his place in the pattern of his experiences, is paralleled to his
realization of the truth about the rock: he "understood what was
so hauntingly familiar and painful about an isolated and decaying
rock in the middle of the sea" (p. 154).

The pattern the reader, with Pincher, pieces together is the
pattern formed by the flashback sequences in Pincher's mind.
Memories of his past life: his cuckolding of his friend Alfred, his
rape of Mary, his reponsibility for Peter's injury, and Nat's death,
are each a microcosm of his whole life. He watches them as if they
are a film being projected on to the pebbles in front of him. The
first picture is of a jam jar on a table which "was interesting because one could see into a little world there which was quite
separate" (p. 8). In piecing the separate worlds together, the reader
and Pincher come to realize that he is indeed what he always was,
and that "an hour on this rock is a lifetime" (p. 40), all the experiences of the book have happened in a moment, but a moment which
is the microcosm of a whole life.

The techniques of characterization Golding uses in this novel
are very similar to those he uses in *Lord of the Flies*; the characters
function midway between realism and allegory. Mary is the girl

Pincher rapes and Nat marries, but she is also the Virgin Mary; Pincher's rape of her is presumptuous in terms of the allegory, too, then. He acts as God. Nathaniel is the Christ figure, and his name is always juxtaposed with Christ's in Pincher's exclamations: "Nat! Nathaniel! For Christ's sake! Nathaniel! Help!" (p. 12). Martin, who was baptized Christopher, has destroyed Christ—in the form of Nat —rather than carried him as his name implies and has literally become his nickname, Pincher. But in brief snatches of description or dialogue Golding keeps every character functioning on the human level also, even as the reader is beginning to see the allegorical pattern. Mary remains the rather uninteresting girl with "the remote and unconquered face" (p. 130); Nat, the gentle, concerned friend.

Through allegorical characterization Golding makes the reader relate his microcosmic world of Pincher on the rock to Christian mythology, and through references to Prometheus to Greek mythology also. Oldsey and Weintraub point out the extent to which the reader is invited to relate the novel to a cultural macrocosm, claiming that the book has echoes of Bierce, of Hemingway, of *King Lear*, of *Paradise Lost*, of Eliot, of Conrad, and of a minor adventure story called *Pincher Martin*.[40] As Nat says to Pincher, "our lives must reach right back to the roots of time, be a trail through history" (p. 138). And in a good fable they must be seen to.

Many critics have commented that the title of Golding's fourth novel, *Free Fall*, has both a theological and a scientific significance, but Golding himself has, as usual, expressed it best: "Everybody has translated this in terms of theology; well, okay, you can do it that way, which is why it's not a bad title, but it is in fact a scientific term. It is where your gravity has gone, it is a man in a space ship who has no gravity; things don't fall or lift, they float about; he is completely divorced from the other idea of a thing up *there* and centered on *there* in which he lives."[41] Sammy Mountjoy, narrator of *Free Fall*, has more insight and perhaps more conscience than Pincher Martin, but basically his is Pincher's problem. He is islanded, trapped in himself, "completely divorced from the other idea of a thing up there."

There are images of cells everywhere. The whole novel can be read as taking place in a prison cell where Sammy is held by the Germans in World War II. Dr. Halde, his interrogator, tells him, "You do not believe in anything enough to suffer for it or be glad.

There is no point at which something has knocked on your door and taken possession of you. You possess yourself" (p. 144). Since he recognizes no reality beyond himself, for Sammy, as for Pincher, other people are merely objects for his use. He knows the way out is to make contact with something beyond himself, to build a bridge; he wants to know what it is like to be Beatrice, for example, but finds himself doomed to isolation: "Our loneliness . . . is the loneliness of that dark thing that sees as at the atom furnace by reflection, feels by remote control and hears only words phoned to it in a foreign tongue. To communicate is our passion and our despair" (p. 8).

The novel is Sammy's attempt to build the bridge, to find his place in a reality beyond himself. One way in which he attempts this is to search for the pattern of his own life, particularly for the moment when he lost his freedom. As in *The Inheritors*, loss of freedom is equated with loss of innocence, with self-consciousness; like Lok's people, Sammy begins in Paradise, here a slum area known as Paradise Hill. On looking back he sees himself and his friend Johnny as "two points of perception, wandering in Paradise. I can only guess our innocence, not experience it" (p. 45). As a child he was fully integrated with his world, spontaneous, free, a quality which the best of his later paintings capture. As Kinkead-Weekes and Gregor say, in this novel "Golding is questioning the nature of understanding itself."[42]

Golding establishes a relationship between an understanding of others and an ability to manipulate them. A series of characters in the novel—Philip Arnold, who "knew about people" (p. 49), Miss Pringle, "a past-master of crowd psychology and momentum" (p. 195), and Dr. Halde, Sammy's tormentor at the prison camp—suggests that for Golding, here as elsewhere, the price of understanding can be too high. Sammy's loss of freedom comes when he recognizes that he can make a choice, that he has the power to manipulate events. Told by his headmaster that one can have anything one is prepared to pay the price for, he makes a Faustian bargain for Beatrice Ifor:

> "What is important to you?"
> "Beatrice Ifor."
> "She thinks you depraved already. She dislikes you."

"If I want something enough I can always get it provided
I am willing to make the appropriate sacrifice."
"What will you sacrifice?"
"Everything." (p. 236)

Sammy attempts to build the bridge from his island also in the
sense of trying to find unity in the outer reality. Golding represents
the apparent chaos of the world in the two teachers of the young
Sammy, Nick Shales, rationalist and scientist, and Rowena Pringle,
teacher of religion. Baker believes that at the end of the novel
Sammy has not made sense of the dichotomy represented by these
two world views, that he has to remain "uncertain, unsatisfied."[43]
It is important to remember, though, that as children Sammy and
his friends "held both universes in our heads effortlessly" (p. 211),
since this indicates that Golding, if not Sammy, believes in a unified
reality. There is no need to resolve the paradox; in Paradise there
is only harmony. The title of the novel, combining a scientific
and a religious significance in one phrase, also suggests this harmony.

As at the end of *Pincher Martin* though, it is possible to accept
Golding's belief in a patterned universe without believing Sammy
ever finds salvation. Nevertheless, I agree with Oldsey and Weintraub here that an important indication of Sammy's salvation is his
cry for help, his willingness to put self aside and recognize "the
other idea of a thing up there." However ambiguous the final
page of the novel may be, Sammy does leave the cell, his island,
and does, like Pincher, receive compassion. The bridge is, after
all, love, as Sammy recognizes. Commenting on his treatment in a
hospital ward as a child, he writes, "I have searched like all men
for a coherent picture of life and the world, but I cannot write the
last word on that ward without giving it my adult testimony. The
walls were held up by sheer, careful human compassion" (p. 77).
The child Sammy, then, who had chosen Nick Shales's irrational
world for nonrational reasons, because Nick gave love and Rowena
Pringle was cruel, is seen to be right after all. Love is the only truth
that matters: "People are the walls of our room, not philosophies"
(p. 222).

Although *Free Fall* resembles *Pincher Martin* in that the physical
situation of the central character, here a prison cell, is a microcosm

of his spiritual life, it is only in terms of its time scheme a fantasy novel. It takes place in recognizably modern times in familiar English places. The novel has been criticized for its lack of a controlling myth; Babb says that in *Free Fall* Golding "would seem to be running a . . . risk; of including materials that do not eventuate in a realized paradigm of meaning."[44] It has been criticized also for the extent to which Sammy comments on his own experience.[45] This, surely, is perfectly defensible given Golding's thematic concerns in this novel. Sammy's desperate desire to communicate, to find a link with an outside reality, is dramatized very well in those passages of commentary directed to the reader. They are not in fact comments upon the action, but rather the essential action of the book itself. As the book progresses and the reader comes closer to Sammy in sharing his search for a pattern, they become fewer in number. Sammy no longer tells the reader at the end, "we share nothing but our sense of division" (p. 10). Sammy's communication with the reader is in itself a sign of health, a bridge built.

For there is a pattern in Sammy's experiences as related in the novel; Hynes is wrong in saying, "the scenes do not compose a myth or fable."[46] The experience of reading *Free Fall* is, like that of reading Golding's other novels, a piecing together of a puzzle, a working from the microcosm to the macrocosm. Each scene of the novel illustrates a paradox: the world of feeling is not parallel to the rational world. Sammy's mother lies to him when he asks who his father was, inventing different stories every time he asks. The little boy is told lies, but emotionally given the truth. His search for his place in the world, which the questions about his father represent, is answered every time his mother shows her love for him. The older girl, Evie, who takes him to school, lies to him too, but holds his hand. When his passion for Beatrice is fulfilled sexually, he feels farther from her than ever; in his head he loves her, but he feels no real emotion. The pattern is clearest, of course, in the conflict between Nick's world and Miss Pringle's: "The beauty of Miss Pringle's cosmos was vitiated because she was a bitch. Nick's stunted universe was irradiated by his love of people" (p. 226).

The existence of a pattern is underscored by parallel events and characters the reader is invited to compare. The boy Sammy laughs at the retarded girl, Minnie, who urinates on the classroom floor; the man Sammy mourns Beatrice who does the same thing on the floor of the hospital. As I mentioned above, Philip Arnold, Rowena Pringle, and Dr. Halde share a knowledge of people enabling them to exploit them. But it is only one side of people, their weaknesses, that they know; love and compassion are unknown to each of these three. The commandant's final comment, "The Herr Doctor does not know about peoples" (p. 253), is in that sense true.

Babb has demonstrated the extent certain paragraphs of the novel turn out to be microcosms of the whole story.[47] The language of *Free Fall* is as dense metaphorically as that of the earlier novels. Here too Golding gives one the sense in which this particular situation is all inclusive; the reader is taken to worlds beyond the novel and is left with the feeling that these worlds may well be infinite. As in other novels of nightmare the reader moves towards infinity. A passage in which Sammy discusses what the Germans wish him to endure in the dark cell literally refers to the possible discovery of a corpse in the center of the room, but has both sexual and religious overtones: "We want you to feel forward over the slope and spread your fingers till you have found the sole of a shoe. Will you go on then, pull gently and find that the sole resists? Will you, under the erected hair in the blindness, deduce without more effort the rigor, the body curled there like a frozen foetus? How long will you wait?" (p. 175). All man's, as well as all Sammy's, experience is here; the womb, sexual intercourse, the search for meaning, death. Golding's language confirms his belief in a unified cosmos.

Oldsey and Weintraub mention literary echoes of Poe's "The Pit and the Pendulum," of Orwell: *1984*, and of *Pincher Martin* but stress that *Free Fall* can be read most successfully as a comment on Camus' *The Fall*: "Golding reverses one of the basic existential tenets: man's position in the universe is not absurd; the universe itself is not; but man's proclivity toward self, toward sin without a concept of atonement, can make him absurd."[48]

The Spire is thematically and technically the culmination of Golding's four earlier novels. Here the central character is Jocelin, Dean of a medieval English cathedral, whose driving ambition is to build a spire taller than any built before. Unlike Sammy Mount-joy and Pincher Martin, he is a religious but not for that reason

any less subject to their vices. Like them he sacrifices people—
ultimately in Golding's scheme equivalent to selling his soul—to
achieve his ambition, justifying it on the grounds that his ambition
is a vision of God's will. He uses an adulterous passion between
his master builder Roger and the wife of a church official, Pangall,
to keep the builder on the job; he prevents Roger from getting work
elsewhere; he is responsible for Goody Pangall's death which results from the affair; he allows workmen to die attempting to
achieve the impossible; he neglects church services; he makes an
unsuitable boy a canon in exchange for his father's gift of timber
for the spire. As Jocelin himself puts it at the end, "I traded a stone
hammer for four people" (p. 212). He succeeds in manipulating
others because he, like Philip Arnold, Rowena Pringle, and Dr.
Halde, know how to exploit people. Indeed he takes pride in this
fact: "I know them all, know what they are doing and will do,
know what they have done" (p. 2). The action of the novel is like the
action of *Pincher Martin* and *Free Fall*, that of the central character's
gradual discovery of the meaning of his life. Jocelin, too, is islanded,
"locked in his head" (p. 83), and looking back says to Roger Mason,
"I was driven too. I was in some net or other" (p. 200).

The metaphorical implications of Jocelin's spire are multiple,
but the most important is the significance of the spire as a symbol
for man's reaching towards another world, in religious terms
Heaven, in an attempt to understand it. The building of the spire,
then, is a metaphor for Camus' premise that man seeks meaning.
When Jocelin climbs the spire, he shouts, "Up here we are free of
all the confusion" (p. 96), and on a second climb asks numerous
questions: "What's this called? And this?" (p. 139). The movements
of the mind are frequently described in terms of climbing: he asks
Roger, "What's a man's mind, Roger? Is it the whole building . . . ?" (p. 203); the questions of his confessor "Wormed
over him, expanded, became a mountain. He saw to what a height
a mind must climb, ladder after ladder, if it were to answer, so he
prepared once more to climb" (p. 160).

It is not that the search for meaning is in itself wrong in Golding's terms, but the motive for the search is all important. It may
be vision, a true search; it may be presumption, mere will. Jocelin
believes he is fulfilling a mission that began when he was first
chosen Dean by God. The action of the novel questions this as-

sumption: Jocelin's position as Dean was in fact given him as a sort of joke by his aunt, then mistress of the king; the spire may have inadequate foundations. As T. S. Eliot demonstrates in *Murder in the Cathedral*, the final temptation of the visionary is pride in the vision, and Jocelin is undoubtedly proud. A deacon says, "He thinks he is a saint! A man like that!" (p. 7). The face of the Holy Spirit carved on the spire is to be Jocelin's; he believes his will and God's are synonomous: "You'll see how I shall thrust you upward by my will. It's God's will in this business" (p. 33). For Golding, to forget oneself in another reality is the chief good; it is indeed necessary for salvation. But Jocelin thrusts himself up, makes himself God.

Jocelin clearly comes to realize his folly. He recognizes that God is indeed love—"If I could go back, I would take God as lying between people and to be found there" (p. 210)—and at the end, dying, apparently calls upon God for help as do Sammy and perhaps, although not willingly, Pincher. In this novel Golding answers the problem critics raise about *Free Fall*, that Sammy himself does not fully recognize the unity he seeks. The answer he gives is that of Anthony Burgess and Iris Murdoch, the other novelists of nightmare: some mystery is both inevitable and necessary. "God knows where God may be" (p. 212), says Jocelin at the end. He may indeed mean, as the critics believe, that man cannot find where God is. But the words can also be read more optimistically to mean that even though man does not know where God is, God indeed does.

The confirmation of God's existence comes finally in the vision of the apple tree given to Jocelin before he dies: "His head swam with the angels, and suddenly he understood there was more to the apple tree than one branch. It was there beyond the wall, bursting up with cloud and scatter, laying hold of the earth and the air, a fountain, a marvel, an apple tree" (p. 195). As Babb points out, the tree includes the divine and the secular, the earth and the sky; it "manifests a miraculous totality."[19] But the tree is an apple tree and must carry overtones of the Garden of Eden. The transformed apple tree is a perfect image for Golding's concept of salvation. Man, a child, lives alongside the apple tree in innocence; adult, he eats of its fruit and falls into sin as he gains self-consciousness and knowledge. But knowledge is also the way forward to salvation; man must see that he is part of a macrocosm, that the tree touches earth and heaven. In this way the original sin may be transcended, the tree transformed.

The spire is the symbol around which multiple meanings cluster. It is, as Babb says, both a physical fact in the external world and a presence within Jocelin himself.[50] It is simultaneously church spire, male organ, and Jocelin's will as the metaphorical language of the novel indicates: "The model was like a man lying on his back. The nave was his legs placed together, the transepts on either side were his arms outspread. The choir was his body; and the Lady Chapel, where now the services would be held, was his head. And now also, springing, projecting, bursting, erupting from the heart of the building, there was its crown and majesty, the new spire" (p. 2). It is a microcosm gradually expanding for the reader towards an infinity of meanings, including a paradigm of the action of the novel itself.

The plot, too, is an expansion. Kinkead-Weekes and Gregor point out that "The first four chapters are intensive, the next four extensive, as the tower rises and permits wider and wider views. . . . But this is only for a time. The cellarage cannot be ignored by climbing into the tower. 'Up here,' 'out yonder,' 'down there,' turn out to be part one of the other."[51] All is seen to be one; "Everything is there at once."

Golding has said that he would prefer his books to be thought of as "myths of total explanation."[52] Like Anthony Burgess and Iris Murdoch, Golding refutes the Sartrean view of man as an alienated being in absurd relation to the universe with what amounts to a leap of faith. He believes that there is meaning, unity, but recognizes this is unprovable. Redemption from the Post-existential dilemma, nevertheless, lies in each man's recognition of his place in the universal scheme. Like Iris Murdoch, he frequently defines this recognition as love. What convinces his reader is not the logic of his argument, but his techniques, those of the novelists of nightmare. He forces the reader outward from the island of a particular situation over the bridges that lead in all directions. Only from the macrocosm can one see that the island is a microcosm of everything else. Golding, as Kermode says, "has found in experience and embodies in his own myths the truths that inform all others."[53]

In an attempt to distinguish between two forms of contemporary fantasy fiction it is inevitable that some distortion has taken place, that the differences between the novelists of number and the novelists of nightmare have been stressed, the similarities underestimated. Yet it is important to remember that novels of number and novels of nightmare are both forms of fantasy and are both contemporary. They share many surface similarities; they reflect the same post-war world with all its violence, mechanization, loneliness, and desperate people. Vonnegut's picture of contemporary society in *Player Piano* is not very different from Burgess's view of it in *The Wanting Seed*. The novelists of number and the novelists of nightmare see the same universe, chaotic, apparently meaningless, and apparently insensible to man's desire for unity. It is the world as defined in Camus' *The Myth of Sisyphus* and Sartre's *Being and Nothingness*.

The difference between the novelists of number and the novelists of nightmare lies in how they choose to regard this vision. The Post-existentialist novelist of number believes his own perceptions and concludes that there is no meaning to his relationship with the universe, no essence to the reality we perceive and therefore no ethical absolutes. The novelist of nightmare, on the other hand, chooses to have faith that there is a unity, a shared essential reality, even if its nature is not fully decipherable by man.

But it is wrong to conclude that the novelist of nightmare is therefore more optimistic than the novelist of number. Only in the ultimate sense is this so. Man may be more significant in a novel of nightmare than in a novel of number, but he is not necessarily happier. Given the choice between life in Barth's world of relative pleasures and life in Burgess's world, where every joy is balanced by violent suffering, one might well choose Barth's. It is probably easier to be Todd Andrews in the world of *The Floating Opera* than Alex in the world of *A Clockwork Orange*, even if one's life has ultimately less significance.

The values Barth, like other novelists of number, chooses to affirm are, of course, merely relative, ways of getting by. For example, love for other people is a "good" for Heller, Barth, Purdy, and Vonnegut, but it is no answer to the Post-existential dilemma. It may make life more bearable; it can not give it meaning. The values the novelist of nightmare affirms, on the other hand, are ways to salvation. The novelist of nightmare is overtly didactic; he claims, unlike the novelist of number, to have the answer, to show us the way. Love, in the novels of Murdoch and Golding, is not merely a way of getting by but a form of recognition of a significant outer reality. It is an absolute good, a refutation of the Post-existential dilemma.

So the novelist of nightmare writes myths, those greatest of teaching devices, fictional constructs which explain man's relationship to his universe. Art, then, is of supreme importance to the novelist of nightmare; it is itself in part the means to salvation for both writer and reader. As the reader recognizes the relationship between an initial Golding situation and the macrocosm of which it is a part, as he solves the puzzle of a Burgess novel, as he reacts in wonder to the "ordinary" world of Iris Murdoch, he constructs the pattern of a universe. How, then, can he deny the possibility of a unified reality?

This elevation of art to the level of religious salvation links the novelist of nightmare to an earlier twentieth-century British tradition, that of Virginia Woolf, E. M. Forster, and Joyce himself. This continuing tradition is perhaps one of the reasons that nightmare appears to be primarily a British form. Even if one extends the list to include other writers, Muriel Spark, for example, or Doris Lessing, one still finds oneself adding the names of British writers. I can think of only one British novelist of number, Nigel Dennis, whose *Cards of Identity* and *A House in Order* are clearly examples of the form, unless of course one includes Beckett. It seems that when the British novelist was faced with the Post-existential dilemma he turned to an older tradition and adapted it to contemporary uses. I don't mean to suggest that Virginia Woolf, for example, wrote fantasy fables—there is much about the novels of nightmare that is exclusively contemporary—but it would probably be valid to describe many of her novels as myths.

But this does not really explain why the British novelist of nightmare should react one way and the American novelist of number another. For the novelists of number are primarily American rather than British; one can add Pynchon, Burroughs, Barthelme to the list and be hard put to find an American novelist of nightmare, though arguments can perhaps be made to include Bellow and Percy. Why should the American novelist be more willing to accept the pessimistic aspects of the Existentialist premises than the British? Why should Sartre and Camus themselves be able to transform these same premises into affirmative humanism and not the postwar novelist of number? We can't, of course, know, but it is possible to speculate.

Is it possible that the ability to transcend the absurdity of the human condition is connected to that sense of a collective spirit Camus defines in *The Rebel*: "In the absurdist experience, suffering is individual. But from the moment when a movement of rebellion begins, suffering is seen as a collective experience"?[1] For Sartre and Camus the heroics of Existentialism were born in the struggles of the Resistance; a common enemy provided a sense of the collective human spirit, made commitment possible. "The hero," as Hassan points out, "has always embodied the collective wish of his race."[2] Is it possible that the second world war provided for the British this very sense of a collective human wish which made them able to transcend, in feeling at least, premises which for American writers were confirmation of despair? The immediacy of World War II certainly turned the shared suffering of the British into a collective resistance.

Is it true to say that postwar America has not really had a comparable resistance until very recently? Is it significant that almost no novelists of number are Jewish—Bruce Jay Friedman is a notable exception—while many of the greatest contemporary American novelists are? Or Black? Indeed the American novel that seems to be closest to a novel of nightmare is Ralph Ellison's *Invisible Man*. Is it true, then, that those writers who have experienced a resistance, known a collective rebellion, whether or not manifested in violence, against a common enemy, are not Post-existentialists? Perhaps.[3] These kind of generalizations are, of course, inevitably simplistic. Exceptions will undoubtedly be found. For example, the theory does not explain at all why other French writers, notably the playwrights, Ionesco, Genet, are Post-existential in spirit when Sartre and Camus are not.

If the theory has any validity, the most important conclusion to be drawn is that the novel of number carries the seeds of its own destruction. Resistance will come; it has perhaps already. The novel of number is by its very nature a limited form, anyway, since it depends for its effects on the frustration of its readers' expectations of realism. When these expectations change, as in time they must and to some extent are beginning to already, the form obviously cannot function in the same way.

This is not to minimize the value of what the novelists of number have done. Both novelists of nightmare and those of number—though most of all the novelists of number—have forced us to look at and talk about fiction in a new way. We can no longer talk about it as if it is an attempt to reflect a given reality, social or psychological. The primary reality which concerns the novelists of number and of nightmare is the reality of the act of reading. To talk about them we have to develop a language to define their effect upon us. And in developing this language how can we fail to discover new ways of talking about all fiction?

Notes to the Preface

1. See, for example, David D. Galloway, *The Absurd Hero in American Fiction: Updike, Styron, Bellow, Salinger* (Austin: Univ. of Texas Press, 1970); Jerry Bryant, *The Open Decision* (New York: Macmillan, Free Press, 1970); Ihab Hassan, *Radical Innocence* (Princeton: Princeton Univ. Press, 1961).

2. Raymond Olderman, *Beyond the Wasteland: A Study of the American Novel in the Nineteen-Sixties* (New Haven: Yale Univ. Press, 1972), p. 14.

3. *Ibid.*, p. 22.

4. *Ibid.*

5. Albert Camus, *The Myth of Sisyphus and Other Essays*, trans. Justin O'Brien (1942; rpt. New York: Vintage, 1955), p. 11.

6. In *The Literature of Silence* (New York: Alfred A. Knopf, 1967), Ihab Hassan pointed out that these techniques have been discussed by French critics but largely ignored by Americans. Since then they have received more attention. See, for example, Robert Scholes, *The Fabulators* (New York: Oxford Univ. Press, 1967); Max F. Schulz, *Black Humor Fiction of the Sixties: A Pluralistic Definition of Man and his World* (Athens: Ohio Univ. Press, 1973); Helen Weinberg, *The New Novel in America: The Kafkan Mode in Contemporary Fiction* (Ithaca, N.Y.: Cornell Univ. Press, 1970).

7. Richard Kostelanetz says that in the last twenty years has appeared "the flowering of the absurd theater, the beginnings of the absurd novel." *On Contemporary Fiction*, ed. Richard Kostelanetz (New York: Avon, 1964), xxvii.

8. Martin Esslin, *The Theatre of the Absurd* (Garden City, N.Y.: Doubleday, 1961), p. 305.

9. John W. Hunt, "Comic Escape and Anti-Vision: Joseph Heller's *Catch-22*," *Adversity and Grace: Studies in Recent American Literature*, ed. Nathan A. Scott, Jr. (Chicago: Univ. of Chicago Press, 1968), pp. 91-98.

10. Ihab Hassan, "Joyce-Beckett: A Scenario in Eight Scenes and a Voice," *Journal of Modern Literature*, 1, no. 1(1970), 7-18.

11. Hassan appears to have altered Sewell's distinction which was fourfold: Number versus Dream; Logic versus Nightmare. The opposite of Number in Sewell's scheme is not Nightmare but Dream; the opposite of Nightmare is Logic.

12. Hassan, "Joyce-Beckett," p. 13.

13. *The Literature of Silence*, p. 13.

14. Ian Watt, *The Rise of the Novel: Studies in Defoe, Richardson and Fielding* (Berkeley: Univ. of California Press, 1957), p. 32.

15. Arthur Mizener, "The New Romance," *The Southern Review*, 8(1972), 106-117.

16. Quoted by Wayne Booth, *The Rhetoric of Fiction* (Chicago: Univ. of Chicago Press, 1961), p. 30.

17. Eugène Ionesco, *Notes and Counter Notes: Writings on the Theater*, trans. Donald Watson (New York: Grove, 1964), p. 144.

18. Hassan, "Joyce-Beckett," p. 17.

19. *Ibid.*, p. 12.

20. *Ibid.*, p. 11.

21. *Ibid.*, p. 16: "The language itself is insanely jocular—jocular yet organic."

22. *Ibid.*, p. 12.

Notes to the Introduction

1. Alain Robbe-Grillet, *For a New Novel*, trans. Richard Howard (1963; rpt. New York: Grove, 1965), p. 32.

2. In *Counter-Statement*, Kenneth Burke points out that for many readers "dealing with life" has become synonomous with preserving some of the realistic conventions of nineteenth-century prose fiction.

3. My reading is based on Dickens' second ending to *Great Expectations*.

4. See, for example, Mark Spilka, *Dickens and Kafka: A Mutual Interpretation* (Bloomington: Indiana Univ. Press, 1963).

5. Camus, p. 11.

6. *Ibid.*, p. 13.

7. *Ibid.*, p. 38.

8. *Ibid.*, p. 5.

9. *Ibid.*, p. 11.

10. *Ibid.*

11. Jean-Paul Sartre, *Nausea*, trans. Lloyd Alexander (1938; rpt. New York: New Directions, 1964).

12. Booth, p. 20.

13. Northrop Frye, *Anatomy of Criticism* (Princeton: Princeton Univ. Press, 1957), p. 134. Cf. The black humorists' "immediate point of departure has been the novel, a form which we view with certain realistic expectations." Robert Scholes, *The Fabulators*, p. 39.

14. Roger H. Smith, *Daedalus* (Winter 1963), 155-165.

15. Booth, pp. 71-73.

16. Richard Poirier, *The Performing Self: Compositions and Decompositions in the Language of Contemporary Life* (New York: Oxford Univ. Press, 1971).

17. Iris Murdoch, *Sartre, Romantic Rationalist* (1953; rpt New Haven: Yale Univ. Press, 1959), p. 85.

18. Robbe Grillet, p. 27.

19. Booth, p. 129. Cf. John Bayley, "Character and Consciousness," *New Literary History*, 5(1974), 225 235.

20. Jean-Paul Sartre, *Being and Nothingness*, trans. Hazel E. Barnes, (1943: rpt. New York: Philosophical Library, 1956), p. 238.

21. Camus, p. 10.

22. *Ibid.*

23. Frederic Jameson, "Metacommentary," *PMLA*, 86 (January 1971), 9-17. Cf. Booth, p. 126 ff.

24. Eugène Ionesco, *Four Plays*, trans. Donald M Allen (New York: Grove, 1958), p. 115.

25. Camus, p. 8.

26. Samuel Beckett, *Waiting for Godot* (New York: Grove, 1954), p. 29.

27. Ionesco, *Four Plays*, p. 48.

28. N. F. Simpson, *One Way Pendulum* (New York: Grove, 1960), p. 61.

29. Samuel Beckett, *Watt* (New York: Grove, 1953), p. 81.

30. As George Steiner points out "Wittgenstein's entire work starts out by asking whether there is any verifiable relation between the word and the fact. That which we call fact may well be a veil spun by language to shroud the mind from reality. Wittgenstein compels us to wonder whether reality can be *spoken of*, when speech is merely a kind of infinite regression, words being spoken of other words." "The Retreat from the Word," *The Listener*, 14 and 21 July 1960.

31. Harold Pinter, *The Caretaker and The Dumb Waiter* (New York: Grove, 1960), p. 97.

32. Camus, p. 44.

33. *Ibid.*, p. 40.

34. Murdoch, p. 59.

35. Camus, *The Rebel*, trans. Anthony Bower (1951; rpt. New York: Vintage, 1956), p. 24.

36. *Ibid.*, p. 22.

37. Sartre, *Being and Nothingness*, p. 43.

38. Camus, *The Rebel*, p. 259.

39. *Ibid.*, p. 253.

40. Jean-Paul Sartre, *What is Literature?* trans. Bernard Frechtman (1949; New York: Washington Square Press, 1966), p. 24.

41. *Ibid.*, pp. 28-29.

42. Howard M. Harper, Jr., "Trends in Recent American Fiction," *Contemporary Literature*, 12 (Spring 1971), 204-229.

43. See particularly John Barth, *Giles Goat-Boy* and *Lost in the Funhouse;* James Purdy, *Cabot Wright Begins*; John Fowles, *The French Lieutenant's Woman*; Samuel Beckett, *Three Novels*; Anthony Burgess, *MF*; Saul Bellow, *Herzog*; Philip Roth, *Portnoy's Complaint*; Joyce Carol Oates, *Expensive People*; Bernard Malamud, *Pictures of Fidelman*.

44. John Barth, *Lost in the Funhouse* (1968; rpt. New York: Bantam, 1969), p. 94.

Notes to Chapter One

1. Heller himself has said that *Catch-22* is "about the contemporary regimented business society depicted against the background of universal sorrow and inevitable death that is the lot of all of us." "Joseph Heller Replies," *The Realist*, 50 (May 1964), p. 30.

2. Richard Lehan and Jerry Patch argue that there are two sources of the absurd in modern literature: the Existentialist view of Sartre and Camus, and the over-structured, bureaucratic world of Kafka. *Catch-22*, they claim, derives from Kafka. "Catch-22: The Making of a Novel," *The Minnesota Review*, 7(1967), 238-244. I shall attempt to demonstrate that these two views of the absurd are not as profoundly different as Lehan and Patch suggest.

3. These elements of fantasy have led such critics as Minna Doskow, Sanford Pinsker and Victor J. Milne to examine the book as myth and allegory, an approach Heller does not dispute: Paul Krassner, "An Impolite Interview with Joseph Heller,"

The Realist, 39 (Nov. 1962), 18-26, 28-31. This approach, however, does not account for those fantasy techniques of logic and language, perhaps the most interesting aspects of the novel.

4. Joseph Heller, *Catch-22* (1955, 1961; rpt. New York: Dell, 1962), p. 108. All page references in the text are to this edition.

5. Thomas Blues, "The Moral Structure of *Catch-22*," *Studies in the Novel*, 3 (Spring 1971), 64-79.

6. Frederick R. Karl, "Only Fools Walk in Darkness," *Contemporary American Novelists*, ed. Harry T. Moore (Carbondale: Southern Illinois Univ. Press, 1964), p. 136.

7. The ending of *Catch-22* has caused much critical disagreement. Some critics see it as a major flaw in the novel; see, for example, "Joseph Waldmeir, "Two Novels of the Absurd: Heller and Kesey," *Wisconsin Studies in Contemporary Literature*, 5(1964), 192-196; Sanford Pinsker, "Heller's *Catch-22*: The Protest of a *Puer Eternis*," *Critique*, 7 (1965), 150-162. Howard Stark sees it as ironic, "*Catch-22*: The Ultimate Irony," *Critical Essays on Catch-22*, ed. James Nagel (Encino, Calif.: Dickenson, 1974). Among others, James Mellard agrees with me that it expresses the final achievement of Yossarian's "freedom and maturity," "*Catch-22: Déjà vu* and the Labyrinth of Memory," *Bucknell Review*, 16(1968), 44.

8. Krassner, "An Impolite Interview."

9. *Ibid.*

10. Karl, pp. 137-138.

11. *Ibid.*, p. 136.

12. *Ibid.*, p. 137.

13. Heller has commented on this change in tone in the Krassner interview.

14. In the interview with Krassner, Heller states that Céline was a major influence on *Catch-22*.

15. For a full discussion of this technique see James Mellard.

16. For discussions of the structure of *Catch-22*, see Jan Solomon, "The Structure of Joseph Heller's *Catch-22*," *Critique*, 9, No. 2 (1967), 46-57; Doug Gaukroger, "Time Structure in *Catch-22*" *Critique*, 12, No. 2 (1970), 70-85.

17. For a full discussion of characterization in *Catch-22*, see Jess Ritter, "What Manner of Men Are These," *Critical Essays on Catch-22*.

18. For a comparison between Heller's techniques and those of Lewis Carroll, see Caroline Gordon and Jeanne Richardson, "Flies in Their Eyes? A Note on Joseph Heller's *Catch-22*," *The Southern Review*, 3 (1967), 96-105.

19. Robert Protherough, "The Sanity of *Catch-22*," *The Human World*, 3 (May 1971), 59-70, makes some interesting comments on the language techniques of the novel.

20. Ian Watt, *The Rise of the Novel*, p. 30.

212/*Number and Nightmare*

Notes to Chapter Two

1. John Barth, *The Floating Opera* (1956; rpt. New York: Avon Books, n.d.); *End of the Road* (1958; rpt. New York: Avon Books, 1960); *The Sot-Weed Factor* (1960; rpt. New York: Grosset and Dunlap, 1964); *Giles Goat-Boy* (1966; rpt. Greenwich, Conn.: Fawcett Crest, 1968); *Lost in the Funhouse* (1968; rpt. New York: Bantam Books, 1969); *Chimera* (1972; rpt. Greenwich, Conn.: 1973). All page references in the text are to the more recent editions listed here.

2. Leslie Fiedler, "John Barth: An Eccentric Genius," *On Contemporary Literature*, p. 239.

3. *Ibid.*, p. 240.

4. John Barth, "The Literature of Exhaustion," *The Atlantic*, 220 (1967), 29-34.

5. *Ibid.*, p. 33.

6. *Ibid.*, p. 31.

7. Hassan, "Joyce-Beckett," pp. 11 and 15. I do not mean to suggest that this theory is uniquely Barth's, though the idea of repeating one's predecessors has been more fully investigated in poetry than in fiction. In *The Anxiety of Influence* (New York: Oxford Univ. Press, 1973), Harold Bloom's sixth stage of the poet's attempt to free his creative impulse, "Apophrades," sounds very much like Barth's theory: "the uncanny effect is that the new poem's achievement makes it seem to us, not as though the precursor were writing it, but as though the later poet himself had written the precursor's characteristic work" (p. 16). However, Bloom demonstrates that the poet is struggling to produce original work; Barth, on the other hand, uses the past to unmake the present, not the present to remake the past. Barth's emphasis is on the supremacy of time; Bloom's poet conquers time.

8. "The Literature of Exhaustion," p. 33.

9. In the original version, published later, Jeannine does not rally him and mere chance saves his life.

10. "The Literature of Exhaustion," p. 34.

11. *Ibid.*, p. 33.

12. *Ibid.* There is, of course, an actual seventeenth-century satirical poem called *The Sot-Weed Factor.*

13. See Scholes, pp. 148-149, for a thorough examination of the significance of this basic metaphor.

14. John Barth, "An Interview," *Wisconsin Studies in Contemporary Literature*, 6 (Winter 1965), 8.

15. Scholes, p. 152.

16. "The Literature of Exhaustion," p. 32.

Notes to Chapter Three

1. "63: Dream Palace" in *Color of Darkness and Children Is All* (1957; rpt. New York: Avon Books, 1965); *Malcolm* (1959; rpt. New York: Avon Books, 1960); *The Nephew* (1960; rpt. New York: Avon Books, 1962); *Cabot Wright Begins* (1964, rpt. New York: Avon Books, 1965); *Eustace Chisholm and the Works* (New York: Farrar, Straus, Giroux, 1967); *Jeremy's Version* New York: Doubleday, 1970); *The House of the Solitary Maggot* (New York: Doubleday, 1974). All page references in the text are to the most recent editions listed here.

2. *Cabot Wright Begins* is an exception to this generalization.

3. Bettina Schwarzschild, *The Not-Right House: Essays on James Purdy* (Columbia: Univ. of Missouri Press, 1968), p. 50.

4. Hassan, *The Literature of Silence*, p. 136.

5. This is also a favorite technique of Vonnegut's.

6. The similarities between Purdy and Albee are numerous as is testified to by Albee's adaptation of *Malcolm* for the stage.

Notes to Chapter Four

1. *Player Piano* (1952; rpt. New York: Avon Books, 1967); *The Sirens of Titan* (1959; rpt. New York: Dell, 1970); *Mother Night* (1961, rpt. New York: Avon Books, 1967); *Cat's Cradle* (1963; rpt. New York: Dell, 1965); *God Bless You, Mr. Rosewater* (1965; rpt. New York: Dell, 1970); *Slaughterhouse-Five or the Children's Crusade* (1969; rpt. New York: Dell, n.d.); *Breakfast of Champions* (New York: Delacorte, 1973). All page references in the text are to the most recent editions listed here.

2. See, for example, C. D. Bryan, "Kurt Vonnegut on Target," *New Republic*, 8 October 1966, pp. 21-22, 24-26; Jerry Bryant, *The Open Decision* (New York: The Free Press, 1970), p. 303.

3. Scholes, *The Fabulators*, p. 40.

4. Bryan, p. 21: "All the anger, the shame, the shock, the guilt, the compassion, the irony, the control to produce great satire are there . . . why, then, does Vonnegut settle for such lovely, literate, amusing attacks upon such simple targets as scientists, engineers, computer technicians . . . ?"

5. Bryant, p. 310.

6. Robert Scholes, "A Talk with Kurt Vonnegut, Jr.," *The Vonnegut Statement*, ed. Jerome Klinkowitz and John Somer (New York: Delacorte, 1973), p. 106.

7. Scholes, *The Fabulators*, p. 41.

8. Frye, *Anatomy of Criticism*, p. 223.

9. Scholes, *The Fabulators*, p. 41.

10. *The Sirens of Titan.* p. 8.

11. *Ibid.*, p. 229.

12. *Slaughterhouse-Five*, p. 66.

13. Dan Wakefield, "In Vonnegut's Karass," *The Vonnegut Statement*, p. 70.

14. Scholes, "A Talk with Kurt Vonnegut, Jr.," p. 108.

15. *Ibid.*, p. 106.

16. See, for example, the following discussion of Eliot Rosewater.

17. James Mellard, "The Modes of Vonnegut's Fiction," *The Vonnegut Statement*, p. 187.

18. Scholes, *The Fabulators*, p. 45.

19. The Dahomean people of Africa call a worker of benevolent magic a "Bokono."

20. Lionel Boyd Johnson, who made himself Bokonon by inventing lies for people to live by, is surely a caricature of Lyndon Baines Johnson. This can be taken as further evidence that Vonnegut did not intend us to treat Bokononism with the reverence given to it by so many critics.

21. Gleen Meeter, "Vonnegut's Formal and Moral Otherworldliness: *Cat's Cradle* and *Slaughterhouse-Five*," *The Vonnegut Statement*, pp. 210-212, points out that *Slaughterhouse-Five* contains many suggestions of "the futility of realism in fiction," and sees the sensibility behind Tralfamadorian art as "stolen from Ian Watt's *Rise of the Novel* . . . read in reverse."

22. J. Michael Crichton, "Sci-Fi and Vonnegut," *New Republic*, 26 April 1969, pp. 33-35.

23. That we are not to agree with Trout is emphasized by the fact that this title is that of General Groes' memoir about the Manhattan Engineering District, the A-Bomb project, of which he was director.

24. Quoted in *Time*, 29 June 1970, p. 8.

Notes to Chapter Five

1. Ihab Hassan, "Joyce-Beckett," p. 12.

2. *Ibid.*, p. 17.

3. *Ibid.*, p. 12.

4. Anthony Burgess, *Re Joyce* (1965; rpt. New York: Ballantine Books, 1966), p. 110.

5. *Ibid.*, p. 22.

6. *Ibid.*

7. Hassan, "Joyce-Beckett," p. ll.

8. *The Right to an Answer* (1960; rpt. New York: Ballantine Books, 1966); *The Doctor is Sick* (1960; rpt. New York: Ballantine Books, 1967); *Devil of a State* (1962; rpt. New York: Ballantine Books, 1965); *A Clockwork Orange* (1962; rpt. New York: Ballantine Books, 1965); *The Wanting Seed* (1962; rpt. New York: Ballantine Books, 1964), *Honey for the Bears* (1963, rpt. New York. Ballantine Books, 1965), *Nothing Like the Sun* (1964; rpt. New York: Ballantine Books, 1965); *The Eve of St. Venus* (1964; rpt. New York: Ballantine Books, 1971); *The Long Day Wanes: A Trilogy* (1964; rpt. New York: Ballantine Books, 1966); *A Vision of Battlements* (1965; rpt. New York: Ballantine Books, 1966); *Tremor of Intent* (1966; rpt. New York: Ballantine Books, 1967); *Enderby* (1963, 1968; rpt. New York: Ballantine Books, 1960); *MF* (New York: Alfred A. Knopf, 1971) *Napoleon Symphony* (New York: Alfred A. Knopf, 1974). All page references in the text are to the most recent editions listed here.

9. *Inside Mr. Enderby* (later incorporated into *Enderby*); *One Hand Clapping*.

10. Thomas Churchill, "An Interview with Anthony Burgess," *The Malahat Review*, 17 (1971), 103-127.

11. *Ibid.*, p. 115

12. *Nothing Like the Sun*, p. 38.

13. *Tremor of Intent*, p. 114.

14. Greene, p. 84.

15. The novel has become far less "fantastic" even in the relatively short time since Burgess wrote it. It is now once again possible to talk seriously of B. F. Skinner's ideas on social conditioning, for example, as a possible way of controlling behavior. Children are given drugs to keep them quiet in school.

16. Churchill, p. 10.

17. *Ibid.*, p. 116.

18. *Ibid.*, p. 110.

19. *Tremor of Intent* is perhaps closer to Hunt's novels than to Fleming's in that, like Burgess, Hunt is an opponent of the Pelagian view and also writes ideological fables.

20. Geoffrey Aggeler, "Between God and Non-god: Anthony Burgess' *Tremor of Intent*," *The Malahat Review*, 17 (1971), 90-102.

21. Burgess, like Enderby, prefers Catholicism to Protestantism and, also like Enderby, finds it necessary to be a lapsed Catholic. Artists must create their own myths.

22. Churchill, p. 126.

23. Jim Hicks, "Eclectic Author of his own Five-Foot Shelf," *Life*, 25 October 1968, pp. 89-98.

24. *Re Joyce*, pp. 26-27.

25. *Ibid.*, p. 342.

26. Maurice Merleau-Ponty, "From Mauss to Claude Lévi-Strauss," *Signs*, trans. Richard Claverton McCleary (Evanston, Ill.: Northwestern Univ. Press, 1964), p. 118.

27. Claude Lévi-Strauss, *Structural Anthropology*, trans. Claire Jacobson and Brooke Grandfest Schoepf (New York: Basic Books, 1963), p. 216.

28. In a chapter in which he discusses Claude Lévi-Strauss, George Steiner comments: "According to the Neo-Platonic and Johannine metaphor, in the beginning was the Word; but if this *Logos*, this act and essence of God is, in the last analysis, total communication, the word that creates its own context and truth of being—then what of *zoon phonanta*, man, the speaking animal? He too creates words and creates with words. Can there be coexistence other than charged with mutual torment and rebellion between the totality of the *Logos* and the living, world-creating fragments of our own speech? Does the act of speech which defines man, not also go beyond him in rivalry to God?" *Language and Silence* (New York: Atheneum, 1967), p. 37.

29. Similarly the death of Gonzi parallels the sickness of Miles; the death of monters is compensated for by the lameness of man.

30. It is worth noting that "yearning for Chapter Zero of the Book of Genesis" is exactly what Vonnegut does in *The Sirens of Titan*.

Notes to Chapter Six

1. *Under the Net* (London: Chatto and Windus, 1954); *The Flight from the Enchanter* (London: Chatto and Windus, 1956); *The Sandcastle* (London: Chatto and Windus, 1958); *The Bell* (London: Chatto and Windus, 1958); *A Severed Head* (New York: Viking, 1961); *An Unofficial Rose* (London: Chatto and Windus, 1962); *The Unicorn* (New York: Viking, 1963); *The Italian Girl* (New York: Viking, 1964); *The Red and the Green* (New York: Viking, 1965); *The Time of the Angels* (New York: Viking, 1966); *The Nice and the Good* (New York: Viking, 1968); *Bruno's Dream* (New York: Viking, 1970); *A Fairly Honourable Defeat* (New York: Viking, 1970); *An Accidental Man* (New York: Viking, 1972); *The Black Prince* (New York: Viking, 1973); *The Sacred and Profane Love Machine* (New York: Viking, 1974). All page references in the text are to the editions listed here.

2. Bernard F. Dick, "The Novels of Iris Murdoch: A Formula for Enchantment," *Bucknell Review*, 14 (May 1966), 66-81.

3. Peter Wolfe, *The Disciplined Heart: Iris Murdoch and her Novels*. (Columbia: Univ. of Missouri Press, 1966), p. 19.

4. G. S. Fraser, *The Modern Writer and his World* (1964; rpt. Baltimore, Maryland: Penguin Books, 1964), p. 185.

5. George Whiteside. "The Novels of Iris Murdoch," *Critique*, 7 (1964), 27-47.

6. Richard Wasson, "Notes on a New Sensibility," *Partisan Review*, 36 (1969), 460-477.

7. Frederick J. Hoffman, "Iris Murdoch: The Reality of Persons," *Critique*, 7 (1964), 48-57.

8. William Van O'Connor, "Iris Murdoch: The Formal and the Contingent," *Critique*, 3 (Winter-Spring 1960), 34-46.

9. Cyrena Norman Pondrom, "Iris Murdoch: An Existentialist?" *Comparative Literature Studies*, 5 (1968), 403-419.

10. A. S. Byatt, *Degrees of Freedom: The Novels of Iris Murdoch* (London: Chatto and Windus, 1965).

11. See, for example, *Under the Net*: "The Bounty Belfounder studio is situated in a suburb of Southern London where contingency reaches the point of nausea" (p. 156).

12. Iris Murdoch, "The Sublime and the Beautiful Revisited," *Yale Review*, 49 (December 1959), 247-271.

13. *Ibid.*

14. *Ibid.*, p. 255.

15. Iris Murdoch, "Mass, Might and Myth," *Spectator*, 7 (September 1962), p. 337.

16. *Sartre, Romantic Rationalist* (1953; rpt. New Haven: Yale Univ. Press, 1959), p. 5.

17. Iris Murdoch, "The Sublime and the Good," *Chicago Review*, 13 (Autumn 1959), 42-55.

18. Pondrom explains the difference between Murdoch and Sartre and Camus: "The contingency of the world is revealed to Camus in the experience of absurdity, in the meeting of the rational mind and irrational universe, but this contingency has something of the flavor of a mindless cosmic conspiracy . . . the succession of events in her books are unexpected, but they are not malign. Her contingency is accidental, random, not conspiratorial. Although she would probably agree with Sartre and Camus that it is the task of man to create value in a contingent world, she . . .would not charge the cosmos with the sin of withholdiing meaning" (p. 409).

19. Iris Murdoch, "Against Dryness: A Polemical Sketch," *Encounter*, 16 (January 1961), p. 18.

20. "The Sublime and the Good," p. 51.

21. Whiteside, p. 29.

22. "The Sublime and the Beautiful Revisted," p. 270.

23. "Against Dryness," p. 19.

24. "The Sublime and the Beautiful Revisted," p. 254.

25. "The Sublime and the Good," p. 50.

26. *Sartre, Romantic Rationalist*, p. 112.

27. *Ibid.*, p. 94.

28. Fraser, p. 187.

29. "The Sublime and the Beautiful Revisited," p. 271.

30. *Ibid.*, p. 257.

31. *Ibid.*, p. 269.

32. Ann Culley, "Theory and Practice: Characterization in the Novels of Iris Murdoch," *Modern Fiction Studies*, 15 (Autumn 1969), 343.

33. Linda Kuehl, "Iris Murdoch: The Novelist as Magician/The Magician as Artist," *Modern Fiction Studies*, 15 (Autumn 1969), 343.

34. Pondrom, p. 405.

35. *Ibid.*, p. 404.

36. Harold Hobson, "Lunch with Iris Murdoch," *The Sunday Times* (London), 11 March 1962, p. 28.

37. Fraser, p. 185.

38. Byatt, p. 181. It is interesting to note that critics frequently employ the analogy of puzzles or games in describing both Anthony Burgess's and Iris Murdoch's novels. See, for example, Dick: "One constantly thinks of a chessboard where figures are continually being moved along and occasionally defying all rules of the game by occupying the same square" (p. 67).

39. One could argue convincingly that her most realistic novels, *The Sandcastle, The Red and the Green, An Unofficial Rose*, are her least successful.

40. *Sartre, Romantic Rationalist*, pp. 108-109.

41. James Gindin, *Postwar British Fiction: New Accents and Attitudes* (Berkeley: Univ. of California Press, 1962), p. 186.

42. G. S. Fraser, "Iris Murdoch: The Solidity of the Normal," *International Literary Annual*, 2 (1959), 37-54.

43. "The Sublime and the Beautiful Revisited," p. 260.

Notes to Chapter Seven

1. *Lord of the Flies* (1954; rpt. New York: Putnam's, Capricorn Books, 1959); *The Inheritors* (1955; rpt. New York: Pocket Books, Cardinal Edition, 1963);

Pincher Martin (1956; rpt. New York: Putnam's, Capricorn Books, 1962); *Free Fall* (London: Faber and Faber, 1959); *The Spire* (1964; rtp. New York: Pocket Books, Cardinal Edition, 1964); *The Pyramid* (1966; rpt. New York: Harcourt, Brace and World, Harvest Books, 1967). All page references in the text are to the most recent editions listed here.

2. James R. Baker, *William Golding* (New York: St. Martin's Press, 1965), p. 15.

3. Bernard F. Dick, *William Golding* (New York: Twayne, 1967), p. 73.

4. *Ibid.*, p. 74.

5. Baker, p. 24.

6. *Ibid.*, p. 40.

7. Jack I. Biles, *Talk: Conversations with William Golding* (New York: Harcourt, Brace and Jovanovich, 1970), p. 75.

8. Mark Kinkead-Weekes and Ian Gregor, *William Golding: A Critical Study* (New York: Harcourt, Brace and Jovanovich, 1968), p. 240.

9. Biles, p. 102.

10. Dick, p. 99.

11. Quoted by Bernard S. Oldsey and Stanley Weintrub, *The Art of William Golding* (1965; rpt. Bloomington: Indiana Univ. Press, 1968), p. 80.

12. Baker, p. 26.

13. *Ibid.*

14. The confusion of Sammy's statements in *Free Fall* with Golding's own beliefs has been a major problem with critical accounts of this novel.

15. Biles, p. 101.

16. *Ibid.*, p. 41.

17. Howard S. Babb, *The Novels of William Golding* (Columbus: Ohio State Univ. Press, 1970), p. 97.

18. Samuel Hynes, *William Golding* (New York: Columbia Univ. Press, 1964), pp. 4-5.

19. I mean here, of course, the most realistic of the five novels I am considering.

20. Kinkead-Weekes and Gregor, p. 194.

21. *Ibid.*, p. 241.

22. *Ibid.*, p. 240.

23. Biles, p. 19.

24. Frank Kermode and William Golding, "The Meaning of It All," *Books and Bookmen*, 5 (October, 1959), 9-10.

25. James R. Baker, *William Golding's Lord of the Flies: A Casebook*, ed. James R. Baker and Arthur P. Ziegler, Jr. (New York: Putnam's, 1964), XXIII.

26. *Ibid.*, p. 190.

27. *Ibid.*, pp. 190-191.

28. Biles, p. 12.

29. Baker, *William Golding*, p. 13.

30. Casebook, pp. 200-201.

31. Hynes, p. 5.

32. This material is so well known that there is little point in repeating it here. See Oldsey and Weintraub and Carl Niemeyer, "The Coral Island Revisited," *College English*, 22 (1961), 241-245. It is perhaps worth noting that *Lord of the Flies* reverses a whole tradition of children's adventure stories of the nineteenth and twentieth centuries in which children, bereft of adult supervision, prove themselves morally mature.

33. Frank Kermode, "The Novels of William Golding," *International Literary Annual*, 3 (1961), 11-29.

34. Letter to John Peter, quoted in "Postscript [to "The Fables of William Golding']," *William Golding's Lord of the Flies: A Sourcebook*, ed. William Nelson (New York: Odyssey Press, 1963), p. 34.

35. The title of the first American edition of the novel, *The Two Deaths of Christopher Martin*, revealed the truth right away.

36. Baker, *William Golding*, p. 38.

37. "Pincher Martin," *Radio Times*, 138 (March 21, 1958), p. 8.

38. Quoted in Archie Campbell, "William Golding: *Pincher Martin*," in *From the Fifties* (BBC. Sound Radio Drama Series), ed. Michael Bakewell and Eric Evans (London, 1961), p. 34.

39. Frank Kermode, "William Golding," *On Contemporary Literature*, p. 374.

40. Oldsey and Weintraub, p. 76.

41. Biles, p. 81.

42. Kinkead-Weekes and Gregor, p. 165.

43. Baker, *William Golding*, p. 68.

44. Babb, p. 99.

45. Both Hynes and Kermode make this criticism.

46. Hynes, p. 39.

47. Babb, pp. 119 ff.

48. Oldsey and Weintraub, pp. 116 and 121.

49. Babb, p. 161.

50. *Ibid.*, p. 137.

51. Kinkead-Weekes and Gregor, p. 212.

52. *On Contemporary Literature*, p. 369.

53. *Ibid.*, p. 381.

Notes to Afterthoughts

1. Camus, *The Rebel*, p. 22.

2. Hassan, *Radical Innocence*, p. 326.

3. In *After Alienation* (New York: World Publishing Company, 1962), Marcus Klein discusses five American novelists who have come to terms with the Post-existential dilemma: Bellow, Ellison, Baldwin, Morris and Malamud. With the exception of Wright Morris, they are all either Jewish or Black.

(No attempt has been made to list every work referred to in the text or the complete works of any author. The critical material has been limited to that which has influenced this study.)

Part One: General Background

A. On Existentialism

Barrett, William. *Irrational Man*. Garden City, N.Y. Doubleday, 1958.
Bauer, George H. *Sartre and the Artist*. Chicago: Univ. of Chicago Press, 1969.
Bree, Germaine. *Camus and Sartre, Crisis and Commitment*. Boston: Delacorte, 1972.
Camus, Albert. *The Exile and the Kingdom*. Trans. Justin O'Brien. 1957; rpt. New York: Vintage Books, 1957.
_____. *The Fall*. Trans. Justin O'Brien, 1956, rpt. New York: Vintage Books, 1956.

————. *The Myth of Sisyphus*. Trans. Justin O'Brien. 1942; rpt. New York: Vintage Books, 1955.

————. *The Plague*. Trans. Stuart Gilbert. 1947; rpt. New York: Modern Library, 1948.

————. *The Rebel*. Trans. Anthony Bower. 1951; rpt. New York: Vintage Books, 1956.

————. *The Stranger*. Trans. Stuart Gilbert. 1942; rpt. New York: Vintage Books, 1946.

Collins, James. *The Existentialists*. Chicago: Univ. of Chicago Press, 1952.

Cruikshank, John. *Albert Camus and the Literature of Revolt*. New York: Oxford Univ. Press, 1959.

Elbrecht, Joyce. "*The Stranger* and Camus' Transcendental Existentialism." *Hartford Studies in Literature*, 4 (1972), 59-80.

Fallico, Arturo B. *Art and Existentialism*. Englewood Cliffs, N.J.: Prentice-Hall, 1962.

Freeman, E. *The Theatre of Albert Camus: A Critical Study*. London: Barnes and Noble, 1971.

Greene, Norman. *Jean-Paul Sartre: The Existentialist Ethic*. Ann Arbor: Univ. of Michigan Press, 1960.

Hanna, Thomas. *The Lyrical Existentialists*. New York: Atheneum, 1962.

Kern, Edith. *Existential Thought and Fictional Technique: Kierkegaard, Sartre, Beckett*. New Haven: Yale Univ. Press, 1970.

Lazere, Donald. *The Unique Creation of Albert Camus*. New Haven: Yale Univ. Press, 1973.

Leiber, Justin. "Linguistic Analysis and Existentialism." *Philosophy and Phenomenological Research*, 32 (1971), 47-56.

McMahon, Joseph. *Human Being: The World of Jean-Paul Sartre*. Chicago: Univ. of Chicago Press, 1971.

McCall, Dorothy. *The Theatre of Jean-Paul Sartre*. New York: Columbia Univ. Press, 1969.

O'Brien, Connor Cruise. *Albert Camus of Europe and America*. New York: Viking, 1970.

Onimus, Jean. *Albert Camus and Christianity*. Trans. Emmett Parker. University, Ala.: University of Alabama Press, 1970.

Peterson, Carol. *Albert Camus*. Trans. Alexander Gode. New York: Frederick Ungar, 1969.

Quillot, Roger. *The Sea and Prisons: A Commentary on the Life and*

Thought of Albert Camus. Trans. Emmett Parker. University, Ala.: Univ. of Alabama Press, 1970.

Sartre, Jean-Paul. *The Age of Reason.* Trans. Eric Sutton. 1945; rpt. New York: Alfred A. Knopf, 1947.

_____ . *Being and Nothingness.* Trans. Hazel E. Barnes. 1943; rpt. New York: Philosophical Library, 1956.

_____ . *Nausea.* Trans. Lloyd Alexander. 1938; rpt. New York: New Directions, 1964.

_____ . *The Reprieve.* Trans. Eric Sutton. 1945; rpt. New York: Alfred A. Knopf, 1947.

_____ . *Troubled Sleep.* Trans. Gerard Hopkins. 1949; rpt. New York: Alfred A. Knopf, 1951.

_____ . *What Is Literature?* Trans. Bernard Frechtman. 1949; rpt. New York: Washington Square Press, 1966.

_____ . *The Words.* Bernard Frechtman. 1964; rpt. New York: Braziller, 1964.

Sheridan, James F. *Sartre: The Radical Conversion.* Athens: Ohio Univ. Press, 1969.

Suhl, Benjamin. *Jean-Paul Sartre: The Philosopher as Literary Critic.* New York: Columbia Univ. Press, 1970.

Thody, Philip. *Sartre: A Biographical Introduction.* New York: Scribner's, 1972.

Warnock, Mary, ed. *Sartre: A Collection of Critical Essays.* New York: Anchor Books, 1971.

B. On the Theory of Fiction.

Allott, Miriam. *Novelists on the Novel.* New York: Columbia Univ. Press, 1959.

Auerbach, Erich. *Mimesis: The Representation of Reality in Western Literature.* Trans. Willard Trask. Princeton: Princeton Univ. Press, 1953.

Bayley, John. "Character and Consciousness." *New Literary History*, 5 (1974), 225-235.

Booth, Wayne C. *The Rhetoric of Fiction.* Chicago: Univ. of Chicago Press, 1961.

Daiches, David. *The Novel and the Modern World.* Rev. Ed. Cambridge: Cambridge Univ. Press, 1960.

Forster, E. M. *Aspects of the Novel.* London: Edward Arnold, 1927.

Frye, Northrop. *Anatomy of Criticism: Four Essays.* Princeton: Princeton Univ. Press, 1957.

Iser, Wolfgang. *The Implied Reader: Patterns of Communication in Prose Fiction From Bunyan to Beckett.* Baltimore: Johns Hopkins Univ. Press, 1974.

————. "The Reading Process: A Phenomenological Approach." *New Literary History,* 3 (1972), 279-299.

James, Henry. *The Art of the Novel.* Ed. R. P. Blackmur. New York: Scribner's, 1934.

Kraft, Quentin G. "Against Realism: Some Thoughts on Fiction, Story, and Reality." *College English,* 31 (1969), 344-354.

Kuspit, Donald B. "Fiction and Phenomenology." *Philosophy and Phenomenlogical Research,* 29 (1968), 16-23.

Levin, Harry. *The Gates of Horn: A Study of Five French Realists.* London: Oxford Univ. Press, 1963.

Lubbock, Percy *The Craft of Fiction.* London: Jonathan Cape, 1921.

New Literary History, 3 (1971). Issue devoted to "Modernism and Postmodernism."

Robbe-Grillet, Alain. *For a New Novel: Essays on Fiction.* Trans. Richard Howard. New York: Grove, 1965.

Scholes, Robert, ed. *Approaches to the Novel: Materials for a Poetics.* San Francisco: Chandler, 1961.

Tillotson, Kathleen. *The Tale and the Teller.* London: Rupert Hart-Davis, 1959.

Trilling, Lionel. *The Liberal Imagination.* New York: Viking, 1950.

Watt, Ian. *The Rise of the Novel: Studies in Defoe, Richardson and Fielding.* Berkeley: Univ. of Calif. Press, 1957.

Warren, Austin and Rene Wellek. *The Theory of Literature.* New York: Harcourt, Brace and World, 1956.

C. On Contemporary Literature.

Abel, Lionel. *Metatheatre.* New York: Hill and Wang, 1963.

Aldridge, John W. *Time to Murder and Create.* New York: McKay, 1966.

Barnes, Hazel. *The Literature of Possibility.* Lincoln: Univ. of Nebraska Press.

Bergonzi, Bernard. *The Situation of the Novel*. London: Macmillan, 1970.

Bryant, Jerry. *The Open Decision*. New York: The Free Press, 1970.

Clareson, Thomas D., ed. *SF: The Other Side of Realism: Essays on Modern Fantasy and Science Fiction*. Bowling Green, Ohio. Bowling Green Univ. Popular Press, 1972.

Cohn, Ruby. *Dialogue in American Drama*. Bloomington: Indiana Univ. Press, 1971.

Esslin, Martin. *The Theatre of the Absurd*. Garden City, N.Y.: Doubleday, 1961.

Fiedler, Leslie. *The Return of the Vanishing American*. New York: Stein and Day, 1968.

——. *Waiting for the End*. New York: Stein and Day, 1964.

Galloway, David D. *The Absurd Hero in American Fiction*: *Updike, Styron, Bellow, Salinger*. Rev. Ed. Austin: Univ. of Texas Press, 1970.

Gindin, James. "The Fable Begins to Break Down," *Wisconsin Studies in Contemporary Literature*, 8 (Winter 1967), 1-27.

Greenberg, Alvin. "The Novel of Disintegration: Paradoxical Impossibility in Contemporary Fiction." *Wisconsin Studies in Contemporary Literature*, 7(Winter-Spring, 1966), 103-124.

Grossvogel, David I. *The Self-Conscious Stage in Modern French Drama*. New York: Columbia Univ. Press, 1958.

Harper, Howard M. Jr. "Trends in Recent American Fiction." *Contemporary Literature*, 12 (Spring 1971), 204-229.

Harris, Charles B. *Contemporary American Novelists of the Absurd*. New Haven: College and University Press, 1971.

Hassan, Ihab. *The Dismemberment of Orpheus*: *Towards a Post-Modern Literature*. New York: Oxford Univ. Press, 1971.

——. *Liberations*. Middletown, Conn.: Wesleyan Univ. Press, 1971.

——. *The Literature of Silence*. New York: Alfred A. Knopf, 1967.

——. *Radical Innocence*. Princeton: Princeton Univ. Press, 1961.

Hauck, Richard. *A Cheerful Nihilism*: *Confidence and "the Absurd" in American Humorous Fiction*. Bloomington: Indiana Univ. Press, 1971.

Hoffman, Daniel. *Form and Fable in American Fiction*. New York: Oxford Univ. Press, 1961.

Josipovici, Gabriel. *The Word and the Book*: *A Study in Modern Fiction*. London: Macmillan, 1971.

Kazin, Alfred. "Absurdity as Contemporary Style." *Mediterranean Review*, 1 (Spring 1971), 39-46.

Klein, Marcus. *After Alienation*. New York: The World Publishing Co., 1965.

Kostelanetz, Richard, ed. *On Contemporary Literature*. New York: Avon, 1964.

Lebowitz, Naomi. *Humanism and the Absurd in the Modern Novel*. Evanston, Ill.: Northwestern Univ. Press, 1971.

Littlejohn, David. "The Anti-Realist." *Daedalus*, 8 (Spring 1963), 250-264.

Moore, Harry T., ed. *Contemporary American Novelists*. Carbondale. Southern Illinois Univ. Press, 1964.

Olderman, Raymond M. *Beyond the Wasteland: A Study of the American Novel in the Nineteen Sixties*. New Haven: Yale Univ. Press, 1972.

Poirier, Richard. *The Performing Self: Compositions and Decompositions in the Languages of Contemporary Life*. New York: Oxford Univ. Press, 1971.

Pronko, Leonard T. *Avant-Garde: The Experimental Theatre in France*. Berkeley: Univ. of California Press, 1962.

Scholes, Robert. *The Fabulators*. New York: Oxford Univ. Press, 1967.

Schulz, Max F. *Black Humor Fiction of the Sixties: A Pluralistic Definition of Man and his World*. Athens: Ohio Univ. Press, 1967.

Scott, Nathan A. Jr., ed. *Adversity and Grace: Studies in Recent American Literature*. Chicago: Univ. of Chicago Press, 1968.

Sturrock, John. *The French New Novel: Claude Simon, Michel Butor, Alain Robbe-Grillet*. New York: Oxford Univ. Press, 1967.

Tanner, Tony. *City of Words: American Fiction, 1950-1970*. New York: Harper and Row, 1971.

Weinberg, Helen. *The New Novel in America: The Kafkan Mode in Contemporary Fiction*. Ithaca, N.Y.: Cornell Univ. Press, 1970.

Wellwarth, George E. *The Theatre of Protest and Paradox*. New York: New York Univ. Press, 1964.

Whitbread, Thomas B., ed. *Seven Contemporary Authors*. Austin: Univ. of Texas Press, 1966.

Part Two: The Novelists

A. John Barth

Works.

Chimera. 1972; rpt. Greenwich, Conn.: Fawcett Crest, 1973.
End of the Road. 1958; rpt. New York: Avon, 1960.
The Floating Opera. 1956; rpt. New York: Avon, n. d.
Giles Goat-Boy, or the Revised New Syllabus. 1966, rpt. Greenwich,
   Conn.: Fawcett Crest, 1968.
"The Literature of Exhaustion." *Atlantic,* 220 (1967), 29-34.
Lost in the Funhouse. 1968; rpt. New York: Bantam, 1969.
The Sot-Weed Factor. 1960, rpt. New York: Grosset-Dunlap, 1964.

Criticism.

Bean, John C. "John Barth and Festive Comedy: The Failure of
   Imagination in The Sot-Weed Factor." *Xavier University Studies,*
   10 (1971), 3-15.
Bellamy, Joe David. "Algebra and Fire: An Interview with John
   Barth." *The Falcon,* 4 (Spring 1972), 5-15.
Critique, 6, No. 2 (1963). The entire issue is devoted to John Barth
   and John Hawkes.
Enck, John. "John Barth: An Interview." *Wisconsin Studies in Con-
   temporary Literature,* 6 (Winter-Spring 1965), 3-14.
Hirsch, John. "John Barth's Freedom Road." *Mediterranean Review,*
   2 (Spring 1972), 38-47.
Joseph, Gerhard. *John Barth.* Minneapolis: Univ. of Minnesota Press,
   1970.
Kennard, Jean E. "John Barth: Imitations of Imitations." *Mosaic,*
   3 (Winter 1970), 116-131.
Le Clair, Thomas. "John Barth's *The Floating Opera*: Death and
   the Craft of Fiction." *Texas Studies in Literature and Language,*
   14 (1972), 711-730.
Majdiak, Daniel. "Barth and the Representation of Life." *Criticism,*
   13 (Winter 1970), 51-67.

McDonald, James L. "Barth's Syllabus: The Frame of *Giles Goat-boy*." *Critique*, 13, No. 3 (1972), 5-10.

Mercer, Peter. "The Rhetoric of *Giles Goat-Boy*." *Novel*, 4 (1971), 147-158.

Noland, Richard W. "John Barth and the Novel of Comic Nihilism." *Wisconsin Studies in Contemporary Literature*, 7 (Autumn 1966), 239-257.

Pinsker, Sanford. "John Barth: The Teller Who Swallowed his Tale." *Studies in the Twentieth Century*, 10 (Fall 1972), 58-68.

Slethaug, Gordon E. "Barth's Refutation of the Idea of Progress." *Critique*, 13, No. 3 (1972), 11-29.

Tanner, Stephen L. "John Barth's Hamlet." *Southwest Review*, 56 (1971), 347-354.

Tatham, Campbell. "John Barth and the Aesthetics of Artifice." *Contemporary Literature*, 12 (1971), 60-73.

————. "The Gilesian Monomyth: Some Remarks on the Structure of *Giles Goat-Boy*." *Genre*, 3 (1970), 364-375.

Tilton, John W. "*Giles Goat-Boy*: An Interpretation." *Bucknell Review*, 18 (Spring 1970), 92-119.

B. Anthony Burgess

Works

A Clockwork Orange. 1962; rpt. New York: Ballantine, 1965.

Devil of a State. 1962; rpt. New York: Ballantine,

The Doctor is Sick. 1960; rpt. New York: Ballantine, 1967.

Enderby. 1963, 1968; rpt. New York: Ballantine, 1969.

The Eve of St. Venus. 1964; rpt. New York: Ballantine, 1971.

Honey for the Bears. 1963; rpt. New York: Ballantine, 1965.

The Long Day Wanes: A Malayan Trilogy. 1964; rpt. New York: Ballantine: 1966.

MF. 1971; rpt. New York: Ballantine, 1972.

Napoleon Symphony. New York: Alfred A, Knopf, 1974.

Nothing Like the Sun. 1964; rpt. New York: Ballantine, 1965.

One Hand Clapping. 1963; rpt. New York: Ballantine, 1973.

Re Joyce. 1965; rpt. New York: Ballantine, 1966.

The Right to an Answer. 1960; rpt. New York: Ballantine, 1966.
Shakespeare. London: Jonathan Cape, 1970.
Tremor of Intent. 1966; rpt. New York: Ballantine, 1967.
A Vision of Battlements. 1965; rpt. New York: Ballatine, 1966.
The Wanting Seed. 1962; rpt. New York: Ballantine, 1964.

Criticism.

Aggeler, Geoffrey. "Between God and Not-god: Anthony Burgess' *Tremor of Intent.*" *Malahat Review*, 17 (1971), 90-102
_____ . "Incest and the Artist: Anthony Burgess' *MF* as Summation." *Modern Fiction Studies*, 18 (1972), 529-543.
_____ . "Mr. Enderby and Mr. Burgess," *Malahat Review*, 10 (1969), 104-110.
Anderson, Ken. "A Note on a Clockwork Orange." *Notes on Contemporary Literature*, 2 (November 1972), 5-7.
Brophy, Elizabeth. "*A Clockwork Orange*: English and Nadsat." *Notes on Contemporary Literature*, 2 (March 1972), 4-6.
Bunting, Charles. "An Interview in New York with Anthony Burgess." *Studies in the Novel*, 5 (1973), 504-529.
Churchill, Thomas. "An Interview with Anthony Burgess." *Malahat Review*, 17 (1971), 103-127.
Connelly, Wayne C. "Optimism in Burgess's *A Clockwork Orange.*" *Extrapolation*, 14 (December 1972), 25-29.
Cullinan, John. "Anthony Burgess' *A Clockwork Orange*. Two Versions." *English Language Notes*, 9 (1972), 287-292.
_____ . "Anthony Burgess' 'The Muse'; A Sort of SF Story." *Studies in Short Fiction*, 9 (1972), 213-220.
De Vitis, A. A. *Anthony Burgess.* New York: Twayne, 1972.
Evans, Robert O. "Nadsat: The Argot and its Implications in Anthony Burgess' *A Clockwork Orange.*" *Journal of Modern Literature*, 1 (1971), 406-410.
Friedman, Melvin J. "Anthony Burgess and James Joyce: A Literary Confrontation." *Literary Criterion*, 9, No. 4 (1971), 71-83.
Kates, George. "Politics and Modernity: The Strategies of Desperation." *New Literary History*, 3 (1971), 93-111.
LeClair, Thomas. "Essential Opposition: The Novels of Anthony Burgess." *Critique*, 12, No. 3 (1971), 77-94.

Morris, Robert K. *The Consolations of Ambiguity: An Essay on the Novels of Anthony Burgess.* Columbia: Univ. of Missouri Press, 1971.

Page, Malcolm. "Anthony Burgess: The Author as Performer." *West Coast Review*, 4, No. 3 (1970), 21-24.

Pritchard, William H. "Burgess vs. Scholes." *Novel*, 2 (1969), 164-167.

C. *William Golding*

Works.

The Brass Butterfly. 1958; rpt. in *The Genius of the Later English Theatre.* New York: New York: New American Library, 1962.

Free Fall. 1959; rpt. New York: Harcourt, Brace and World, 1962.

The Hot Gates and Other Occasional Pieces. New York: Harcourt, Brace and World, 1965.

The Inheritors. 1955; rpt. New York: Pocket Books, 1963.

Lord of the Flies. 1954; rpt. New York: Putnam's 1959.

Pincher Martin. 1956; rpt. New York: Putnam's 1962.

Poems. London: The McMillan Co., 1934.

The Pyramid. 1966; rpt. New York: Harcourt, Brace and World, 1967.

The Spire. 1964; rpt. New York: Pocket Books, 1964.

Criticism

Adriaens, Mark. "Style in W. Golding's *The Inheritors.*" *English Studies,* 51 (February 1971), 16-30.

Babb, Howard. *The Novels of William Golding.* Columbus: Ohio State Univ. Press, 1970.

Baker, James. R. "The Decline of *Lord of the Flies.*" *South Atlantic Quarterly*, 59(1971), 446-460.

———. *William Golding.* New York: St. Martin's Press, 1965.

Biles, Jack. "Literary Sources and William Golding." *South Atlantic Bulletin*, 37, No. 2 (1972), 29-36.

———. *Talk: Conversations with William Golding.* New York: Harcourt, Brace and Jovanovich, 1970.

Cox, C. B. "Lord of the Flies." *Critical Quarterly*, 2 (Summer 1960), 112-117.

Crane, John K. "Golding and Bergson: The Free Fall of Free Will." *Bulletin of the Rocky Mountain Language Association*, 26 (1972), 136-141.

Davies, Cecil W. "The Novels Foreshadowed: Some Recurring Themes in the Early Poems of William Golding." *English*, 17 (1969), 86-89.

Delbaere-Garant, Jeanne. "The Evil Plant in William Golding's *The Spire*." *Revue des langues vivantes*, 35 (1969), 623-631.

_____. "From the Cellar to the Rock: A Recurrent Pattern in William Golding's Novels." *Modern Fiction Studies*, 17 (Winter 1971-1972), 501-512.

_____. "William Golding's *Pincher Martin*." *English Studies*, 51 (1971), 538-544.

Dick, Bernard F. *William Golding*. New York: Twayne, 1967.

Ditlevsen, Torben. "Civilization and Culture or *Pro Civitate Dei*: William Golding's *Lord of the Flies*." *Language and Literature*, 1, No. 3 (1972), 20-38.

Fackler, Herbert V. "Paleontology and Paradise Lost: A Study of Golding's Modifications of Fact in *The Inheritors*." *Ball State University Forum*, 10, No. 3 (1969), 64-66.

Freedman, Ralph. "The New Realism: The Fancy of William Golding." *Perspective*, 10 (Summer-Autumn 1959), 118-128.

Hodson, Leighton. *Golding*. Edinburgh: Oliver and Boyd, 1969.

Hollahan, Eugene. "Running in Circles: A Major Motif in Lord of the Flies." *Studies in the Novel*, 2 (Spring 1971), 22-30.

Hynes, Samuel. *William Golding*. New York: Columbia Univ. Press, 1964.

Kermode, Frank. "Coral Island." *The Spectator*, 201 (1958), 257.

_____. and William Golding. "The Meaning of it All." *Books and Bookmen*, 5 (October 1959), 9-10.

_____. "The Novels of William Golding." *International Literary Annual*, 3 (1961), 11-29.

Kinkead-Weekes, Mark and Ian Gregor. *William Golding: A Critical Study*. New York: Harcourt, Brace and Jovanovich, 1968.

Nelson, William. *William Golding's Lord of the Flies: A Source Book*. New York: Odyssey Press, 1963.

Niemeyer, Carl. "The Coral Island Revisited." *College English*, 22 (1961), 241-245.

Oldsey, Bernard S. and Stanley Weintraub. *The Art of William Golding*. 1965; rpt. Bloomington: Indiana Univ. Press, 1968.
Peter, John. "The Fables of William Golding." *Kenyon Review*, 19 (1957), 577-592.
Spitz, David. "Power and Authority: An Interpretation of Golding's *Lord of the Flies*." *Antioch Review*, 30 (Spring 1971), 21-33.
Stinson, John J. "Trying to Exorcise the Beast: The Grotesque in the Fiction of William Golding." *Cithara*, 2, No. 1 (1971), 3-30.
Walters, Margaret. "Two Fabulists: Golding and Camus." *Melbourne Critical Review*, 4 (1961), 18-29.
Whitehead, Lee M. "The Moment Out of Time. Golding's *Pincher Martin*." *Contemporary Literature*, 12 (Winter 1971), 18-41.

D. Joseph Heller

Works

Catch-22. 1955, 1961; rpt. New York: Dell, 1962.
Something Happened. New York: Harper and Row, 1974.
We Bombed in New Haven. 1967; rpt. New York: Dell, 1969.

Criticism

Day, Douglas. "*Catch-22*; A Manifesto for Anarchists." *Caroline Quarterly*, 15 (Summer 1963), 86-92.
Frost, Lucy. "Violence in the Eternal City: *Catch-22* as a Critique of American Culture." *Meanjin Quarterly*, 30 (December 1971), 447-453.
Galloway, David D. "Clown and Saint: The Hero in Current American Fiction." *Critique*, 7 (1965), 46-65.
Henry, G. B. McK. "Significant Corn: *Catch-22*," *Melbourne Critical Review*, 9 (1966), 133-144.
Kiley, Frederick and Walter McDonald, eds. *A Catch-22 Casebook*. New York: Thomas Y. Crowell, 1973.
Krassner, Paul. "An Impolite Interview with Joseph Heller." *The Realist*, 39 (Nov. 1962), 18-31.

McDonald, James L. "I See Everything Twice: The Structure of Joseph Heller's *Catch-22*." *University Review*, 34 (1968), 175-180.

McNamara, Eugene. "The Absurd Style in Contemporary American Literature." *Humanities Association Bulletin*, 19 (Winter 1968), 44-49.

Milne, Victor J. "Heller's 'Bologniad': A Theological Perspective on *Catch-22*." *Critique*, 12, No. 3 (1970), 50-69.

Monk, Donald. "An Experiment in Therapy: A Study of *Catch-22*." *The London Review*, 2 (Autumn 1967), 12-19.

Nagel, James, ed. *Critical Essays on Catch-22*. Encino, Calif.: Dickenson, 1974.

Nelson, Thomas. "Theme and Structure in *Catch-22*." *Renascence*, 23 (1971), 173-182.

Orr, Richard W. "Flat Characters in *Catch-22*." *Notes on Contemporary Literature*, 1, No. 1 (1971), 4.

Pinsker, Sanford. "Heller's *Catch-22*: The Protest of a *Puer Eternis*." *Critique*, 7 (1965), 150-162.

Scotto, Robert M., ed. *Joseph Heller's Catch-22: A Critical Edition*. New York: Dell, 1973.

Solomon, Eric. "From Christ in Flanders to *Catch-22*: An Approach to War Fiction." *Texas Studies in Language and Literature*, 11 (1969), 851-866.

Thomas, W. K. " 'What Difference Does it Make?" Logic in *Catch-22*." *Dalhousie Review*, 50 (1971), 488-495.

Way, Brian. "Formal Experiment and Social Discontent: Joseph Heller's *Catch-22*." *Journal of American Studies*, 2 (1968), 253-270.

E. Iris Murdoch

Works

An Accidental Man. 1971; rpt. New York: Warner, 1973.

"Against Dryness: A Polemical Sketch." *Encounter*, 16 (January, 1961), 18.

The Bell. 1958; rpt. New York: Avon, 1966.

The Black Prince. 1973; rpt. New York: Warner, 1974.

Bruno's Dream. 1969; rpt. New York: Dell, 1970.
A Fairly Honourable Defeat. 1970; rpt. New York: Warner, 1973.
The Italian Girl. 1964; rpt. New York: Avon, 1965.
The Nice and The Good. 1968; rpt. New York: Avon, 1969.
The Red and the Green. 1965, rpt. New York: Avon, 1966.
The Sacred and the Profane Love Machine. New York: Viking, 1974.
The Sandcastle. 1958; rpt. New York: Warner, 1973.
The Sovreignty of Good. 1970; rpt. New York: Schoken Books, 1971.
Sartre, Romantic Rationalist. 1953; rpt. New Haven: Yale Univ. Press, 1959.
"The Sublime and the Beautiful Revisited," *Yale Review*, 49 (December 1959), 247-271.
"The Sublime and the Good," *Chicago Review*, 13 (Autumn 1959), 42-55.
A Severed Head. 1961; rpt. New York: Avon, 1966.
The Time of the Angels. 1966; rpt. New York: Avon, 1967.
Under the Net. 1954; rpt. New York: Avon, 1967.
The Unicorn. 1963; rpt. New York: Avon, 1964.
An Unofficial Rose. 1962; rpt. New York: Warner, 1973.

Criticism

Byatt, A. S. *Degrees of Freedom: The Novels of Iris Murdoch.* London: Chatto and Windus, 1965.
Dick, Bernard F. "The Novels of Iris Murdoch: A Formula for Enchantment." *Bucknell Review*, 14 (May 1966), 66-81.
Fraser, G. S. "Iris Murdoch: The Solidity of the Normal." *International Literary Annual*, 2 (1959), 37-54.
German, Howard"The Range of Allusions in the Novels of Iris Murdoch." *Journal of Modern Literature*, 2 (1971), 57-85.
Hoffman, Frederick. "Iris Murdoch; The Reality of Persons." *Critique*, 7, No. 2 (1964), 48-57.
Hoskins, Robert. "Iris Murdoch's Midsummer Nightmare." *Twentieth Century Literature*, 18 (1972), 191-198.
Kogan, Pauline. "Beyond Solipsism to Irrationalism: A Study of Iris Murdoch's Novels." *Literature and Ideology*, 2 (1969), 47-69.
Majdiak, Daniel. "Romanticism in the Aesthetics of Iris Murdoch." *Texas Studies in Literature and Language*, 14 (1972), 359-375.
O'Connor, William Van. "Iris Murdoch: The Formal and the Contingent." *Critique*, 3, No. 1 (1960), 34-46.

Pondrom, Cyrena Norman. "Iris Murdoch; An Existentialist?" *Comparative Literature Studies*, 5 (1968), 403-419.

Thomson, P. W. "Iris Murdoch's Honest Puppetry: The Characters of Bruno's Dream." *Critical Quarterly*, 11 (1969), 277-283.

Vickery, John B. "The Dilemmas of Language: Sartre's *La nausée* and Iris Murdoch's *Under the Net*." *Journal of Narrative Technique*, 1 (1971), 69-76.

Whiteside, George. "The Novels of Iris Murdoch." *Critique*, 7, No. 2 (1964), 27-47.

Wolfe, Peter. *The Disciplined Heart: Iris Murdoch and Her Novels.* Columbia: Univ. of Missouri Press, 1966.

F. *James Purdy*

Works

Cabot Wright Begins. 1964; rpt. New York: Avon, 1965.

Children Is All. 1962; rpt. New York: Avon, 1965.

Color of Darkness. 1957; rpt. New York: Avon, 1965.

Eustace Chisholm and the Works. 1967; rpt. New York: Bantam, 1967.

The House of the Solitary Maggot. New York: Doubleday, 1974.

Jeremy's Version. 1970; rpt. New York: Bantam, 1971.

Malcolm. 1959; rpt. New York: Avon, 1960.

The Nephew. 1960; rpt. New York: Avon, 1962.

Criticism

Baldanza, Frank. "Playing House for Keeps with James Purdy." *Contemporary Literature*, 11 (Autumn 1970), 488-510.

Bush, George E. "James Purdy." *Bulletin of Bibliography*, 28 (1971). 5-6.

Pease, Donald. "James Purdy: Shaman in Nowhere Land." *The Fifties: Fiction, Poetry, Drama,* ed. Warren French. Deland, Florida: Everett/Edwards, 1970.

Schwarzschild, Bettina. *The Not-Right House: Essays on James Purdy.* Columbia: Univ. of Missouri Press, 1968.

G. Kurt Vonnegut, Jr.

Works

Breakfast of Champions. 1973; rpt. New York: Dell, 1974.
Canary in a Cat House. New York: Fawcett, 1961.
Cat's Cradle. 1963, rpt. New York: Dell, 1965.
God Bless You, Mr. Rosewater. 1965; rpt. New York: Dell, 1970.
Happy Birthday, Wanda June. 1971; rpt. New York: Dell, 1971.
Mother Night. 1961, 1962; rpt. New York: Dell, 1972.
Player Piano. 1952; rpt. New York: Dell, 1972.
Sirens of Titan. 1959; rpt. New York: Dell, 1970.
Slaughterhouse-Five. 1969; rpt. New York: Dell, 1971.
Welcome to the Monkey House. 1968; rpt. New York: Dell, 1970.

Criticism

Bodtke, Richard. "Great Sorrows: Small Joys: The World of Kurt Vonnegut, Jr." *Cross Currents*, 20 (Winter 1970), 120-125.

Bryan, C. D. B. "Kurt Vonnegut, Head Bokononist." *New York Times Book Review*, 6 April 1969, pp. 2, 25.

————. "Kurt Vonnegut on Target." *New Republic*, 8 October 1966, pp. 21-22, 24-26.

Carson, Ronald. "Kurt Vonnegut: Matter-of-Fact-Moralist." *Listening*, 6 (Autumn 1971), 182-195.

Clancy, L. J. " 'If the Accident Will': The Novels of Kurt Vonnegut." *Meanjin Quarterly*, 30 (1971), 37-47.

Crichton, J. Michael, "Sci-Fi and Vonnegut." *The New Republic*, 26 April 1969, pp. 33-35.

Critique, 12, No. 3 (1971). The entire issue is devoted to Vonnegut.

Demott, Benjamin. "Vonnegut's Otherworldly Laughter." *Saturday Review*, 54 (May 1971), 29-32, 38.

Engel, David. "On the Question of Foma: A Study of the Novels of Kurt Vonnegut, Jr." *Riverside Quarterly*, 5 (February 1972), 119-128.

Fiedler, Leslie. "The Divine Stupidity of Kurt Vonnegut." *Esquire*, 74 (September 1970), 195-197, 199-200, 202-204.

Goldsmith, David, *Kurt Vonnegut: Fantasist of Fire and Ice.* Bowling Green, Ohio: Bowling Green Univ. Popular Press, 1972.

Klinkowitz, Jerome and John Somer, eds. *The Vonnegut Statement*: *Essays on the Life and Work of Kurt Vonnegut, Jr.* New York: Delacorte, 1973.

"Kurt Vonnegut, Jr.: A Symposium." *Summary*, 1, No. 2 (1971).

Leff, Leonard. "Science and Destruction in Vonnegut's *Cat's Cradle*." *Rectangle*, 46 (Spring 1971), 28-32.

May, John R. "Vonnegut's Humor and the Limits of Hope." *Twentieth Century Literature*, 18 (January 1972), 25-36.

Palmer, Raymond C. "Vonnegut's Major Concerns." *Iowa English Yearbook*, 14 (1969), 3-10.

Reed, Peter J. *Kurt Vonnegut, Jr.* New York: Warner, 1972.

Scholes, Robert J. " 'Mithridates, He Died Old': Black Humor and Kurt Vonnegut, Jr." *The Hollins Critic*, 3 (October 1966), 1-12.

Wolfe, G. K. "Vonnegut and the Metaphor of Science Fiction." *Journal of Popular Culture*, 5 (Spring 1972), 964-969.